ABOUT TH

Lars Muhl was born in Aarl
Royal Academy of Music,
konservatorium) from 1974 to ___ , ___ . For many years, he was
a successful singer-songwriter – first as a band member, and
then from 1986 as a solo artist. In 1996, he was awarded the
WCM's Songwriters Million Certificate.

The author has had a great interest in spirituality from a
very young age, and, concurrently with his music, he studied
the world's religions and esoteric knowledge. Then, in 1996,
he was struck down by an unexplained illness, which neither
doctors nor alternative therapists could diagnose. This was
the start of a completely new existence and the beginning of
that quest he has so grippingly described in *The Seer*. In 1999
Lars Muhl decided to leave music to concentrate fully on his
spiritual interests.

Lars Muhl has studied Aramaic, the language of Jesus, and
has spent many years writing and lecturing on spirituality
throughout the world. In 2003 he started Hearts and Hands,
a non-profit and apolitical aid organization based on the
voluntary work of various therapists. The aim is to help
people who are suffering from life crises such as cancer and
stress-related illnesses. In 2009 Lars Muhl and his wife Githa
Ben-David founded the Gilalai Institute for Energy and
Consciousness.

THE GRAIL

VOLUME 3 OF THE ⊙ MANUSCRIPT

LARS MUHL

WATKINS

Sharing Wisdom Since 1893

This edition first published in the UK and USA 2017 by
Watkins, an imprint of Watkins Media Limited
Unit 11, Shepperton House
89-93 Shepperton Road
London N1 3DF

enquiries@watkinspublishing.com

Design and typography copyright © Watkins Media Limited 2017

Text copyright © Lars Muhl 2017

Designed and typeset by Donald Sommerville

Printed and bound in the United Kingdom

A CIP record for this book is available from the British Library

ISBN: 978-1-78678-082-9

www.watkinspublishing.com

'There is light within people of light,
and they shine it upon the whole world.
If they don't shine it, what darkness!'

Yeshua, *The Gospel of Thomas*

Prologue

A few years ago an old Spanish manuscript was handed over to me. The title was *San Gral* and the author was stated to be *Kansbar.*

The man who gave it to me was first my teacher and then later my friend. In the time between he suffered the indignity of fulfilling the doubtful but archetypal role as my spiritual father. It followed, of course, that I played the role of the dutiful son who, however, never succeeded in totally satisfying his father. The relationship had the classic conflict situation built into it: first the idolization of the father, followed by the inevitable, symbolic patricide.

The old Spanish manuscript is about 400 pages long. It is of no literary value. The contents are more or less uninteresting, at least to the untrained eye. If there is anything in it at all of the slightest interest it is to be found between the lines. And the little the zealous reader may find there is only for the few to whom it has any meaning at all.

Reading the dedication of the manuscript you immediately get the feeling that the contents are a matter between the one in the dedication who is handing the manuscript over and the one who is receiving it. In this case *Kansbar* and *Flegetanis*.

The manuscript is dated, 'Alhambra, 1001', and the dedication reads as follows:

'Kansbar is not my real name. But due to the secrets I have been chosen to guard, I have taken this old Persian name. Kansbar the Chosen One. Kansbar the Wise. Kansbar the Seer. Kansbar the Protector of the Grail. I am getting old. For many years I have been searching for the one who is to take over this duty after me – but in vain. Only now do I remember the day I met Flegetanis, an itinerant Moorish singer, in a marketplace in a small town on the coast of Andalusia. This manuscript is for him. This is the story of the Grail.'

At the beginning I didn't know what to do with the manuscript. Apart from a slight curiosity, I just felt a childish pride that I had been found worthy to guard it. Not until I started reading it, finding that the contents did not live up to the promises of the dedication, did my new-found worthiness evaporate like dew in the morning sun.

For two years, the manuscript stayed untouched in the bookcase in my study collecting dust, until the day the sun sent a pale ray on to it as if it wanted to lead my attention to it once more.

Thus, it was totally without any kind of expectation that I opened the yellowed manuscript again. The moment I took it in my hands it seemed that the light in the room changed. I hesitated and looked up from the empty page.

The empty page?

Outside, the sun was pale and low in the sky. Apparently nothing had changed in the room. Only the book. I turned a page. Not a letter. Not a single word. I turned another one, and yet another, only to see that apparently nothing was written in it. Instead, some neat, almost transparent characters appeared on the paper. The strange symbols and signs seemed to move, and the more I looked at them the more the signs danced in front of my eyes, almost teasingly and diabolically.

I sat for a long time, unfocused and ruminating about the strange thing I had just experienced. When once again I looked at the manuscript, the original text was suddenly there on the pages. I leafed through it and saw that, apparently, the text was intact again. Was all this simply a figment of my imagination?

Then it suddenly dawned on me that, although the contents of the manuscript in itself were insignificant, it nevertheless constituted a protective veil, a kind of key to an otherwise closed world. Not until later did I understand that the manuscript was simply a metaphor, a mirror or a gate to another dimension.

The information that the manuscript communicated was only a pale shadow of a much deeper knowledge. The ordinary text told a local story from Andalusia, mainly about two characters, Kansbar and Flegetanis. The inexplicable signs behind the text, somehow, were the key to this deeper knowledge. However, it was a kind of knowledge which only reveals itself to those who are ready for it. The manuscript, then, was a metaphor for a possibility that is to be found in man himself: an access to the so-called Akasha files in the great, ethereal, universal memory.

I turned a page and started reading.

PART I
SYLVIA

1

The train cut like a knife through the European dusk. The rain whipped against the windows of the compartment.

'God is peeing,' said a small boy sitting on the seat opposite me with his sister.

'Carl!'

Their mother looked apologetically at me while she leaned toward her son and wiped his mouth with a paper napkin.

'God doesn't pee,' his sister answered, 'He cries.'

It was not a fanfare of a statement, just a quiet establishment of a fact with a faint exclamation mark behind it. Like a stifled breath with an immediate, checkmating effect.

'He must be very sad, then,' the mother sighed resignedly with an empty look at the steamed-up window, before hiding once more behind a women's magazine.

The girl put her head on her brother's shoulder, uncomplaining. Sitting there, they constituted the silent protest of a whole generation against the thoughtless rejection of that Holy of Holies: people's divine and frail ability to be present.

I smiled sympathetically at them and leaned back in my seat hoping to get some sleep.

In the bag beside me lay the result of two years of intense work, the manuscript for the book about Mary Magdalene, the forgotten, feminine power. But it was also the result of the breaking up of a life. For two years I had more or less roamed about with no other fixed point than the manuscript. In a small house in the Andalusian mountains, at Gare du Nord in Paris, at the Hôtel Costes in Montségur. Line by line, piece by piece, at haphazard lay-bys, changing hotel rooms and busy railway stations, wherever it was possible to sit with my laptop on my knees.

The work was done and I was on my way to Denmark, tired like Methuselah. There was a fear deep in my consciousness whether or not the pieces would fit together. Would there be coherence in chaos? That was all I had time to think before falling asleep to the sound of the tears of God, which drummed against the window, drawing momentous patterns on the back of my eyelids.

There is a small town, Bélesta, in the valley of love, *Val d'amour*, in the Pyrenees. In this town there is a child who cries a tear each time a leaf falls to the ground prematurely. The child mourns the ignorance of man. Mourns the ever-present ignorance about the true essence of man. Mourns the spiritual blindness of man.

There is a church in this town. Deep in the darkness of the crypt below the church there is a basin in the floor filled with the tears of this child, and they constitute holy water in which the pilgrims may bathe their eyes and regain their sight.

Is it not a paradox then, that the Christian Church, at least on a symbolic level, hides its true power in the unconscious?

The churches in Cathar country hoard many secrets, which have only now begun to see the light of day. There was a time, in my efforts to uncover some of them, that I thought it was all about revealing the misanthropy and mendacity of the Catholic Church. Nothing could be further from the truth. Through the years, the Church has committed many irreparable atrocities. One is almost tired just thinking about having to name them all. But how could the Church have been any different, considering the fact that it is a product of the limitations of man himself? Just like all the other churches and religions of the world. Whether a new-born child is initiated as Hindu, Buddhist, Muslim, Jew, Christian or atheist depends solely on the choice of the parents or the circumstances decided by the specific culture. No man and no church, however, decide the true cosmic identity of the child. This, in turn, is for all of us.

I believed that my journey was almost over. In reality, it was just about to begin, but I had no idea about that at the time. My focus was only on completing the Magdalene manuscript. Although I was the one who had written it down, it felt more like a gift that I had been allowed to bring home than something I personally had created. It filled me with a deep gratitude but also with a strange emptiness, another kind of emptiness than the one you normally experience each time you finish something.

Intuition has many roads. Basically you might say that if man doesn't use it, intuition doesn't use man. At best, my journey was an example of what may happen when you let yourself be guided by an inner voice, let go of the material reality and travel into the landscape of the soul, which basically is always accessible but seldom visited, and is usually hidden by the limitations of the specific personality.

Meeting the Seer had taught me about some of the innumerable levels surrounding us, as well as the numerous traps that the seeker far too easily may be caught in. I had visited the underworld and met my personal shadows, as well as a long series of collective demons hiding there, on my astral journeys. I got in contact with the Oracle on my journey to Toledo, an inner voice I could contact if need be, if my balance was reasonably good. But this was all just school, and lessons to be learnt. On a decisive level I was still tied and full of fear. I still had to relate to my basic loneliness, and the temporary separation from the Seer didn't make the situation any easier.

During one of our sessions at Montségur, in the middle of the culmination of our conflict and in order to correct me, he doggedly told me that I was nothing more than an errand boy for the Board of Directors. The fact that he was talking about the Board of Directors of the Grand Lighting Company Upstairs did not relieve the tension between us. Since then, his words had come back to me again and again, and at this moment they were sounding louder than ever. There was no evading it: the time was ripe for me to take up my inheritance. I was left to my own devices.

The train protested in all its couplings. From far away the screeching sound from the brakes woke me up from my sleep. I opened my eyes. The neon tube in the ceiling was turned off. The mother with the two children had gone. Instead, I caught a glimpse of a figure in the seat directly opposite me surrounded by a strange, blurred light. The light was not sufficiently clear for me to see whether it was a man or a woman. The figure sat totally motionless and I squinted in order to penetrate the invisible veil between us. But I didn't succeed.

I wanted to say something and had the feeling that my mouth moved, but for some inexplicable reason not a sound came out of it. Oddly enough, this seemed more or less natural. No words were needed. That which under normal circumstances would have been very frustrating, now changed to total acceptance. Not until then did I notice how peace ruled in the inner void. I leaned back again and surrendered to the rocking motion of the train. I was not alone.

I slowly dozed off and floated back through time until I woke up in the year 1982. It was the year that, together with Warm Guns, I recorded the album *Italiano Moderno* in the Eden studio in London. It was one of the days when the legendary songwriter and producer Nick Lowe was visiting the studio. We were listening to the recordings of the day over a beer when suddenly he pointed to an ad in *Time Out*. It said, '*Psychic Readings*'.

'Have you ever had a *reading*?' he asked.

I shook my head. But I knew immediately that I had to try it.

Two hours later I found myself in front of the old domicile of the College of Psychic Studies in the centre of London. Outside, a small queue of housewives, punks and a businessman from the City were waiting. A ticket was £2 and I was shown to a room on the second floor.

I was met by a young woman. We said hello and she asked me in. Apart from that, we didn't speak. She then asked for my wristwatch. When I had given it to her she held it in

7

her hands and slipped into a trance-like state with her eyes closed. After a while she started talking in a subdued voice:

'Your little sister sends you her greetings. She says that it is time to let go of your sadness and your feelings of guilt because of what happened when you were children. She is now married to a man who spent his childhood in the same part of the town where you lived. He died almost at the same time as your sister, as he ran out in front of a car together with a boy of his own age. Now, he and your sister have married and have a family.'

The young woman was silent for a while before she continued:

'Your grandparents send you greetings. One of them, and you yourself know who it is because you have his broken pocketwatch at home in a desk drawer, is saying that your father is ill and that you ought to tell him that he must change his life.'

Once more, the woman went silent, turning my watch over in her hands.

'Some day you'll stop your present occupation because you'll realize that there is another kind of music of a different and much greater value. You'll be working with healing. In the course of time you'll get in contact with people who will have great influence on you and your true work. One of them is called Sylvia. When the time comes, she will have something to tell you which you must pass on. Be vigilant and do not forget your inner force. Do not forget your real destiny.'

I don't know how long I slept but it seemed like just a few moments. That is why it surprised me that the stranger was no longer in the compartment and I had not heard him leaving.

I started thinking about the idea of *home*. Where does man belong? Where do we come from? Where are we going?

8

Where do the homeless at Hamburg Central Station actually live? Where the well-to-do travelling first class?

If *home* is where the heart is – where do we all live then?

Where was *my own* heart?

Where is it now – while I'm writing this?

I have visited thousands of places. I have wandered in endless deserts. I now see how often I left my heart for other places, things, ideas, trinkets or the company of others. All in the hope of finding some meaning, a little peace and confirmation that after all, I was loved. All the while forgetting that everything that I was looking for was to be found in the heart I had left behind.

All right. I may have received more help than most people. But not everything that I did was received very well. And there are reasons for that.

My book about Mary Magdalene was published practically in secret. Without a single review the first edition sold out within a month. The fifth edition was published within a year – yet another element of proof that, after all, there is another reality, a hidden network far away from the focus of the press and people as such.

On the other hand, my book wasn't about a nobody. After two thousand years of oblivion, Mary Magdalene and her true relationship with Yeshua were starting to be manifest in the minds of more and more people all over the world. The result was a whole series of books on the subject, the latest one being Dan Brown's novel *The Da Vinci Code*, which broke through the media barrier with a bang and fascinated millions of readers.

My own interest in Magdalene as a hidden feminine archetype started in the mid-1980s. This was after meeting some of the gospels in the Nag Hammadi scrolls as well as *The Gospel of Mary* and the Gnostic writings *Pistis Sophia*.

Not only did these take me to the heart of a heretical past but they also gave me contact with tracks pointing towards a history which seemed to have deeper things to say to us than sensational revelations and intricate criminal riddles.

Reality always surpasses any kind of colourful fiction.

Thus it was, during a talk at the Theosophical Society in Copenhagen, that a sixty-year-old gentleman asked me a question which would turn out to have a significant impact on the work I had started with *Mary Magdalene*:

'Lars! The last picture in your new book is of a woman. But this is the only one in the book which does not have a title or an explanation. Would you care to tell us where you got the picture and who it is in it?'

The question was heaven-sent. I had just been talking about the fact that you have to challenge your intuition and ask some questions that otherwise you wouldn't be able to answer, thus sharpening the energetic senses and the access to the Akasha files.

I explained, which was the actual truth, that it had been given to me some time in 1983 by an acquaintance, the philosopher John Engelbrecht, and that he told me that it had been channelled by three psychic monks. The picture portrayed Mary, that is the Virgin Mary. I later understood that it just as much depicted Mary Magdalene. But since I didn't have any real evidence that this was the case I placed the picture without any further information attached to it. The picture was a kind of distress signal.

The man now stood up:

'It may then be interesting for you to know that it was my mother who took the picture back to Denmark in 1960, and that it is true that it was channelled by three psychics.'

The man paused before playing his trump card:

The Crucifix in Bélesta

'Furthermore, I can actually tell you that it really depicts Mary Magdalene.'

A sigh went through the crowd. I couldn't have asked for more convincing evidence of the power of intuition. It spoke its own clear language.

After the talk I tried in vain to find the man among the audience to get more information about his mother. Something in me told me that this was important, but the crowd of people who wanted to ask me questions was too large.

Later that evening in my hotel room, I experienced a strange phenomenon of light. At first I thought that it was the light bulb in the lamp on the writing desk which was about to go. Later I found out that it hadn't been turned on at all. A faintly pulsating ball of light, about the size of a tennis ball, was hanging in the air. The ball changed colour to a pale blue with a purple circle around it and a radiating purple cross in it. At the same time I sensed that there was another person in the room. It seemed only to last for a minute, but when I checked my watch an hour had passed. I had experienced time disappearing like this before. What was new in this was the fact that apparently no kind of meaning, message or any other kind of information was linked to it. Where had this segment of time gone to, and what had happened in the meantime?

I had experienced the radiating symbol of the cross before. It happened during a visit to the small town of Belcaire in the Pyrenees, where the Seer and I wanted to do some investigation. A life-size crucifix was raised next to a war memorial commemorating the fallen sons of the town. As I was meditating in front of it, a small pale blue ball showed itself. It was surrounded by the same purple circle with the purple cross in it. Most of all it looked like a soap bubble hovering in front of the feet of the Crucified One. I managed to take a picture of it at the time.

My phone rang a week after my public talk. It turned out to be the gentleman, Hasse Smerlov, whose mother had brought the picture of Mary Magdalene to Denmark:

'Well, I'm sorry to call you now, but I didn't want to disturb you after the talk. I just wanted to tell you that my mother is still alive and that she would very much like to meet you. She is getting old, and she is not too well physically. But then again, she is probably of a sounder mind than most people. But you ought to experience this yourself. If you've got pen and paper I'll give you her address.'

I fumbled for a pen and almost overturned a cup of coffee before finding a stub of pencil.

'Right,' I said.

'Her name is Sylvia. She lives . . .'

That was all I got. Just one word stayed in the air like the sound of a secret bell with very pure overtones creating strange harmonies, and with a very deep sub-harmonic sound within myself:

Sylvia!

'I'm sorry, what was the name again?'

'My mother's name is Sylvia.'

He paused in order to give me time to write. I wrote the name and address in my notebook as if in a trance, and I hardly remember saying goodbye to him when I woke up in front of the telephone, the receiver having been replaced.

Could this be the very same Sylvia whom the English medium 23 years earlier had predicted that I should meet because she had something to tell me?

All this happened at a time when my astral travels were decreasing and were instead replaced by moments where I 'fell out of time', so to speak. I could be walking down the street when suddenly I found myself in another time or at another level. The surroundings were more or less the same. I almost imperceptibly slipped into a synchronized reality which affected my sense of time and the daylight around me.

During these 'dropouts' I become surrounded by an ethereal net of dancing particles of light, mutually reflecting each other, and adding life to everything as far as I could see. I have the feeling that I'm in the morphic field, the sparkling blueprint behind the visible, material reality. Sometimes the experience is so intense that I clearly see the little, radiating, maintaining and creating angel-beings, the Guardians of Light, manifesting themselves as thousands of sparks, or as an eternal net of small crystals in the air around us.

There were days when these experiences had such an overwhelming, physical effect that I could do nothing but stay in bed all day long. I usually experienced severe pains in my medulla oblongata, just where the upper part of the central nervous system fuses into your brain. At other times this phenomenon was followed by a pain in my solar plexus as well as loss of all energy. There was no doubt that these symptoms were suspiciously close to the ones I had experienced ten years earlier and which had kept me in bed for three years, until I met the Seer. I thought that maybe the old disease was returning because I had been separated from the Seer.

No.

This was different.

The accustomed feeling of iron and lead was no longer part of the symptoms. This had something to do with a lack of clarity, some blockage in me, which had to be removed before the cosmic forces could flow freely. I was no longer the unconscious cause of, and paralysed witness to, my own funeral.

I see no reason to cultivate suffering. On the other hand, however, I have no doubt that the moment the one who suffers understands the cleansing of the pain and realizes its liberating effect, the seemingly meaningless becomes meaningful. To say it plainly, there is a hell of a difference between understanding the deeper essence of suffering and not doing so.

These 'dropouts' put me in a frame of mind where it was no longer possible to make any appointments or plan anything at all. I more or less unwillingly had to give up all control and I realized how much conscious or unconscious energy we spend on controlling everything, and also that this focus on control stems from one thing only: fear. Letting go of this may in itself be anxiety-making.

I had a dream the night before meeting Sylvia. I'm walking along a road, and I cannot see where it is leading. No one else is about, and the peace of Paradise reigns over the enchanted landscape. However, I sense that the idyll is hiding something demonic, something which leaves an ominous impression, but, nevertheless, I'm totally calm and confident.

After a while the road splits into two minor roads, and I am in doubt about which one to take. A figure is approaching on the left one. At first it is only a dot on the horizon, but shortly after the Seer is standing in front of me in his well-known pose and with his pilgrim's staff in front of him.

Then another figure is approaching on the road to the right of me. This one is also just a dot in the distance. When it gets closer, I see that it is an image of myself. This image is also holding a pilgrim's staff in front of it.

The situation seems to be locked. Something is keeping me down while I'm facing the Seer to the left and the image of myself to the right, until I realize that both images are projections of some blockages in me. These two figures are now standing there, guarding a threshold and blocking the way. I stand in front of them desperately trying to find a solution. I undoubtedly have to pass them by, because they are both representing old forms that I do not need any more, the essence of which, however, I must acknowledge before they can be dissolved and no longer constitute a hindrance on the road. But how? Which road should I choose?

Standing there, totally paralysed, I see a blue angel in the sky above the two roads. It approaches very quickly, and I'm suddenly lifted from the ground while a voice is saying:

'Let not yourself be led astray. Both roads are leading back to old limitations. You have come a long way along these roads, but now the time has come to let go of the old.'

The angel is carrying me in its arms and we disappear through the air above the two figures.

It was snowing when I got off the train at Charlottenlund to the north of Copenhagen. Big soft snowflakes were floating down from heavy clouds like manna from Heaven. The air was filled with crystals. My senses were honed to such a degree that I looked right through the people I passed on the street. It wasn't the blockages or limitations of each person I noticed, it was solely the highest qualities. They appeared as radiating patterns in the ethereal aura. It was striking, however, that none of them seemed to be aware of the help that surrounded them.

An elderly gentleman, who was waiting for someone, had an age-old, pulsating and reddish-golden crown hovering over his head. The crown reflected a longing – a longing for the woman he had been married to for thirty years but who had recently gone to another world. The longing was now transformed and presented itself as patience.

A couple walking hand in hand: a nacreous triangle embracing them, dissolving the jealousy between them.

A young girl, lost in her own thoughts: a small, radiating tiara just in front of her budding breasts – the fireflies' celebratory dance to the awakening eros.

A pregnant woman: a sparkling filigree of light embracing her and the new life in her womb.

A woman who tried to hide her tears in vain, glittering like diamonds on her cheeks: a faint pulsating cross on her stomach; the sadness over the lost lover, the image of the empty bed; sorrow as the redeemer of a new life.

The apartment houses in the bohemian quarter. The transparent door. Top floor. Initiation.

I rang the door bell and heard the faint ringing somewhere in the apartment. Eternity. I knocked on the door. Then I heard a faint noise in the corridor. The door opened:

The blue angel.

2

The blue angel was standing in the doorway disguised as an elderly lady in her eighties.

There was an aura about her, radiating like suns and moons in endless Milky Ways, the clear and genial eyes of a young girl laughing out at me, filled with warmth, care and love looking through the eyes of the elderly woman, who was not of this world.

'What took you so long?' she laughed, 'better late than never. Good to see you. Do come in.'

Her words rolled out like a red carpet, and stepping over the threshold I knew that I was stepping into the world I had been looking for for such a long time, but which I had stopped believing really existed. Somehow, I felt that this might be the most important step I had ever taken on my long journey home.

The woman wore a blue dress with a matching blue hat.

In the living room a certain order reigned in the chaotic display of books, ring binders and documents in stacks on tables and bookshelves. We sat down in two armchairs on each side of a low table with room only for two cups into which she poured steaming, delicious-smelling hot tea.

'Oh Lars, would you please get the two pastries I got for us. They are in the kitchen. I'm not as agile as I used to be.'

I got up and managed to find my way between books and documents. In the kitchen were two pieces of Christmas pastry big enough for at least twelve people.

'Well, both of them are for you,' she shouted from the living room. 'A young man like you must have some sustenance. I myself do not eat anything these days.'

The laughter in her voice filled the air, a sound of bells ringing through me as I cut a piece off the cake and balanced it into the living room on an exquisitely cut crystal plate.

'I have waited for this moment to arrive much longer than you'll ever know,' she said, when we again sat opposite each other.

'I haven't read your books yet, but when my son showed me the picture of Mary in the *Magdalene* book I realized that the messenger I have been waiting for, for forty years, had finally shown himself. Actually, I was close to giving up hope. The Board Upstairs know how often I have prayed that you should show yourself. The picture of Mary has constantly been a smoke signal. And now we've both got our answer.'

Her voice was pure and clear and filled with sunshine.

'Did you yourself know what was going on?' she asked curiously.

I told her about the medium in London who many years ago had predicted that I should meet Sylvia. I told her about meeting the Seer and working with him, and also about the unexpected power that had been released in me when we broke our liaison. Power that I wasn't too sure I would be able to handle. I finally told her about my intuition, when the book was finished and was on its way to the printers, telling me to place the picture of Mary after the last chapter without really knowing why.

As I was telling her about this, she sat with an innocent smile on her lips humming away as if she already knew. When I had finished my story, she said:

'Everything is fine. Everything is exactly as it is supposed to be.

'An unbroken chain of arrivals and departures, recognitions and acknowledgements. What are we if not travellers, meeting and parting, crying and laughing, dancing and dying in an eternal cycle. Travelling souls in time and space. A cup cannot contain an ocean. A cloud cannot be captured in a bag. The acknowledgement of eternity cannot be contained in one single human being. That is why God created more than one individual. And among those, the grail-rider must acquire the greatest burden of cognition, that is the knowledge about his own origin, his task and destination. Everything you have gone through so far, your victories and your downfalls, have been necessary steps on the way bringing you here. You often mistake your direction until you learn to decipher the signs, but we all get there in the end. About you and the Seer, you must remember that when one door closes another always opens. Some day you'll meet again, perhaps not in this life but then in another, where you'll finish the task you took upon yourselves a long time ago. The energies you are exposed to at the moment are cleansing for you. The cosmic power can only manifest itself on earth through flesh and blood, and through an immaculate being. I myself am only being kept alive long enough to be able to pass on my knowledge to you.'

Sylvia – The Blue Angel

'What knowledge is that?' I asked.

She looked at me inquisitively as if for a moment she doubted that I was the one she had expected. Then she said:

'If I say MU-energy, what do you say?'

The question hovered in the silence between us. Thoughts flashed through my mind. MU-energy. It sounded familiar, but I didn't feel that I could give her a satisfactory answer here and now. Was it a test?

'Well, it can wait,' she said, while her look burned through the crippled remains of my defence system.'

'Instead, it may interest you to know how long ago it was that Mary Magdalene came into my possession.'

I nodded eagerly.

'As a young woman, I was invited by a Dutch High Priestess to Montségur in the Pyrenees. I understand you have also been through a difficult schooling there.'

I nodded in confirmation and she continued:

'At the time I didn't know anything about the area and its power. There were twelve of us, all women, who had been asked to come to the Castle of Montségur. We received an initiation there, which because of my vow of silence I cannot tell you. Not yet. Maybe later. We'll see.'

She paused as if to find the right words.

'After the initiation, which lasted for three days and three nights, the newly initiated priestesses each received one of the Cathar castles in the area. When the High Priestess found out that there was no castle for me I was driven to the church in Rennes-le-Château. This then was under my dominion.'

She paused again to let her words sink in, looking directly at me before continuing:

'I take it for granted that you are aware that I'm talking about the Church of Mary Magdalene.'

I nodded my assent. This was too good to be true.

'As we drove into the small town I immediately felt the presence of a powerful energy which, however, I couldn't explain at the time. But stepping into the Church of Mary Magdalene I almost fainted, that is how much it affected me. The church was in a rather miserable condition at the time. It was before they freshened up the restoration made by the renowned priest, Saunière, and once more veiled some of the clues to the secret which many adventurers are looking for in vain, in Rennes-le-Château and the surrounding area.'

'What kind of clues?'

She didn't answer but smiled secretively and looked at me with eyes that penetrated spheres and seemed to look into unknown universes. An alternating golden and purple light radiated around her. A white, pulsating crown of crystal hovered above her head.

'There is much focus on Rennes-le-Château at the moment. Mostly for the wrong reasons. You see, the need for spiritual entertainment is the result of a deeply rooted indolence and neurotic dependence on matter and fear, which create a desire for a quick release, encourage easy solutions and lead directly to astral delusions. Thus one may actually keep playing on the surface of the spiritual amusement park for all eternity. It turns into illusion instead of intuition, ravings instead of a creative imagination, hallucinations instead of a visionary creativity. There is nothing wrong in wanting transformation. But you must have the courage to look into your own reasons, in order to understand what stems from old wounds, fear, inferiority and ties to things and other people and what is based on a real inner scrutiny, acknowledgement and certainty.'

Her ocean-like look embraced me gently as she continued her explanation:

'Ultimately, it all boils down to a lack of love and a lack of knowledge of the true powers of the soul. It is really rather trite, but nevertheless true.'

She motioned towards the kitchen:

'More cake?'

I shook my head, declining. It was remarkable how easily she alternated between the wise, seeing High Priestess and the kind elderly lady who was concerned about my welfare.

'I'm glad you came. You and I have much to do, but time is running short.'

In spite of her obvious care for me, I sensed that there was still something that barred the flow of communication between us. Apparently, she read my thoughts, because shortly afterwards she said:

'Don't lose heart, but I must make sure that you possess the necessary qualifications before communicating the knowledge which is hidden behind forty years of silence.'

She had barely finished speaking the last sentence when an indescribable peace embraced me. The being in front of me, who, until then, had looked like an elderly lady, seemed to dissolve. Instead, I was now looking into a constellation of stars, which can only be described as angel-like. I was then lifted, softly but firmly, as if by a giant hand and pulled through the floating wall of crystals, on through ethereal light, into the astral spheres, like an endless breathing, breaking through level after level, until I was pulled through the last veil of limitation into a kind of flowing being that can only be described as *freedom*, only, however, to be drawn back again through the worlds, back into the living room where I came to with a sigh, facing Sylvia and her warm smile. Everything went so fast that there was no time at all to reflect on it. It was like a test, which was supposed to tell me something about my present spiritual state of mind. A white rose manifested itself between us. It slowly floated down on to the table in front of me.

'It symbolizes your soul,' she said looking at me intently. We sat quietly in the silence, then she continued:

'It is important that you work on your grounding. I know the feeling of being insecure, the way you feel right now. That is why I also know how important it is that you re-establish a solid foundation. You must begin the decisive part of your Grail journey. Here you'll learn about the secret of the imprisoned princess who must be liberated, and the dragon, which must be conquered before the prince may lift his cup and drink the elixir of eternal life. You'll understand the metaphorical truth of the legend of the Grail as well as all its allegorical meanings. You'll only be able to learn the true knowledge and to present it purely by taking this journey yourself.

'Is it possible for you to reveal some of the knowledge you received during your initiation at Montségur?'

The moment I asked the question I knew how inappropriate it was. Her almost inaudible sigh was a clear confirmation of this fact.

'If I revealed this, it would remove the most important motivation for you to go at all.'

'Where does this journey go, then?'

'At the physical level to the land of the Cathars. At the inner level to the Castle of the Grail in your heart.'

'Why exactly the land of the Cathars?'

'Because it plays a central role in some of your latest incarnations, partly as a priest and partly as a troubadour. You carry a copy of it in your innermost self.'

'Is there a special power in that area securing my success?'

'Yes. Just as it is the case everywhere where a special energy has been accumulated through the ages. You may also go to

Jerusalem or Assisi, Lourdes or Damascus. There is a power on Iceland for example, which is about to be discovered now. You could also stay here in Denmark. There are lots of suitable places, but remember that these places are expressions of an inner reality more than they are expressions of external destinations. Neither *Shambhala* nor *Shangri-La* are places, but solely states of mind. Each person is a gate to the cosmos. But it presupposes that the person in question is willing to be responsible and concentrate on this acknowledgement. It is important to understand this.'

'Your own initiation, has that got something to do with my journey?'

She shook her head leniently:

'It is quite touching that you try to extort my secrets from me so innocently by pretending not to know. But you are not very convincing. There is no reason why we should continue to test each other. Let us get down to business.'

The blue angel was still hovering above my head. Then it disappeared faster than the eye could follow it. I couldn't help thinking that this performance was just another way for Sylvia to test me.

'As of today, nothing will be the same. You must expect that your physical expression will change, from the level of the cells to your physical appearance. New energies shall flow, and some of them will seem rather heavy and arduous because they come from unknown universes and because you are still battling with some personal limitations. Somehow, it is a paradox, since it is only by letting go of your worldly ties that the energies may flow freely. On the other hand, it is also necessary to stay grounded. It is thus a matter of keeping a very delicate balance, which you must find and sustain.'

A triangle became visible while she was talking. To the right on the bottom line Sylvia was standing, and there

Sylvia after her initiation

was an image of myself to the left. At the top of the triangle together we both manifested the angel-like being.

'Please notice that the triangle you see is the missing top of the Great Pyramid. Thus, although we are standing at the bottom, it is the bottom of the small pyramid constituting the upper part of the big pyramid. This makes quite a difference. Between us we are creating the angel at the point of the pyramid who, as of now, shall be your protector. This is how man, in pairs or in groups, may manifest angel-like thought forms to the benefit of mankind. This is white magic or true alchemy.'

She got up with some difficulty and slowly disappeared in the darkness between her stacks of books. She reappeared ten minutes later with a piece of paper, which she placed on the table in front of me. I picked it up. It turned out to be a napkin with a strange symbol and the letters MU written upon it, apparently scribbled in haste with a ballpoint pen.

'Makes you think, doesn't it?'

'But what is it supposed to be?' I asked.

She didn't answer, but instead she asked me:

'Did anything out of the ordinary happen to you on the twentieth of April?'

I tried to think of something but couldn't remember the day in question. I brought out my diary and found the date. Bingo!

'This was the day my book about Mary Magdalene was published.'

She chuckled happily:

'I was in hospital on that day. A nurse served me coffee and cake. The napkin in front of you was on the plate.'

Our eyes met and we couldn't help laughing. The image of the young girl appeared among the multitude of stars. It lasted for a moment only, then it disappeared.

'The Board Upstairs have been busy,' she said when she recovered her breath.

She reached for the teapot and poured me some tea.

'What is the significance of the symbol in combination with MU?' I asked.

'I'm not fully aware of that yet. But, as you know, MU is the ethereal continent of the first souls on earth, Le-MU-ria. MU is the ancient sign for water in all shapes in ancient Egypt. In the Greek alphabet *mu* is the centre, or what is situated in the middle, between the beginning, *alpha* and the end, *omega*. MU is the highest mode of vibration of the element and the idea of *water*. It is *living water*, the prerequisite for *the transforming fire*, which is promulgated by Zarathustra and, thus, by Yeshua. The MU-energy is the higher ether, where water and fire meet.

'MU is the Buddhist's mystical word for the elimination of any kind of temptation. MU is the cleansing of souls.'

The words were like little candles in the air, an age-old knowledge which only needed the right impulse in order to manifest itself.

'Your own name is an allegory on the mystery you are here to solve and pass on. Parts of it are obvious. The two first letters in your last name make MU. But I'm not so sure that you would be able to bear everything about the secret woven into your name in your present condition.'

I wanted to contradict her but she continued instead:

'You are an old soul. But an old soul which has fallen deeply in earlier days. Your being consists of a very beautiful and radiating centre. There is a lot of love and healing in you. But you also possess a self-destructive element, a part of you which you haven't accepted yet and which must be taken care of. If you can do this, nothing will be able to stop you in your mission of the soul.'

Her words were an echo thrown back from an unknown wall somewhere in the past. In spite of the promising prospects, the warning was still clear.

'You'll find the princess where the dragon is. Find the princess and you'll find the dragon. And where you find them, you'll also find the Grail. The three of them are inextricably united.'

'Which princess?'

'The princess within yourself. The feminine aspect within the man. But there is also a woman waiting somewhere out there. If men and women only knew the possibilities they possess when they are together. The initiated ones in antiquity always worked in pairs. Just as Simon the Magus had his Helen and Yeshua his Mariam, Paul had his Thekla. Not many Christians are aware of this. When they established the Church in the year 325 it was first and foremost a political act, with the purpose of stopping the autonomous gnostic and mystical society which was flowering at the time of Yeshua and in the years after his ceremonial death. When they established the Church they also adopted the dogmas and some of the rites of the Mithras cult and the Ishtar/ Isis tradition, which fitted the political agenda under new headings and names. The rest was silenced. In this way they literally threw out the wisdom aspect, Sophia, with the bath water. The symbolic Second Coming happens through Sophia, that is the higher Sophia aspect, which is secret. Find her and you have found the princess. It's happening now. The Second Coming of the higher Sophia aspect is not just a collective matter but also a process, which each and every one of us must go through. That is why so many people, and especially those who work spiritually, experience that these are turbulent times. This implies a confrontation with the old. All that limits us. And that is hard for most people. Look around. Have you noticed how many men and women leave each other in this day and age? Not because something is wrong with any of them. They simply started their relationship on the wrong foundation. People now must enter into true relationships. This is how it is at all levels. Not just between man and woman but also ties within the family, friendships, and the old teacher/student relationships are also broken because of the new which is on the way.'

She looked closely at me as if she had seen something and was now wondering if she should tell me. Then she said:

'Step out of the old circle. It is always painful to say goodbye to a teacher. Even more so when he has become a kind of spiritual father. But everything has its time. The Seer has taught you much. There is a lot to be thankful for. On the other hand, you have also given him the best of you. Now you must realize that your time with him may be over for now. Take upon yourself whatever springs from the fact that you do not owe anyone anything, and there's nothing you haven't got. Let it go. Otherwise your common gestalt will break you down. The pact you have made will protect you if you live up to its innermost command which builds on mutual respect.'

Her words were like a velvet glove holding my heart to the light, in order to reveal the sorrow, so that it could find its way out. I now saw it disappear into the air like a bird on the horizon on its way to the freedom it had waited for, for such a long time.

'In spite of all the knowledge you have acquired in the course of time you must accept the fact that now you stand here empty-handed. Otherwise you'll not be pliable enough and therefore not able to move others. Be strong in your compliance. Only thus can you cope with that which has become rigid. Clay is shaped like a cup and is then heated in the kiln to make it durable. Still, it is the empty space in the cup which enables it to contain something.'

She reached across the table and put a hand on my arm.

'If you are a cup, let the content be love.'

We sat in a cathedral of silence, embraced by her wisdom.

'A knight of the Grail is an idealist. He knows that true love may be tough in its excoriated honesty. But do remember, that the knight of the Grail, although he may laugh at the folly of man, nevertheless attempts to lessen the suffering, which is a result of it. This does not mean that he takes the responsibility away from other people – it only means that he takes his own upon himself.'

Something inexplicable was manifesting itself around us. It seemed like a third entity born from the unity of our souls. From far away, the pealing of a church bell was heard in the living room underlining the exalted mood.

'The difference between the two of us is that you must work in the open while I must work secretively. But. please be aware, that not everything should be revealed. There are still secrets that may be misused, and will be, if revealed.

'There will always be weak souls waiting to exploit those secrets for personal gain. Just look at the many so-called teachers and gurus seducing gullible souls with promises of initiation and other tomfoolery, convinced of their own excellence. That is why you must be careful what you reveal.'

Although the tea had long turned cold she took a sip before continuing:

'You must accept that our future contact will happen telepathically. Are you familiar with telepathy?'

I was pondering the question, when she helped me by saying:

'I know that you communicate with your oracle, Miriam,

33

and I therefore take it for granted that you and I may find a frequency enabling us to keep in contact.'

She opened her arms:

'Do not worry about it. All will happen just as it has been planned.'

Apparently, she worked from a preconceived plan. But she didn't say anything about the one who had conceived it. Something told me that she didn't tell me everything but kept certain things hidden, either because she didn't think that I was ready to understand them or that she wanted to be certain that I was worthy of her trust. I had experienced many things in my life, but this woman was something out of the ordinary. Like the Seer, Sylvia was of another world.

'Just now, the hosts of Heaven are gathering. This fact has an effect at all levels including the level of the human cell. It turns everything upside down. The changes that many have prophesied are happening right now. We are actually in the middle of it. It is a tough time that will accelerate in years to come and will affect all of us without exception. No one will escape this cosmic trial, which for man will mean the option of unlimited possibilities or total destruction. This is the choice we are faced with. The choice between the lower self's insatiable lust for power, things and entertainment or of living up to the spiritual aspirations of the higher Self. This is the choice we must be willing to make each and every day. Possibly each and every minute.'

Time was running out. I sensed that the audience was almost over. I therefore seized the moment:

'You must give me a sign or something to go on.'

The question did not seem to take her by surprise. And once more she replied with another question:

'What do you know about the seven veils?'

'The seven veils?'

'Yes, the seven veils.'

All kinds of thoughts were running through my head. I automatically thought of Helen Blavatsky's first major work, *Isis Unveiled*.

'Has it got anything to do with Blavatsky?'

She looked surprised at me:

'That was an interesting connection. Both yes and no. I'm sure that Blavatsky was one of the higher Sophia aspects of our time. But the secret of the seven veils goes back much further. You yourself have opened part of the secret in your book about Magdalene. Look in the Gospel of Matthew. Read about Salome dancing the Dance of the Seven Veils in order to satisfy her stepfather Herod's lechery – in return for the severed head of John the Baptist.'

'Can you give me more?'

She couldn't help laughing at my insatiability.

'Some get the impression that the dance was a kind of vulgar striptease. Instead, the Dance of the Seven Veils was an integrated part of the holy drama predicting the death of the Anointed One and the descent into the underworld, in which the Goddess took off one piece of clothing each time the Anointed One passed one of the seven gates of the underworld.

She got up.

'But there is much more. There are depths to this mystery that must be brought into the open. This is the task.'

We said our goodbyes in the hall. It was as if I had always known Sylvia, and I had to struggle with an old sadness coming out of the darkness, threatening to make my tears run freely. I kissed her on the cheek and the young girl's laughter was singing in my soul as I walked down the stairs and into the world in order to find the dragon, the princess and the Holy Grail.

3

Sylvia's laughter followed me all the way to the station. Her tone mingled with mine and together new, strange patterns were formed. One of these led to a door in my subconscious. Above it was written, in invisible ink, 'The door is on the inside.'

Thoughts of unknown origin poured forth from hidden nooks and crannies. What was the secret that Sylvia claimed was woven into my name and which apparently would make me understand the deeper meaning of my life?

I put my faith in the angel.

It was dark when I got off at Nørreport Station and walked along Kongens Have towards Bredgade where I was going to stay overnight with friends. The snow had spread its sound-muffling carpet everywhere and the spirits appeared for a short moment before disappearing into the silent night once more. Nothing can remove the sense of time like snow and darkness in a world where the continuing flow of memory images constantly rivets people to their horizontal reality.

I was meditating to the noise of the snow under my shoes when suddenly I had the feeling that I wasn't alone. It sounded as if someone was literally walking in my footsteps. Another pair of steps, the sound of which came just seconds after mine. I stopped short in the cone of light from a street lamp. The steps behind me stopped as well. Slowly I turned around. Nothing to be seen. Still, I had no doubt that someone was there.

'Who are you? What do you want?' I heard myself asking.

Silence.

'I know you are there. Tell me who you are.'

Still no answer.

I stood stock still, staring, challenging, into the cone of light.

Then I demonstratively shook my head and turned around in order to continue my walk. But before I had time to react, my feet disappeared from under me and I fell to the ground. A terrible stab of pain ran all the way up through my left side.

'If you want to be free you must let go of the fear of walking alone.'

The voice spoke directly to me.

'Until you can do that you cannot know who I am.'

I wanted to reach out towards the figure I sensed was standing over me. But I didn't take hold of anything but the cold air.

Somewhere someone laughed.

What was happening to me? After the separation from the Seer and my meeting with Sylvia I was moving into another sphere where all my old preferences and fixed points, in fact, all of my old and well-known world, were slowly coming apart. It was like floating about in a room without any walls, floor or ceiling. Even the structure of the cells in my body seemed looser, exactly as Sylvia had predicted. There was literally more 'contact', more transparency than at any other time. I moved more than ever before between the worlds and with much more agility. And no matter where I was, I had this inexplicable feeling of being observed and protected. However, it didn't necessarily make it any easier to be in the world. It could be very difficult to find any kind of meaning in ordinary human life. It was hard not to notice that the games played by people in the so-called visible world were as primitive as ever. The only difference was that they were expressed in a more sophisticated manner than before. That was almost the hardest part.

It was bitterly cold when, towards the end of March, I packed my car and drove south to Montségur.

Jutland was wrapped in frost and a cold mist. It got milder in Hamburg. It was springtime between Kassel and Frankfurt, and when late at night I got to Mulhouse and turned into France I passed the magical border between despondency and melancholy.

I found a corner in a lay-by outside Dijon where I could get a few hours' sleep. I woke up at 4 a.m. and continued south before the busy morning traffic took over the motorway. The light changed outside Nîmes and, driving with an open window, I could smell the salty Mediterranean in Montpellier. I stopped at a pavement café in Narbonne to get some lunch. It was so warm in there that I had to take off my jacket.

I was in a hurry. Inside me I had the feeling I was running out of time. Although it was an old time, it was in itself a reminder that there was something I had to do. The motorway of the old time led directly to my own inner wasteland, the ultimate cul-de-sac. It was a place I knew all too well. The ever-returning memory images of laconically smiling and distorted masks, behind which the pent-up and petrified identities are hiding. Identities, all of which represent old and fatal ties. Imprisonment. Limitation. Everybody, just like me, the enslaved result of the daily bombing raids from manipulating archetypes in a sick society. Buy this, buy that. It is no good where you are right now! Come over here! This is where the party is! A world filled with perverts. Famous for a day. The total corruption of values. The heartless animal: industry and its lobbyists. The faceless elite: the stockmarket's sense of cool cash. God's Chosen Ones: the stockholders, whose greed is surpassed only by the unforgivable stupidity and ignorance of man. The callous view of man, the callous society. The total burn-out of the essence of the soul. From sun up to sun down, the eternal undermining of the true human being, the higher Self. And why? For what reason? Fear? Money? Power? Control? Comfort? Boredom? The total nightmare: absurdity sold as common sense and the freedom of choice.

Suddenly I saw it. I saw it right there at a pavement café in Narbonne, that I myself was one of the stockholders with quite a few shares in hopelessness.

'Your days are numbered.'

I turned around. But the only person I could see was seated a few tables away reading a newspaper.

The Voice.

Well, life only lasts fifteen minutes. And you cannot take man's incarnation to a life on earth for granted. Life is a gift. Isn't it important then how we use it?

It was time to find another way.

In a flash I saw the young, dark-haired waitress adjusting her short skirt as she stood in the shade of the awning. There was something familiar about her movements as she turned to adjust the seams of her net stockings. Shortly after, she stepped out into the sun on her high heels and I imagined how awkward it must be to walk on them. It was like a silent movie lasting a few seconds only, but played over and over again. It was the adjustment of her stockings and the moment when she stepped into the sun and turned towards me. I tried to ignore it but the image wouldn't go away and I put it down to my fragile and changeable state of mind between the physical and ethereal realities.

I closed my eyes and pulled all my senses back to the centre. There, I found myself standing in front of a door at the end of a long corridor. A sign was hanging above the door like a diabolical smile from the hereafter bearing the well-known text, 'The door is on the inside.' Wherever this door may be, this one was ajar. I slowly pushed it open and stepped into a small square in another time. I saw right away that it was the same square where moments ago I had had lunch, served by a young and beautiful woman in high-heeled shoes. I stopped in order to get my bearings. Around me, people were moving about dressed in foreign, medieval clothes. Hesitatingly, I stepped into the open square, squinting a little because of the bright sun. No one seemed to take any notice of me. Then I saw that the people were concentrating on something else. The atmosphere was hectic and, apparently, something important was about to happen. I let myself be carried along by the crowd, through a narrow passageway and on to a somewhat larger square where hundreds of people were already gathered. In the middle of the square a large bonfire was prepared but had not yet been lit. To the right the people of the Church were standing with their crosses and pompous gowns. I saw their postured piety out of which the demons of fear and self-righteousness swarmed into the air around them. And I saw that it is exactly this kind of piety that is devoid of any kind of kindness and compassion. The ecclesiastical head was sitting on a throne. Cold and without showing any sign of sympathy. An audible sigh went through the crowd as a primitive cart entered the square, pulled by a single horse. The figure of a woman was standing on the cart with her head bowed. She was scorned by the mob with shouts, which were more degrading to those who shouted than to the woman they were aimed at. The cart stopped in front of the Church dignitary who said to the prisoner:

'What do you want: Heaven or Hell?'

The woman didn't answer, she was already somewhere else.

Someone threw a stone, hitting the woman on the back of her leg. The blow made her turn around and take hold of her thigh while the crowd cheered with malicious pleasure.

The Church dignitary now stood up and shouted:

'Well, what'll it be?'

Without waiting for the woman to answer he continued:

'Let your silence be the Lord's writing on the wall. By that you have judged yourself!'

Addressing the guards he said cynically, as if the woman was already dead and he was talking about refuse:

'Burn her!'

The sight of the tall, thin dignitary froze my heart. The pronounced features framing a cold smile, the result of an unspeakable fear and a barren heart. His eyes met mine for a split second. At first he looked confused, then he looked straight through me as if looking into a distant future. I wanted to say something but the words stuck in my throat.

41

Running back to the square in order to find the door through which I had entered moments ago, I heard the heartless laughter of the crowd, and before I hurriedly walked back through the long corridor, I sensed the smell of burning human flesh from the stake of the Inquisition.

I opened my eyes. The young waitress was twisting her body in order to adjust the seam on the back of one of her thighs. Then she turned around and stepped into the sunshine heading for me.

'*Que souhaites-tu? Le Paradis ou l'Enfer?* What would you like: Heaven or Hell?' she asked standing in front of me.

I sat totally paralysed. She handed me the menu, smiled at me and said:

'You have the choice of our heavenly yoghurt brunch with goat's cheese and fresh fruit or you may choose the diablo brunch with seasoned cheese and chilli sausage.'

I couldn't say a word. I just stared at the menu while beads of sweat formed on my upper lip.

'Well, what'll it be?'

She impatiently waved the menu in front of me but I still couldn't say a word.

'You look like someone who'd like our diablo,' she said turning about and walked away.

I wanted to protest but she didn't hear me.

'*Un diablo!*' she shouted into the shadows.

I could hear the hidden Self behind the sounds of the world like blood rushing in my veins, the orchestra of the forgotten language, the simple music of which is like the ocean. Not the sound of melancholy waves against the shore – far more *the sound of no shore* – as an old dervish once said.

You cannot run away from the past. The past, just like the future, is forever present *now*. All you can do is laugh and cry, swim in the sea, filled with loss, lust and longing for land, or walk on the water, full of love, without any expectations, knowing that only the death within you is longing for the beach of dreams.

'There you are,' the young waitress said with a smile, placing the diablo brunch in front of me.'

'*Bon appétit!*'

I watched her as she walked back into the shadows.

'*Ephatah, ephatah, ephatah, ephatah*,' I prayed intensely and immediately felt how my heart opened wide and how a silvery line came out from it trying to connect to the woman. My faith in the Power was unconditional. This also was one of the results of my state of mind. The whole square immediately turned into a holy room where the most blessed and total peace ruled. A radiating face appeared in the darkness. The young woman smiled at me. Her eyes were filled with forgiveness. She saw the one I had been and the one I was now. It was not the Church dignitary she recognized but God in his most humble disguise, she saw and greeted me with the best of her: an open heart.

I got up and went inside in order to pay at the bar. She was drying some glasses, which she then placed on a shelf above the counter.

'It has got nothing to do with the quality of the food, that I didn't touch it,' I said, 'but I'm a vegetarian.'

She looked at me curiously as if trying to find out who I was and where I came from. I gave her my credit card. She took it and looked at it. She then tried to pronounce my name but, of course, it sounded totally wrong, though very charming with a French accent.

'Las Myll!'

She tasted the two syllables and looked at me questioningly, and then she broke into a catching laughter.

She tried to imitate my own pronunciation but it sounded just as funny and charming as her first try. She handed me the credit card.

'You are not going to pay for something you haven't ordered,' she said in a low voice.

'You don't always get what you want, but always what you need. And this was just what I needed,' I answered.

We just stood there without trying to end the moment as if we both knew that there was a deeper meaning to this. I broke the silence: 'Let the payment be the symbol of an account that has been made up.'

She hesitated before taking my card back and running it through the machine on the counter.

'Where are you going?' she asked.

'Montségur,' I answered.

'How long are you going to be away?'

'A couple of weeks, I guess. There is a lot to be done.'

Standing there, something suddenly struck me:

'Excuse me, but what is your name?'

She smiled. She then took a card and a pen and slowly wrote the letters down. She handed me the card. It said, 'Belo Bar.' Above it I read the name she had written in a fine spidery writing: *Marie Périllos*.

I thanked her:

'I may drop by on my way back.'

'May?'

This incident took place at a time when I didn't yet know the significance of our meeting. The incident, however, was food for new thoughts, and on the motorway between Narbonne and Perpignan I finally realized that the existence I had considered for the last fifty years to be *mine* was nothing but a speck of dust in an unlimited universe with no end and no beginning.

I began to understand that a self is nothing but a moment's ripple on the endless ocean, and that this self is but one of innumerable expressions of the necessary limitations of the individual. Possibly because we are not yet sufficiently mature to be able to contain the frightening truth about our own unlimited divinity. Imagine the responsibility. This may be the reason why man is so busy constructing his own reality as a parallel to Creation. And are most of man's constructions in reality diversions away from the naked self?

Could the only difference between the constructions of the materialist and the mystic be in the wording?

I thought about Sylvia's words about the monumental change that man is in the middle of right now. 'Even your physical expression will change,' she had said. This was also true. When, now and then, I stole a furtive look in the mirror I was alarmed to see a stranger looking back at me, just as surprised and confused as I was looking at him.

I turned off the motorway outside Perpignan and followed D117 into the land of the Cathars, the beloved Shangri-La of my worldly soul. At once a feeling of freedom took hold of me as I realized that I wasn't going anywhere in particular and wasn't expected at a certain time. It struck me that for the first time in six years, I wasn't going to meet the Seer at this place which had come to mean so much to both of us. I was free to do what I wanted. There were so many places I didn't know and had never seen.

I took my foot off the accelerator at that moment, let go of time and floated into Grail country. Outside, the countryside moved by in slow motion. Estagel, Maury, St-Paul, Lavagnac.

In Quillan I took the usual road towards Foix. Nothing strange about that. The car slowly crawled through one hairpin bend after the other. When I reached the top and was just getting close to the road to Belcaire I felt a force pulling that way. A willpower other than my own insisted.

A sunbeam cut through the spruce trees outside and exploded inside the car. It was almost like in the movies when people are visited by extraterrestrial beings. Surprised, I turned my head towards the passenger seat but it was empty. I nevertheless had the feeling that someone else was in the car with me.

Estagel, Belcaire, Camurac, Prades. Over Col de Marmare and Col de Chioula. Ax-les-Thermes.

The sun was setting. In the Pyrenees it happens within a few moments.

The car continued south. A short distance outside the town I got an impulse to turn off.

A sign pointed towards Orlu.

The road ran through a valley. To my right a rather large lake. In the dusk I could see the moon's reflection on the surface of the water. After fifteen minutes' driving, the road ended in a gravelled open space. I parked between some trees and stepped out of the car. I stood for a moment in order to get my bearings, not knowing anything other than the fact that I had decided to follow my intuition, or the power that showed the way. A path disappeared into the darkness between the trees. I followed it and began my ascent.

It was as if I was carried upwards. My sense of time had been cancelled. An inexplicable power rushed through me. It is difficult to explain, but if I should describe some of its contents I cannot get any closer to it than the word *information*. Not just information as pragmatic knowledge, but a kind of certainty, which cannot be explained. This piece of information didn't come from a specific place. It came from within, was everywhere around me and was a kind of *non-local*, here-there-and-everywhere state of mind.

The invisible hands of the power pushed me gently between the trees and into an open space on a plateau where a totally unexpected sight was waiting for me. As far as I could see, a strange-looking water reservoir with odd dimensions stretched out in front of me. This unreal sea looked like something that must have fallen from the sky, if it wasn't the sky itself. The moon was placed on the mirror-like surface like a ripe fruit from a foreign universe, a gate to other realities, and I had no doubt at all that it was wide open at this moment. The Voice spoke to me. But I understood that it is always accessible for those who have ears with which to listen and are able to read in the universal memory of man.

'There is one memory only.'

A thousand thoughts came to my mind. I knew, of course, the reality of Akasha. However, the moment the Voice spoke, I became painfully aware of my limited knowledge. The Akasha files are the memory of eternity containing everything which happens and everything which has ever happened. They are like a photographic film of all our desires and experiences here on earth.

Akasha is the ethereal memory of everything created. Here, all thoughts that have been thought throughout time are stored. From this point in time, those thoughts have the possibility of reacting retrospectively and of being expressed as archetypal material that has an effect on man, either locking him into the old ideas or giving him the option of new possibilities.

'Thoughts are energy creating form leaving imprints on all the various levels.' The Voice spoke to the knowledge I had in me at the time, which now had to give way to another more embracing kind of insight.

'Man is surrounded by cosmic information. It is everywhere at the ethereal level and always within reach. When man has *a bright idea or experiences the closeness of a higher, intuitive presence, it is cosmic information dripping an insignificant drop of its contents on to man. Without being conscious of this fact, man will stay in the regular, drugged and noisy reality cutting himself off from any kind of help from within and from above.'*

I suddenly saw myself trying to water my garden while at the same time standing on the hose. It was the most elementary kind of teaching I had ever received. My self-righteousness and feelings of superiority were blown away in one, single breath. I could actually feel how the qualities in me were drawn out of the darkness. I could feel my defences falling and making room for the certainty of my true identity.

'The degree of chaos in the world is in proportion to the number of chaotic thoughts in the mind of man. All universes result from the energy of thought. Understanding this is a prerequisite for the understanding of the four- or five-dimensional reality. The change happens now. All must prepare for it. New energies are on their way and these energies depend on man.'

Suddenly there was silence. In that instant I understood that it was the small spark of fear in me, with its origin in the collective fire of fear, which had silenced the Voice, or rather had made me deaf to its presence. Something in me started breathing, all the way from my feet and throughout the body. Calm entered immediately.

Heavenly Father-Mother – You Who are everywhere – Hallowed be Thy Name – Thy Kingdom come – Thy Will be done – Here and now and forevermore.

You Who are in me.

'Concurrently with the entrance to the ethereal reality expanding, man will change at all levels. The ethereal reality enables man to think at a higher level, which means that physical genetics will be surged with spiritual genetics. It will have an effect on the DNA of man in such a way that man will be able to

draw sustenance from the light at the ethereal level. The memory of the true origin must be established.'

The breathtaking view was enveloped in a paradisiacal peace. A faint, transparent and radiating being floated across the surface of the water where it slowly faded away into the replica of the moon.

'*You Who are in me.'*

The teaching was over for now. I turned around and walked back to the car. An hour later I was back in Ax-les-Thermes where I took a room in a small hotel on the outskirts of town. There wasn't much fuss, only certainty.

In spite of the journey and the extraordinary experiences, I wasn't in the least tired. On the contrary, I was filled with an inexplicable vitality. But what do you do in a room with nothing but a small table, an uncomfortable chair and an alluring, soft double bed? You lie down and try to fall asleep.

Then I realized that this being was still with me. I got up, turned on the light and looked around. No one there. I then slipped into bed again, turned off the light and felt that someone took my hand and guided me along towards a clear light on the horizon.

'You Who are in me.'

4

The light from the fires formed a golden arch on the pitch-black Mongolian sky. Oyugun turned his horse in the dark and shouted:

'Saran!'

Shortly after he heard a horse in the thickets.

'Hurry up!' he called to her.

In the glow from the fire he faintly saw his little sister Sarangarel's flaming hair flowing against the backlight.

As soon as they were together again they rode towards the fires in the distance. They had been on their way for two weeks in order to participate in the *Sagaalgan*, The festival of the White Moon, where shamans from all over the country gathered in order to perform their old rituals.

It was the first Moon festival for Sarangarel and Oyugun, which meant that they had to go through the necessary initiation. However, she had a somewhat fierce disposition and did not want to submit herself to any kind of authority. Only Oyugun's powers of persuasion had made her agree. Now, close to the goal, she hesitated and tried to delay.

When they were quite near the valley they could hear the noise of a large number of horses galloping through the mountain pass and filling the air with the sound of thunder. Pushing through the thickets they continued along the ridge. Below them was a magnificent view. Seven bonfires burned in the valley and the horses and riders circled the fires, galloping faster and faster. Sarangarel had never seen anything like this. It ignited her own ferocity lying in wait just below the surface, waiting for the right opportunity. But even deeper within her she felt another power sending another kind of song through her, making her insecure but at the same time filling her with hope.

It took them half an hour to find their way down the mountain, through the pass and into the festival area. Close to the fire at the centre, they found a number of tents where shamans who preferred to use song and sound had gathered. They were easily recognizable by their characteristic, long, pointed hats. The singing shamans had a special status giving them certain privileges, but they had to go through the usual initiations just like the other shamans.

Sarangarel and Oyugun were met by one of great father Tenger's servants, Arigh Gal.

'Welcome to Tsagaan Sar,' he said opening his arms. He wanted to say more but stopped as he caught sight of Sarangarel. Rumours of her beauty had gone before her but no one had prepared him for the reality. Oyugun laughed when he saw the shaman blushing. A woman stepped up and took hold of the halter of Sarangarel's horse and led her to the women's quarters.

Oyugun on the other hand immediately rode out and mingled with the other horsemen forming a live circle around the bonfire.

The seven bonfires symbolized Mushin's seven main stars,[*] the seven sisters or the seven virgins who had played an important role in the mythology of the Mongols since the beginning of time. The shamans in particular were very close to the cosmic forces and, especially during the festival of the White Moon, numerous qualities could be received from the Cosmic Council. Any kind of enmity was prohibited. All the gates of cosmos should be kept open and this was only possible in the right kind of spirit.

The festival of the White Moon was also a fertility festival in which seven virgins were symbolically sacrificed to Tenger. At the same time, this was the way the young girls were made familiar with the world of women. In order to be the purest possible sacrifice these virgins had to be menstruating. If a girl who was about to be initiated did not menstruate during the festival she had to wait until the following year. If it didn't happen then either, she would not be able to take on the work of a shaman.

The men rode throughout the night while the women through songs and sounds began finding openings to the ethereal level, which might serve as gates to the world beyond. This could go on for days.

After three days and nights, many of the horsemen, failing to connect with the world of spirits, had dropped out exhausted. However, on the evening of the third day the breakthrough came. The women met in a totally pure and

---

[*] The Pleiades.

52

powerful note that broke through the universe and created an opening. A sigh of relief was audible among the horsemen and the horses staggered to the watering place, ready to fall, where they were taken care of for the rest of the festival. They had given their best. The horse is the most holy animal of the shamans. The horse carries the shaman into the world well protected, and he leaves it again on the Horse of the Sky or the Horse of the Wind in order to co-operate with the spirits in the other worlds.

Seven women and seven men sat round the clock singing the note that the women had found, which made it possible for the three oldest of the shamans to travel to the worlds of the spirits in order to prepare the way for the virgins and the young men who were to be initiated.

Meanwhile they were testing the young virgins in order to find out who could meet the demands, while the young men spent three days and three nights in the caves in the mountains. Sarangarel had been found worthy, but as soon as it was possible she had crawled to the horse-pen under cover of darkness where she had tried to escape on her brother's horse. However, she had been caught by one of the guards who had to get help from two other guards in order to calm her down. As punishment Sarangarel was tied to a pole outside the main tent for a whole day to the amusement of the passers-by who teased her with friendly shouts.

She stamped the ground agitatedly so that sand and gravel flew through the air. She was like a wild and unmanageable stallion, which refused to be broken.

Among the crowd was a young shaman who fell in love with Sarangarel the moment he saw her. He stood there all day without saying a word, but looked at her, passionately, languishing and very much in love. Sarangarel had seen him and looked at him tauntingly, mainly because she found it very humiliating to be stared at like a captive animal.

However, when the sun was on its way down the sky, something peculiar happened. Suddenly the young shaman started singing. It wasn't particularly strange as such but his tone of voice was so pure, soft and compassionate that it struck the heart with such a loving force that no defence could withstand it.

Sarangarel froze in her ropes. All resistance fell to the ground like the dust she had kicked up moments ago. All sounds stopped, within as well as around her. All activity ceased. All interest was focused on the young man singing to the young woman who stood tied to the Tree of Life in the middle of the world. But this was just the beginning of something that those who saw it would never forget. From an unknown place within Sarangarel a sound grew forth. At first it sounded like the painful crying of a wounded animal. Nevertheless, the sound was inexplicably different from anything they had heard before. It cleansed the air of every impurity. Then it changed and became clearer and more free. Those who witnessed it later said that it was as if Sarangarel was transformed in front of them. This unmanageable woman inexplicably turned into a winged being, the likes of which none had ever seen before. The voice of this being stood like a pillar of light among them. Every heart had to open to this force, and it was as if it healed all sorrow, all diseases and all death. Anyone hearing this sound had to leave the old and welcome the new. From all corners of the world all shamans turned to this pillar of sound, which had united with the Tree of Life and miraculously had sown an imperishable seed in their hearts.

*

I woke with a start as if I were torn from one reality and thrown into another. I looked around and remembered that I was in a hotel room in Ax-les-Thermes. Somewhere far away there was a faint echo of a voice singing an unknown song. The events of the previous night came back to me. What was it that had made me go 'astray' and up to the lake, and who was it that spoke to me there? I remembered the radiating being walking on the water and disappearing as quickly again. Everything seemed totally unreal. And yet, I had no doubt that it had happened. I suddenly experienced a burning desire to go back but couldn't remember the way to get there. I tried to reconstruct the route in my thoughts but the details faded away from me. There was no doubt that the experience was connected to my nocturnal journey and the meeting with Sarangarel and the singing shamans. Lying there on the bed I was caught by a deep longing to see her again. The echo from her song still vibrated inside of me and something seemed to be changing. It was as if a totally new opening was created into a long forgotten area of my heart, a small tear through which the song quietly flowed in and embraced the splintered crystal of the universe:

> I AM the light in the heart
> Supplanting every darkness
> And transforming everything into Golden Light
> With the only thing which is real.
> I AM the one who is sending my love into the world
> In order to mend everything which has fallen down
> And to break down bitterness and resistance.
> I AM the endless power of love
> Acting through all that is alive
> With the only thing which is real:
> Forgiveness for ever more.

It felt as if an invisible hand held my heart very gently. I could feel a healing power flowing through my chest.

I stayed in bed that morning watching the dawn sending golden rays into the room. There reigned a very deep feeling of peacefulness, which in turn gave birth to a similar deep feeling of gratitude. What kind of beings had decided to take care of me in this way? Who was the oracle, Miriam, who had revealed herself to me in Toledo and who had stayed close to me and had helped me when I wrote the book about Mary Magdalene? And what kind of beings were looking after me now? Who was Sylvia with whom I had so surprisingly made contact and who apparently had something she was going to pass on to me? Who was the Seer, this extra-universal being who had saved my life? And what about all the people who had been helping me along the way? Not to mention the beings from another reality. Indeed, I had much to be thankful for and, slipping into my silent hour, I sent them all loving thoughts.

After breakfast I decided to drive back towards Belcaire and on to Bélesta where I turned off towards Montségur. I was looking forward to seeing the old village again, situated in the Promised Valley where I had had so many transforming experiences with the Seer, and I couldn't get there fast enough. However, having passed Fougax-et-Barrineuf, a small village about fifteen minutes' drive from Montségur, I spotted a big, yellow-red building, set back from the road on my right. I had seen it so many times when the Seer and I were visiting the area but I had never been inside it.

A sign outside said, 'Om shanti'. The building could very well be a Buddhist or Hindu monastery. Whether or not this was my reason for turning in there I do not know, but something made me do it.

No one seemed to be about. I parked the car and approached with caution. There was a large rack for shoes and boots at the front door. Above it, a big, beautiful bell. I could see a figurine of the Madonna in a window and in the other window another figurine of a saint. It wasn't totally Eastern then.

I carefully knocked on the door. It was ajar and I therefore opened it and went into a small front hall with doors on each side and a wide staircase ahead of me. There were some kitchen sounds behind one of the doors and I was about to knock on it when it was opened.

'Welcome,' a warm voice was saying, 'Can I help you?'

A man of about sixty years of age was standing in front of me. As soon as I saw him I sensed his golden, crystal-like aura, which was clearly connected to this place. I couldn't decide whether it was him who gave the place this fine quality or if it was the other way round. However, as he stood there receiving me so heartily I was inclined to think that he was the bearer of the power. I had the thought that maybe he was yet another sage who had been given the dubious task of showing me the way.

We introduced ourselves. His name was Mar. Shortly after, we were seated in the kitchen together with his wife, Leny, who also possessed a similar radiating, crystal-like aura. They came from Holland and had owned this place, Les Contes, for twelve years. Earlier, it was a guesthouse for poor French children, run by the Catholic Church.

Later, when Mar showed me around, I could see the vastness of the physical framework of Les Contes. One dormitory after another, floor upon floor, and in addition spare rooms and annexes galore. At least 3,000 square metres. There was also an old chapel, which Mar and Leny had made into a meditation hall.

From the mountain, fresh spring water flowed continuously in large quantities into a gigantic water reservoir, supplying drinking water and electricity for Les Contes. Wherever you were in the building, you were constantly surrounded by the sound of trickling water.

In front of the house a big garden was laid out and behind it, a small park.

While Mar was talking I noticed how much he looked like the Seer. As far as I was concerned they might have been brothers. They probably were at some level or other.

'Leny has asked me to show you to your room, if you'll follow me?'

We walked up the stairs in the old main building. Above each door, the old names that the nuns had given the rooms could still be seen. My room was on the second floor. It was called St François d'Assise.

It was a big room containing both a double and a single bed, a small table, a wash basin and the only balcony at Les Contes.

'Margaret Starbird also stayed in this room when she was doing the Magdalene courses in the area,' he said casually before turning about and walking towards the staircase.

'Excuse me,' I said, 'did you say Mary Magdalene?'

'Oh, are you also interested in her?'

'I've just written and published a book about her.'

He smiled as if he would say, 'Who hasn't,' but then he said in the same casual voice as before:

'Of course.'

Our eyes met, and laughter rang throughout the old house.

'Dinner at seven!'

I heard him humming and laughing as he walked down the stairs.

The dining hall was buzzing with voices. Fifteen people were seated around the two refectory tables. I was sitting next to Mar and Leny. We exchanged polite pleasantries and they enquired as to my connection with the area. But I also sensed that another kind of exchange was going on telling my hosts who I was at another level.

'Do you know the Cave of Bethlehem?'

The light cheerfulness suddenly changed, and Mar's intense look and lowered voice had my full attention.

'I've heard about it,' I said. The question took me totally by surprise and my hesitant answer was quite an understatement. For years the Seer and I had looked in vain for this legendary place.

'What have you heard?'

'That it was one of the secret places of initiation for the Cathars and is in the vicinity of Ussat-les-Bains.'

He looked intently at me while I was talking and sat silently for a while before answering:

'The Cave of Bethlehem may or may not have been one of the most secret places of the Cathars; it is not certain. All they know is that the cave was found and excavated in 1938 by one of the most expert contemporary spokesmen of Catharism, Antonin Gadal. They also say, however, that he wasn't totally trustworthy. As far as they know, he did many strange things in order to draw tourists to this, then very poor area.'

'Have you visited the cave?' I asked without being able to hide my enthusiasm any longer.

'Many times,' he said. He was considering how much to tell me, but then he continued:

'No matter whether it is a hoax or not, anyone visiting the cave has to acknowledge that there is a very special energy there. The Rosicrucians ascribed and still ascribe great importance to the place, and I myself have no doubt at all that initiations took place and maybe still take place there. I have had some very special experiences in the cave.'

'What kind of initiations took place there?'

'According to Gadal, the cave was used by the Cathars as a kind of church where the "new Christ" was born and where the initiated one finally obtained the rank of *Parfait*, one who is perfect. In other words a place where the candidate had to leave everything old, his whole past, behind him, in order to step into a new life in Christ. On the eastern wall of the cave a big natural pentagon is imprinted. The candidate had to stand in it while a Cathar priest would read, in all likelihood, from the Gospel of St John before the initiation took place.'

He stopped, got up and left. Shortly after he returned with pen and paper.

'I'll draw you a map so that you may find the place. But do remember to move about very quietly when you find the area.'

After supper some of the guests gathered in a room with an open fireplace entertaining each other with small talk. I especially noticed a mature woman and a young man. The woman looked as if she had had a hard life; it was imprinted on her face, which looked like a Tibetan demon mask. The young man had thick-lensed glasses and a long ponytail and was dressed entirely in black. They were lost in an intense discussion, which sometimes sounded like a severe argument. But for some reason or other something told me that the subject was of importance to me. I caught the odd word but since they were talking very quickly, and in Dutch, I couldn't get the whole of it. I drank my tea, bade everybody good-night and went to my room to get some sleep.

Les Contes

Leny & Mar Van der Velde

I lay for a long time listening to the sound of water surrounding this magical place, which had once been a paradise for poor children.

Or had it?

What had really gone on here?

The water seemed to dissolve the foundation of the building, which floated into the air and disappeared into the universe. I closed my eyes and floated with it.

The sound of children playing filtered into the room. I woke up feeling a bit dizzy after a long night of travelling, where to, I was not too sure.

The cracks in the ceiling and the flowered wallpaper. The light laughter of the children. The busy steps on the stairs. How had it really been here seventy-five years ago? Now I heard the sound of suppressed crying. I got up. It was as if the sound came from just beside the bed.

'Who are you?' I whispered.

Outside, the sun had not yet risen. I walked over to the balcony and looked out. I couldn't see anyone down below. And still, the sound of the children playing was very real.

Against this background the low crying seemed even more heartbreaking. A foggy, grey shadow about the size of a child was sitting huddled at the head of the bed furthest from me in the room. I moved closer very carefully and squatted in front of the small being while I recited the heavenly Aramaic prayer:

> Heavenly Source
> You Who are everywhere
> Thy Kingdom come
> Your will be done
> Here and now and for evermore.
> Fill us with the power of your mercy

> And free us from the fetters with which we bind
>   each other.
> Lead us out of temptation: free us from ourselves
> And give us the strength to be one with You.
> Teach us the true power of forgiveness.
> May this holy moment be the ground
> From which our future actions grow.
> Amen

The room was now completely quiet.

Homesickness!

I lit a candle.

In front of me the little grey cloud slowly dissolved. Between all the grey I sensed some small, sparkling lights dancing around the being, which followed it on its way to the place where it belonged. All the old sounds folded in around me and disappeared the same way.

Outside, the sun was on its way over the mountains.

The only sound in the room was the sound of my own heartbeat.

After breakfast I drove to Tarascon via Ax-les-Thermes until I got to Ussat-les-Bains and Ornolac where I crossed the small bridge across the Ariège river. There was a small church to the right, which didn't seem to be in use any more. Across from it was an old thermal bath. I parked the car outside it and started walking along the road to the right. Just before Villa Bernadac I turned to the left and followed a path into the forest. According to Mar's drawing I was supposed to follow an even smaller path on the left further ahead. I found the path and followed it as shown on the map. I struggled to get through the thickets that closed in around me. The long branches of the wild roses made any progress very difficult. I crawled under a fallen tree, which was also shown on the map, but then lost sight of the path when it split into two and ended in nothing at all.

I worked my way back to the starting point with great difficulty and started over again. This time, after twenty minutes of struggling with the bushes, I ended in front of a steep cliff wall where no further progress seemed possible. Relentlessly, the sun reflected its rays off the face of the cliff and the gorge seemed like a natural oven. Sweat dripping and a crumpled map in hand, which apparently didn't help at all, I was ready to pack it in.

Turning around in order to begin the walk back I looked up for the first time. On a ledge above me the door was clearly visible which, according to Mar's drawing, was the first indication that I was on the right track. The problem, however, was that Mar had made a mistake.

I was very excited when I carefully pulled at the door and opened it with a creaking sound. I continued through a brick gate and started ascending a narrow staircase. Shortly after, I found myself next to an impressive cliff wall with a large opening in front of it. I paused for a while in order to get my bearings before turning to the right and walking to what seemed to be the entrance to the Cave of Bethlehem.

A moment later I stepped inside, holding my breath.

One step below me was an almost rectangular room of about 9 x 3 metres. Close to the entrance was an enormous rock resting on three smaller ones. It looked, more than anything else, like an altar. The famed pentagon was there on the opposite wall, where the candidates had to stand during their initiation. To the left of the entrance was a recess in which, according to legend, the Holy Grail is said to have been placed during ceremonies. The cave was open to the south from which there was an impressive view over the valley and Ornolac.

Mar was right. Whether the cave was an authentic Cathar site or not, it certainly had a very special atmosphere. I sat down on a stone bench close to the altar and fell into the silence of the place.

As I was sitting there it was revealed to me that the most important part of the initiation did not take place at the pentagon in the wall but at the stone altar. This was where the initiated one had to lie down and spend the night in order to give up the small self, so that the higher Self, Christ, might be born and take over the place of the old self. As soon as I understood that I decided to spend the night there myself.

I spent the rest of the day in the area. I picked up my sleeping bag late in the afternoon and some cardboard to lie on.

It was getting dark when I made my bed on the altar and lay down. There was just room enough for me to stretch out on it. A few flickering candles were all I had to keep the bats at bay.

My inner demons, however, could not so easily be kept at bay.

The sounds of the night now took over the cave and the world outside. I wondered whether or not they were the same?

The wind blew out the candles with one gust and filled the cave with an impenetrable darkness. What under other conditions might have sounded like little creeping things, now sounded like animals of hitherto unknown dimensions. A pair of yellow eyes approached through the air and disappeared somewhere below me. I closed my eyes and tried to relax on the uncomfortable bed, but kept twisting and turning in order to find a position that fitted the surface of the stone, which I could clearly feel through the sleeping bag and the cardboard.

I don't know for how long I kept trying to fall asleep but I must have slipped into another state of mind, since suddenly I found myself in another human shape, in another cave, in another country, a long, long time ago.

*

Oyugun was running along the cliff wall while he tried to read the small signs which were supposed to guide him along the way. His sweat blinded him behind the tiger's mask and he had to concentrate in order to keep his balance. Once in a while he stopped to catch his breath and to listen, but the only thing he could hear was his own heart pumping the blood around his young body. He ran for his life. He ran through the faintly lit and winding passages where the torches were placed with so much distance between them that he could just about manage to see where he was running. If they had told him about the circumstances around his initiation he would have been able to prepare for it. But he realized that the uncertainty was an important part of the test.

When Oyugun realized that apparently there was no system in the construction of the maze and that no kind of reason could figure this abomination out, he finally surrendered and ran in the direction shown him by his heart. He almost hovered along, round and round, up and down, down one passageway after another. The heat, however, made him understand that he was getting closer to what must be the centre.

He stopped at the end of a long passageway at the foot of a staircase. He turned his head and looked back, but it didn't seem as if he had missed anything. His heart thundered in his chest and his breath sounded like one of the great bellows by the bonfires at the Moon festival outside.

The Bethlehem Cave

He slowly started to walk towards the opening at the end of the steps where a faint light made long, vague shadows from beings he didn't know.

He stopped again to catch his breath. Then he stepped into a room with four arches forming a symmetrical flower in the ceiling above the altar in the middle of the room. A woman lay on the altar. No other living being was to be seen. He had reached his goal. He knew that all he had to do now was pass the last part of the test.

Carefully he stepped closer.

A young woman wearing a mask in the shape of a snake lay tied to the altar. She was dressed in a thin dress made from snakeskin and decorated with various animal symbols, which barely covered the most intimate parts of her body.

Oyugun gasped when he saw her. The sight fixed him to the spot while chaotic thoughts went through his head. What was the next step?

He watched the young woman. The eyes of the snake met his. Her chest was heaving faster and faster, but otherwise she was calm. He thought for a moment that he caught something in her eyes, something that wanted to guide him or encourage him. But he didn't understand it. He was aware of one thing only: there was no time to waste. He heard the sound of drums and bells from far away and he was sure that they were approaching. Immediately he began untying the woman. When he had set one of her arms free and was beginning to untie the other, he wondered why she didn't move her arm. She only moved slightly when he had untied her legs as well. He thought that maybe she had been drugged, but he also realized that such thoughts were of no avail and didn't lead anywhere. There was only one thing for him to do. He hesitated for moment before reaching out in order to help her out of the snakeskin dress. He fumbled with the lock holding it together at the side, while she was quietly holding on to his wrist. She then let go of him, loosened the dress in front and revealed her breasts to him. Most of all he wanted to discard his own mask and to remove hers as well and to kiss her, but he knew that this was not allowed. The eyes of the snake met his and they said 'come on' to him.

The drums and the bells were not far away now. He tore the rest of the snakeskin away from her in one flowing movement and stared at her open sex lying in front of him like a black and red pearl, the gate of life and death, waiting for him to enter into the Holy of Holies.

He was one single, tight muscle as he slowly entered her. They merged into one single movement and he was caught in a vice, making it impossible for him to pull away. He heard her warm breath behind the mask under him. Somewhere close, the maniacal rhythm and the sharp notes of the bells sounded, chasing an opening to the ethereal level. At that moment his world exploded in an inferno like the Flood breaking all the dams of the world, while he cried out like a delivered animal. He sank on to her, sweating. He sensed the presence of beings in the room.

'Oyugun!'

He looked surprised at the Snake and he seemed to recognize her voice. Then he tore the mask from her face.

'Sarangarel!'

5

'*A part of you is travelling through time and space. However, another part of you is not subject to such limitations. It is on a totally different kind of journey.*'

I opened my eyes slowly. The morning sun bathed my surroundings in a faint purple hue. I was cold and my body was aching. I looked around, bewildered. The Bethlehem Cave.

Oyugun and Sarangarel.

What kind of story was that? Was it about my own past and, if so, why was I confronted with it like that?

And who was it that kept talking to me?

I was disturbed by the fact that it was not possible for me to identify the Voice that kept communicating with me in such rather trite language about the cosmos and the correct meaning of things. This was all stuff that I knew already. Why this insistence? I worked with all aspects of human nature. Especially the psychological, mental and various other dimensions of the soul and spirituality through the humanities and through esoteric knowledge.

'There is a need for transformation at the emotional level more than at the mental level. When you are afraid to enter, it is so easy to demonize the complementary part. Fear is the burden of man. Time is ripe for you to break your mental limitations. This is your great blindness and this is what clouds your true vision. If your emotions are not integrated, your mental field cannot be clean.'

I looked around in the cave. I saw faintly a figure squatting and leaning against the cliff wall next to the opening to the Ornolac valley. It was, however, impossible for me to see who and what it was and what it looked like.

'Who are you?' I blurted out.

I actually sensed that this being smiled at me indulgently. This upset me. There was no answer, but instead the figure continued:

'There are deeper layers. Layers where the body, the psyche, the mind and the senses are simply filters, which must be cleaned before a human being may be infused by the cosmic. In this way a human being may be transformed into a pure, cosmic presence – on earth in its present incarnation.'

I thought that it might be Sylvia who had taken on another character, since it was a complete repetition of some of the things she had told me at our first meeting. Had she not told me that in the future we would communicate telepathically?

'The unusually slow and heavy energies, to which man subjects himself, make it impossible to see clearly. When he nevertheless tries, it may first and foremost be due to his memory of the clearness of his sight before he incarnated. But memory alone is not enough. Memory is only a faint copy of true quality. The higher

ethics are hiding here. The small self has no part in this. That is why it cannot be used as measurement for anything at all. It is above any kind of judgement and is not able to judge or condemn anyone or anything. When man cannot stand himself or the situation he is in, when he is unable to control his surroundings he has a tendency to judge others and to judge that which is going on at the time. However, anyone who judges another, is solely judging himself. And when someone judges himself he has placed himself within the most constricting limitations possible. Power and control are simply expressions of fear and only forgiveness may remove it. Only forgiveness may cut through delusions and restore true vision. I am committed to that, and only to that.'

'I?'

Did I hear correctly? If so, it was the first time I had heard the Voice using *the first person singular* about himself.

The sun was now so bright that I couldn't see if this mysterious being was still sitting at the opening to the cave.

'Are you still here?' I asked in a low voice.

No answer.

Slowly, I got to my feet. I felt as if my body had been torn apart during the night. I realized shortly after that the mysterious being had either left the cave or taken on a shape which was not immediately visible to me. However, I still felt its presence.

I stepped on to the ledge, enjoying the view while I stretched myself and breathed the fresh mountain air. The morning dew lay like an ethereal carpet over the valley and it was pure pleasure to feel the energies surging through me with renewed power. It was like a gift from my unidentified friend. I imagined its gentle, animating laughter, if nothing else then as a happy echo in my own innermost self.

Having packed the car, I drove to Tarascon in order to have breakfast at a café on the banks of the Ariège. Sitting there watching the river, I thought about the long series of thought-constructions which are a result of man's fear of freeing himself from any kind of compensatory and limiting thoughts and illusory dreams. Not just the dream about a painless life, where you walk through it without any kind of strife and with all material wishes fulfilled, but also the dream about the perfect partner, the perfect guru, the perfect spirituality, which are all just constructions meant somehow to make life tolerable for us. Even the conception of suffering, Heaven and Hell, even the conception of a personal God, are constructions, which we have made in order to make our lives meaningful. Nothing wrong with that per se. This is precisely one of the possibilities given to man: free will and the ability to create reality through the power of thought.

Suddenly it was clear to me that the quantum leap that modern man is faced with has something to do with the dissolution of the illusory nature of these constructions, and that we must have the courage to step out of them, until we are finally and totally able to give them up.

The next problem, of course, would be that imagining a life freed from any kind of construction would, in itself, be a construction.

Such a dissolution would be a catastrophe for any kind of foundation on which we build our reality.

I let the question rest. I had now asked it and I was certain that the answer would come in due course.

Meditating on my coffee with a map of the area in my lap I stumbled on the name Notre-Dame-de-Sabart. I could see on the map that it was situated near by. Without thinking too much about it I knew that I had to go there. No doubt at all.

The church was only a five-minute drive from Tarascon.

Stepping out of the car I immediately saw the figures above the entrance. They were clearly visible: Yeshua and

*Mariam and Yeshua greeting visitors outside
Notre-Dame-de-Sabart*

Mariam. One on each side of a stained-glass window. Yeshua to the right and Mariam to the left. They bade the pilgrims welcome with open arms.

It was very peaceful inside. No other visitors were present and for some reason or other I went to the right side of the church. I could see an altar at the end of the aisle. It was as if I was pulled there by an unknown force. I didn't see her before I was very close. The penitent sinner of the church. Mariam Magdal. Kneeling and with the skull and the book at her feet, just like at the altar in the Mary Magdalene Church in Rennes-le-Château.

The skull and the book!

The altar was not very well kept, and contrary to the other figures of saints in the church, there were no candles. Either they had just found the altar and were waiting for the restoration of it or they didn't consider it very interesting.

74

I sat down on the floor to meditate.

Softly, softly.

Heart.

The old road – in His footsteps. Purple. The colours of the clouds. Dust. Light. The unlimited united above my head. The thundering sound of an unknown being flying by me. In His hand: the power to open or to close. Let the wanderer return to the beginning. I stand alone at a crossroads. Open. Closed. Down. Up. An unforgettable moment. An echo from eternity. The sound of the inevitable steps on the stairs – heard through time – and shaking me.

Awake!

> *I AM forgiveness, working here,*
> *Throwing away all doubts and all fear,*
> *Making man forever free*
> *With wings of cosmic victory.*
> *I AM the one who is calling with all my power*
> *For forgiveness each and every hour;*
> *To all life everywhere*
> *I let the grace of forgiveness flow.*

Sarangarel!

I opened my eyes. Deep inside me I was beginning to understand the meaning of my nocturnal journey and the confrontation with the beautiful and also very painful images. I understood that no one is a victim of apparently accidental circumstances.

No circumstances are accidental in the great game!

But why did I have to go back and look at it once more?

'You cannot get to the top of a house unless you take one step at a time. If there are one hundred steps and you only take ninety-eight of them, you'll never know how it is at the top. On the other hand, neither can you skip a step, because then you wouldn't

know the way. If a well is fifty metres deep and your rope is only forty-six metres long, you'll never be able to fill your bucket with water. In the same way man must realize that as long as he cannot raise himself above the reality of the body and the senses, he shall never know anything about the reality of the higher worlds. And the prerequisite for every step is the forgiveness of any kind of judgement. You must forgive yourself.'

Forgiveness. Here we go again. It was slowly getting to be a rather worn concept. I mean, the sound of the word itself was becoming quite nauseating, as it had been misused in so many contexts and had seldom been understood and practised.

The Voice immediately came to my assistance:

'There is forgiveness and then there is Forgiveness. Forgiveness is not just a prayer, but the total giving up of judgement. The moment man understands the depth of these words and makes them his life, he is stepping into a totally different sphere, so totally different from anything he has known before. We are talking of rebirth here. A totally new life. Give up any kind of judgement.

'Every judgement is simply a projection. Do not judge anyone.'

I got up, walked back and bought a candle, lit it and placed it in front of the altar to Mary Magdalene.

Sarangarel's altar.

Women's altar.

The altar to the feminine power.

I stood in silence watching the flame. It flickered slightly in the draught, but I could see that it was strong and could not be quenched. When it finally burnt out, it would continue to burn at another level.

'Forgive me,' I whispered.

I then turned around and walked out.

It was not until I was sitting in the car that I felt how deeply the experience in Notre-Dame-de-Sabart had moved

The Magdalene Altar in Notre-Dame-de-Sabart. Notice the skull and the book.

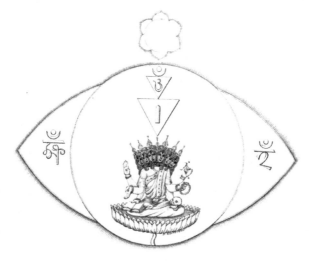

Hakini from Layayoga. Notice the skull and the book. She symbolizes the third eye. She is the moon-white sitting on a wild lotus holding in her six arms a rosary, a drum, a bow, a skull and a book. Her hands symbolize disintegration of fear.
(S S Goswami)

me. It was as if my ethereal body almost vibrated, as if a faint electrical current ran through it like an angel walking through a room. The veils had been pulled aside to reveal the most vulnerable part of me, the strongest part, the unconditional being, the conscious soul in the archetypal feminine centre: Mariam Magdal.

Driving along towards Foix to get some lunch I felt very certain that Mariam somehow had been to France, that her spirit had always been alive in the south of France. I cannot say how I knew, I can only say that it was a kind of certainty originating in the feminine part of my greater being. It was not a matter of history but the archetypal vibration sending its song through time, heralding its message of the arrival of unconditional love and its final reckoning with any kind of intolerance, any kind of abuse, any kind of power and any kind of lie.

As I drove along I juxtaposed the intuitive certainty with the historical background in my mind.

During the time before and after Yeshua, Marseilles was one of the most important cities in the Roman Empire with a thriving commerce and a major concentration of esoteric knowledge. A major Jewish settlement made it more than likely that Jewish, Syrian and other pilgrims, visitors or refugees from Palestine, would come here where tolerance was greater than in many other contemporary parts of the world.

Marseilles was well known for its Athena, Diana, Minerva and Isis temples. In the city you'd see druids, Jewish mystics and Isis priests and priestesses walking freely beside each other under Roman rule.

Legend has it that Mariam Magdal arrived in a boat without sail and oars with her entourage, Lazarus and Martha (brother and sister), Mariam Clophas (Yeshua's aunt),

Mariam Salome (Yohannan's mother) as well as Sara the Egyptian (maid) at a small town not far from Marseilles, Saintes-Maries-de-la-Mer, which at the time of Yeshua was called Ra or Ratis.

It is hard to say whether or not this legend should be taken literally, but there is no doubt that whatever arrived at Ra in a boat without sail and oars it was something which was going to have an enormous impact on the spiritual life of Europe.

Sara the Egyptian later became the great saint of the gypsies, celebrated once a year when the Black Madonna is baptized in the sea.

Isis, Artemis and Cybele were worshipped in Ra as early as the 4th century BC. The first Black Madonna figures in Europe are said to come from here.

Another mystery surfaced when they started delving into this: the Black Madonnas. Who were they and what role did they play?

When I was writing my book about Mary Magdalene I had met these figures time and again, but without finding any answers to the questions raised by these black virgins.

However, one name kept coming up: Isis. It took me by surprise that the Isis tradition, which until now I had been convinced was a strictly Egyptian phenomenon, had been spread across Europe by means of the Roman advance, blending with Celtic and Teutonic traditions. And even more surprising, these heathen traditions were alive a long time after the establishment of Christianity on the European continent. They actually worshipped the Great Mother in various guises, more or less officially, up to the Middle Ages.

Not many Christians are aware that the 'historical' Virgin Mary was not introduced by the Roman Church until the year 470 as a direct result of a public demand to re-establish a female divinity. The successful miscarriage of justice carried out by the Church against Yeshua's better – but dangerous – half, Mariam Magdal, had some unwarranted and, at the time, also unpredictable consequences. As a result, the feminine force had more or less to go underground where, nevertheless, it was able to gather so much power that it is, finally, on its way to breaking down the limitations man has accepted up until now.

It was these kinds of thoughts I contemplated on my way to Foix. This openness to the ethereal reality and its collective memory in my mind was by now so familiar that I realized that in order to keep the channel open I had to refrain from any kind of judgement or critical thought. On the other hand, there was also the demand for sobriety and the courage to be totally honest in relation to the incoming information. On top of this was the question of the personal bits and pieces that should not be involved. It was a very delicate balance and in every way a great paradox – how do you judge something soberly without using the so-called judgement based on reason? It is simply a matter of a totally different kind, and in itself a totally inexplicable kind of certainty, when the so-called judgement, based on reason is completely abandoned.

We are talking about a kind of certainty that not only knows about the ethereal level but also, beyond that, the astral levels. The ability to distinguish between those levels is not only a general prerequisite, but a necessity of life, if you are to keep your balance and have hopes of using the information advantageously.

There are no well-defined borders between the various levels. Everything is integrated and I know of no one who can say where one ends and the other begins. But the starting point itself, the fundamental part, the principal one, cannot

Esclarmonde
(Painting by Peter Fich)

be understood as long as you are solely entrenched in the earthly aspect and the above-mentioned idea of reason.

In spite of all this, it is necessary to know the difference between the ethereal level and the astral level if you are to apply the information you receive usefully.

When man becomes familiar with the reading of the great cosmic memory he is going to wonder, even be shocked, to see that written history, which we have trusted until now, only constitutes part of the truth, since it is only an expression of the version of the writers of history and, usually, the people in power.

You might say that the Church has been the representative of the exoteric (the external, superficial) knowledge which, successfully and for centuries, it made into dogma and historical truths, while the so-called heretics, kabbalists and alchemists, mystics and Rosicrucians represented the esoteric (the concealed and deeper) wisdom living a life in hiding.

The time has come, however, when everything hidden must see the light of day. And this not only goes for the collective unconscious, but for the personal level as well. Each individual must find the courage to look at his own mythology before a lasting healing may be possible. And here, perhaps, lies the greatest challenge for contemporary man. When we wake up, we realize that there are no further escape routes. Many will continue to look for them and grasp at any opportunity to avoid taking responsibility for themselves. But this will only be a short respite. In spite of the innumerable offers of quick relief, man must realize that the promises of short cuts to freedom are just yet another illusion.

The oldest Taoists upheld the principle that the detour would always turn out to be the fastest and most effective road to the goal. I smiled to myself and thought about the scene in my book *Mary Magdalene* in which Yeshua challenges every form of Pharisaic self-righteousness with the words: 'Only the redeemed cannot be saved.'

A judgement or a sad fact?

In Foix I found the cafe in the square where the Seer and I had enjoyed a glass of pastis so many times before. It was usually here we started our work meetings and always here that we ended them with a last aperitif. I ordered a pastis and sent him a friendly thought. The sun had disappeared behind a cloud. It looked like rain. I went and sat under the awning.

Having finished lunch I thought about Sylvia's words about my journey of the Grail, 'The princess is where the snake is. Find the princess and you are close to the Grail.'

The Grail.

One of the oldest and most beloved legends names Montségur as the mountain of the Grail. An old shepherd told me this legend when I came here for the first time in order to meet the Seer.

This is what the old man said:

'When the walls of Montségur were still intact, the Cathars, the pure ones, guarded the Holy Grail there. Montségur was in danger. The armies of Lucifer lay in a circle around the walls. They wanted the Grail so that they could place it in Lucifer's tiara again, from where it had fallen to the earth when the angels were expelled from Heaven. When peril was at its highest a white dove descended from Heaven and split the mountain in two with its beak. Esclarmonde, the female guardian of the Grail, threw the precious holy treasure into the mountain. It then closed again. That is how the Grail was saved. When the devils forced their way into the castle, they were too late. Filled with anger, they burned all the pure ones at the stake in the field below the cliffs and the castle on the *camp de crémats.'*

Tradition has it that 205 Cathars, men, women and children, voluntarily ran singing to the stake. According to the same tradition, they promised to return after 700 years.

Montségur fell in the year 1244. Thus, the 700 years had passed and the time was here – now.

Esclarmonde.

Perhaps she was yet another in the series of female incarnations of the great goddess? Was she, like Magdalene, yet one more of the daughters of Isis?

Esclarmonde was the Duchess of Foix. When the Roman Church instigated the inquisition against the Cathars she became their protector and saint. She was 'the Light of the World' to them.

I drove to Montségur after lunch. Once more I had the sensation that the decision was not mine to make, but that I was more or less being guided along. I had actually planned a whole day for my reunion with the holy mountain. But I had started to accept the fact that the work with the ethereal reality somehow had a mind of its own.

The fine drizzle made mysterious filigree shapes dance before me as I spotted the mountain through the windscreen. As usual, it looked like the ultimate runic letter waiting for the pilgrim who had the courage to climb it in the spirit in which it had been placed there, at one of the most open and holy sites.

I brought out my raincoat and my pilgrim's staff from the boot of the car. Apparently there were no other visitors as the car park was empty.

My heart pounded heavily as I walked through the well-known thicket towards the meadow of Prat, the guardian of nature. For the first time in the seven years I had been coming here, I was alone and had to do what must be done without the help of the Seer.

Slowly I walked to the middle of the meadow to the spot where Prat used to be. I stuck my pilgrim's staff into the ground and took a step toward the holy spot. I closed my eyes and let go of my nervousness. When you are standing here giving your worries to the female guardian of the world, everything external dissolves and, imperceptibly, you slip into the first sphere of the ethereal reality. You, who are everywhere.

You, who are a part of me.

A fine, almost milky veil appeared in front of me. A slightly veiled reality opened up at a point in the air where I had focused my sight, in which the finest filigree of crystals vibrated with a purple hue. Within this net of light I sensed a soft feminine figure, vitalized by beings of fire the size of sparks, which seemed to originate in an unquenchable source of light. I assumed that the figure had to be Prat. But before I had accepted this fact, another being appeared, and I sensed that it was another version of what hitherto had expressed itself through Prat.

The woman was pure light and was surrounded by the salamanders of fire. Then she lifted her hands up above her head as if she was pouring from an unknown source, and I saw that, somehow, she was also made of water.

All the particles of my physical body, all the beings of fire in my ethereal body, all the star material in my astral field were as compass needles exposed to an enormous magnetic force. Everything within and around me pointed to the centre of this radiating being in front of me and, with one voice, asked the question:

'Who are you?'

I did not expect an answer, since at a higher level I knew very well that this being was at such a high-frequency energy level that it must be a higher being.

'I am Esclarmonde!'

The voice sounded like thousands flowers opening to the sun during springtime's first vitalizing hour, a dance leading directly into the centre of the heart's maze.

'Now, as then, anyone who wants to walk the holy paths must choose between Roma or Amor! Choose between the path of the world or that of love!'

ROMA – AMOR!

No compact shapes. Everything soft and pliable. Like seeing everything through a jellyfish held against the light of the sun. A mirage of milky silk and velour. But in a very clear way.

As I came back to the physical reality, the sun sent its rays through the clouds and for a long time I could still see the hectic activity of the little beings of light, sparkling like pearls in the bright air.

After the meeting with Esclarmonde I began ascending the mountain. The first part up to the stele, as usual, was the hardest part. After a short break I continued along the narrow path through the forest. Walking there, I noticed steps behind me once more. I stopped to get my bearings, but no one was there. I thought that perhaps, like myself, the person in question had taken a break, but as soon as I started walking again I could hear the steps like an echo with a very slight delay, only a few metres away. I realized that, once more, it was my invisible friend on the prowl.

I stopped at all the well-known points on my way up, the ethereal openings that I had become familiar with through my work with the Seer. On the ledge where the Oracle is, you only ask the questions to which you have the courage to get the answer. The answers you get here are so direct that you are immediately robbed of any kind of illusion in which you may find yourself at that moment. Catching these answers and passing them on in the most applicable way was what made the Seer such a master in his field.

It was with a certain awe that, an hour later, I approached the entrance to the castle, the Gate of Time. Here you must prepare yourself for the energies activated around the Point of the Grail in the middle of the courtyard. You make yourself free from earlier incarnations and all of your old baggage in the Gate of Time. It works the same way as *The Shaft of the Soul*, as I described in *The Seer*. Images from your personal as well as the collective levels pass in front of you, and the one standing in the Gate cannot control anything at all. You doesn't always get what you want, but always what you need. Or: you often gets what you want, but hardly ever in the shape you had hoped for.

I stayed in the Gate of Time until I was empty of all images. Then I stepped into the courtyard, which seemed strangely empty without the presence of the Seer. I could see him as he took over the Point of the Grail in his familiar way and prepared himself for the work of the day. It was now up to me to attempt to move the energies.

I found the Point of the Grail and drew a circle around myself with my pilgrim's staff. I then put the staff aside, opened my arms and started swirling around. I rested on my left foot while I used my right foot to propel myself around, anti-clockwise. The palm of my right hand turned upwards toward the sky and my left was turned down. Slowly at the beginning, then faster and faster. Round and round until I felt the lines from the corners of the world being sucked into the centre by the centripetal force, the power of which increased with every turn.

The power was focused in the palm of my right hand. Within the centre of this centripetal force a centrifugal one was born, communicating with the external forces, so that an outgoing force was flowing from the middle of the palm of my left hand. The only way to explain this is to ask you to imagine the other side of everyday reality turned inside out so that another synchronous reality becomes visible from behind the veil.

I kept on turning round and round until every kind of limitation was dissolved in a radiating being that manifested itself in the field of tension between my outstretched hands – a pillar of light, or rather a cross of light in the middle of the courtyard.

Then I let go . . .

6

The wheel turns.

Round and round.

The silver string is like an umbilical cord continuing endlessly into the universe. I don't know what is at the end of it. I just see the wheel turning round and round. I am thinking that it may be the Wheel of Life that keeps turning until each and every person has fulfilled his task on earth.

I now see that the wheel is part of a spinning wheel and that a girl of about twelve to thirteen years of age is working it. She is sitting in a room without walls, totally illuminated by the sun, spinning her thread. The girl is dressed in a simple white cotton dress. Its only adornment is a small red fleur-de-lis embroidered on the chest. Only now do I see that it is the girl who is spinning the sunlight. This sight is devoid of sentimentality.

The image fades away and another slowly appears. A heart in a bonfire surrounded by flames. However, it is not burning on the outside. Only the eternal fire burns in the heart. The heart now changes into a fleur-de-lis. The lily burns but does not perish. The heart is burned at the stake but cannot be devoured by the flames.

Then everything becomes heavy and black.

The sun was on its way down behind St-Barthélemy on the other side of the valley as I, slightly dizzy, found my way down the mountain in the dusk.

My thoughts were focused on the darkness I had seen in my vision.

I felt that I was carrying a burden, which was heavier than anything I had carried before. Even the rocks that I had carried up this mountain seven years earlier were nothing to this inexplicable loneliness, which had seized me and reinforced my basic loneliness more than I can say. Something inside me felt as if it was going to burst, and I felt a lump in my throat, an urge to cry which had to be a thousand years old – that is how sad I was, how broken-hearted.

I realized that what had happened in the courtyard was more than I could handle by myself and in my thoughts I asked the Seer and Sylvia for help.

The pictures I had been allowed to see were harsh. But something about the way everything had disappeared into the darkness made me very miserable. The painful loneliness coming from this was impossible to explain. Perhaps it was just difficult for me to understand and accept that when the floodgates open, it is not unproblematic for a person who is not as ready to work with this kind of energy as he should be. When you want to go up, you must be willing to go down, and the heights you may reach are in proportion to the depths into which you have the courage to dive. That's the way it is. I had known this for a long time. But it is also a well-known fact that there is a difference between theory and practice.

Someone must have heard my prayer since the Voice was present once more on my way down:

'*You are not alone, but you have to do this on your own.*'

Period.

I was shaking all over as I walked the rest of the way towards Prat's, or rather Esclarmonde's meadow. All of the Montségur mountain had belonged to Esclarmonde in the thirteenth century. She was the Duchess of Foix and princess and saint to the Cathars. The mountain still belonged to Esclarmonde and it probably always would.

In spite of my state of mind I managed to find the point in the meadow in order to thank her for the insight I had received. Even though I didn't understand the contents of it.

When I got back to the car my legs were shaking so badly that I could hardly stand. I had to hold my car keys with both hands, that is how severely they were shaking. I was cold to the bone.

It was very difficult to get the key into the ignition. When finally I succeeded I turned the heat up all the way. I stayed like this with the engine idling until the car was warm and dry. A sudden inspiration made me turn on the radio and out poured the sound of a well-known voice, Leonard Cohen, singing his song 'Joan of Arc'.

> *It was deep into his fiery heart*
> *He took the dust of Joan of Arc*
> *And then she clearly understood*
> *If he was fire, oh then she must be wood.*

I saw her wince, I saw her cry,
I saw the glory in her eye
Myself I long for love and light
But must it come so cruel, and oh so bright?

'But must it come so cruel, and oh so bright?'

In spite of the state of mind I was in, Cohen's 'haphazard' comment nevertheless made me smile. Yes, dear reader, I certainly am very slow-witted. In spite of the fact that my life for many years has been filled with these wonderful and frightening coincidences, I still wonder and often hear myself repeating the same sentence over and over and over again, 'How strange.'

It seemed as if Cohen's song for Joan of Arc epitomized with a few brilliant words both the moment and eternity. He was truly a troubadour of love. Completely in the old French, esoteric tradition. And according to this tradition the troubadours were closely connected to the Cathars and the Templars. I especially remember one of the stanzas from the tradition of the Grail that I like the most, written by Arnaut Daniel in the twelfth century:

'*With every day do I become a purer and a better person, because I serve the noblest lady in the world and I worship her. I say this openly. I carry in my heart the file with which I cut rare words and make them into rare rhymes because I write about an unknown being.*'

These troubadours were well known for the fact that their poems and songs were filled with a deep esoteric knowledge. Influenced by the Celts and the Gnostics, they worked with four levels representing the elements: the external, historical level, equivalent to the level of earth; a moral level, equivalent to water; a level of the natural sciences, equivalent to air; and finally an ethereal level of fire leading to the highest contemplation. The 'unknown being', to whom they dedicated their songs, was the beloved one, the beautiful and wise Sophia in various shapes, and often incarnated as various beautiful duchesses and ladies of castles. They often developed into amorous erotic relationships between a lady of a castle and a troubadour, and there are numerous examples when a troubadour had to flee headlong from a jealous husband.

The afternoon's experience on Montségur kept me in thrall and at supper I was allowed to sit alone with my thoughts. The other guests at Les Contes had enough sense to notice that I wasn't interested in any kind of small talk. Cohen's song was still in my head. I knew from experience that when I was in a state of openness, nothing happened accidentally. When I turned on my car radio it was not in order to be entertained, but solely because I was meant to. In this case I clearly got an important message.

Joan of Arc.

I had been fascinated by her fate from very early in my life. Like Lawrence of Arabia, Dag Hammarskjöld and Simone Weil, Joan of Arc spoke to an archetypal level in me, which moved me deeply. All four had a very complicated and complex nature combined with a dedication, seen by some as pathological and by others as divine.

Most people have heard about Joan of Arc, but not everybody is aware of her unusual destiny. She was born in the small town of Domrémy on 6 January 1412. At thirteen years old she heard a voice, which she thought belonged to the Archangel Michael. She was in her father's garden at the time, on a summer's afternoon. The voice asked her to seek out Duke Charles of Lorraine and to bring about his appointment as the rightful King of France. At the time France was occupied by the English.

When she was seventeen she was admitted to the presence of Charles and convinced him and his council that she, and she alone, would be able to lead the French troops to victory over the occupation forces, for the simple reason that she was God-sent. And after one month of mental and physical examination the inexplicable happened. Charles pronounced the seventeen-year-old shepherdess leader of the French army in the war against the English.

Joan of Arc succeeded in beating off the enemy and getting Charles crowned king.

On Wednesday 30 May 1431 she was burned at the stake in Rouen after having been betrayed by her own people and subsequently captured by the enemy. During the proceedings dignitaries of the Catholic Church – a number of whom hated her for her great piety and even more so because of the great love of the people for her – tried to get her to admit to heresy. But Joan mastered her rhetoric better than her adversaries. Her words had an authority and authenticity that swept all empty theological arguments and every hypocritical lie aside. Inevitably this led to her death.

What makes the historical sources so extraordinarily credible is the fact that they rest on so many different statements, in which both the words of friends and enemies have been written down and passed on.

What kind of power was expressed through this young woman who apparently could neither read nor write? It is reasonable to claim that she, just like Yeshua, in the course of three years went through the same changes as he did to get to the Christ state of mind. The difference between these two lives is that we know with certainty that Joan was a real person living in the fifteenth century. During the three years in question, she was guided by two saints; in particular St Catherine of Alexandria and St Margaret. They appeared as voices, which in any given situation could advise Joan as to what she should do. According to Joan herself, these voices were never wrong. The few times the promised prophecies did not come true were due only to the hesitation and ignorance of Charles's council.

If one reads the historical sources, and there are many of these, a single statement is repeated again and again: she was purity itself. And this purity made her the messenger of God. Everyone who met her said that she radiated such great piety that she was almost divine. No one could help being moved by her.

This was the official story. But there had to be something else. Something that could guarantee the success of this utopian project. She must truly have had special powers. But what kind, – what were they?

I let the question be for the time being.

After supper most of the guests at Les Contes were going to Carcassonne to enjoy a ballad opera about the troubadours. I declined an invitation to join them since I was too tired. Instead, I brought my tea to the fireplace. To my great surprise the Dutch mother and her son sat there already, lost in conversation. Apparently they were not going on this excursion either.

They fell silent as I entered the room and they got up smiling kindly, and bid me welcome. I immediately realized that this meeting here at the fireplace and at this time was not at all accidental. Thus, I was hardly seated before the conversation started.

'We had better greet each other properly,' the woman said and, offering me her hand, finished her sentence with 'Vivien'.

I answered with 'Lars', and shook her hand.

She pointed to her son who had taken a few steps backwards:

'This is my son, Roderick.'

I offered him my hand, but he just took another step backwards.

'Roderick, you might at least say hello.'

Her voice was not in the least reproachful. She then said to me:

'I'm sorry, but you see, Roderick has to get used to people first. It hasn't been too easy for him.'

'Are you here on holiday?' I asked mainly to be polite.

Once more it was the mother who answered:

'We come here once a year. And we usually stay here for a month at a time. Roderick is of noble birth. He comes from the d'Hautpol family.'

Roderick put his left hand out towards me at these words, as if to underscore his mother's words. On his ring finger he had a large ring which looked as if it was made from gold with a large, black stone in it.

'The family lost all their possessions under circumstances that I shall not bore you with. However, if you are familiar with the history of the region you'll know that the d'Hautpol family owned the old castle in Rennes-le-Château. Unfortunately, the castle is in a ramshackle state today. The family name originates in a small town called Opoul where one of the forefathers slew a dragon in the days of yore. But that is another story.'

I looked closely at Roderick while his mother was talking. He showed no signs of emotion. But it was obvious that he was filled with a pent-up anger being manifested as infantile aggression.

Certainly, I knew something about the d'Hautpols. I had seen the name several times in connection with my studies of the Cathars and the Templars. The name was also mentioned several times in connection with the by now, world-famous priest Saunière and the mystery at Rennes-le-Château.

It was obvious that the mother had told the history of the old, aristocratic family several times to strangers in the past. The question was whether or not I was considered a stranger in this context since the attitude of both mother and son was very direct. It was as if they had something tell *me,* and that somehow they wanted to get it over with.

Without further ado, I turned to Roderick and addressed my question directly to him:

'What have you experienced?'

For a moment the question hovered in the air between us. Apparently it paralysed the mother. Then Roderick answered:

I am a so called *abductee.* I've been taken up.'

'Taken up?'

'Yes, by beings from other realities.'

'UFOs?'

'You may call them that. I would rather call it an abduction into a synchronous reality.'

He stopped as if to give me the opportunity to collect myself. His words, however, did not make me lose my balance. I had studied both UFOs and the so-called abductions and their theories and had formed my own opinion about these phenomena. And the words of Roderick seemed to be very close to these thoughts.

His mother used the rhetorical pause to put in a remark:

'Yes, it's a family weakness, if one can put it that way. For generations we have been abducted by strange beings from other star systems who have used us as guinea pigs.'

We were silent for a while.

'How did you experience this?'

He contemplated my question before answering:

'It is not a very nice story, I can tell you. What I have experienced is beyond the worst nightmares you can imagine. There is so much darkness, so much heavy matter around us and around the earth that sometimes it is difficult to understand how man can continue with life and with evolution.'

'One can also question whether or not this may be called evolution. Do we not primarily still express the most primitive part of our being, although in a much more sophisticated way than we did earlier? As I see it, man is only using about a thousandth of his potential, the rest of which is allowed to stay dormant in the unconscious and is totally wasted.'

He nodded.

'You are right. Perhaps the beings I know are the result of man's heartbreaking ignorance. Perhaps they are something like demons, created by us?'

'In other words, you do not think that we are talking about UFOs as such, with so called *aliens* from other planets?'

'No, not in the normal sense of the word. But I do believe that these beings manifest themselves in various shapes, according to the role they want to play in human consciousness. I believe that this is a part of the seduction. Take the Bugarach Mountain, for example, close to Rennes-le-Château. They say that it is visited by vessels from other planets. Hundreds of people claim to have seen UFOs there.'

'Have you been there?'

He nodded his assent.

'Many times. I have never had this kind of experience at Bugarach but you ought to visit the place. Something is going on there which is out of the ordinary.'

Roderick's tale was certainly exciting. Whether or not it was true, that was another story. I was certainly not in a position where I could decide what was right and what was wrong in this respect. I knew from my own experiences how fragile such experiences are when they are told and passed on. But there was something I had to know:

'When do these abductions happen?'

'At night when I am asleep. As soon as I pass through the R.E.M. sleep, they get me and take me to other levels. And this is not for babies I can assure you.'

It sounded totally like my own nocturnal excursions, the difference being, however, that I did not experience any kind of coercion and I never felt attacked in any way. I was often confronted with difficult sights and heavy decisions, but I never felt that I was subjected to any kind of injustice or experiments. On the contrary, I increasingly had the feeling that I could move about quite freely on the other side.

'Who is abducting you, then?'

'Beings that look exactly like those described by other abductees. Little grey men without ears and noses and with big, slanting eyes without pupils. They seem to be totally devoid of feelings and in many ways quite bestial. For example they do not show any signs of compassion or sentimentality. They are not consciously evil or cold-hearted. They simply do not have the same kind of sentiments as humans do. They are not human, if you know what I mean. They nevertheless seem to be very intelligent in some inexplicable way. I have thought that they may be some kind of robot, made by highly developed beings who do not themselves want to deal with anything as primitive as man.'

He smiled at his own conclusion.

His story made me think. I couldn't help thinking that he might be right about the fact that they were artificially made. But I had no doubt at all that, whatever they were or whoever had made them, they were nevertheless something that occurs in the lower astral fields. The presence of these beings in the energy field of man resulted from conscious and unconscious manipulations with the archetypes, partly by ourselves and partly by those we had elected to manage the world and partly also by outside forces.

The big multinational corporations are managing the external world through the balance of trade and the stock exchange. Taking the risk of sounding paranoid, I suggest the possibility that these corporations have the one single purpose of exploiting all resources, material as well as mental, to the hilt, as long as mammon is the result, no matter the consequences. This doesn't necessarily mean that it is profitable; on the contrary, these institutions somehow are an expression of the collective disease on the earth level, an external expression of the internal state of mind of collective man.

I also believe that the only thing feared by these corporations is that man will wake up and see that he is not free but is kept doped by a long series of undermining activities poisoning modern society, in the shape of a cynical cocktail consisting of equal parts of fear and entertainment. To repeat this fact: these institutions are the external expression of man's collective inner fear of having to be responsible for himself.

I wouldn't be surprised at all if right now there are people working hard to find ways to buy the copyright of people's thoughts, in order to make a profit on them. Imagine a future, dear reader, where poor parents are forced, in advance, to sell the rights to exploit the future thoughts and ideas of their newborn child!

Do you find this improbable?

There are forces in the world that will not stop until the last resource has been exploited and the last drop of blood has been squeezed from life itself. And these forces, again and again, are simply external signs of our own internal state of mind, which we confirm and maintain, when we feel unable to stand our ground and free ourselves from the slavery of normality.

There is so much material excess in the world today that we could solve all the social, humanitarian and environmental problems of the world reasonably quickly. The problem is, of course, that all the riches belong to very few people who do not really want to change the present imbalance of values. And as long as these few are successful in selling the illusion of free elections and democracy to the many, this imbalance will remain.

This external imprisonment, in a way, is a gift, since perhaps it is because of this situation that one day we may understand that freedom must be found inside ourselves.

It was Roderick who broke the silence:

'Did you know that Les Contes is the twelfth *Earth Gate*?'

'Earth Gate?'

I looked at him without understanding. He nodded eagerly:

'Yes, there are thirteen superior Earth Gates on the earth and Les Contes represents Montségur, which is the twelfth.'

'What does that mean?'

'It means that there is a so-called heart meridian on earth consisting of particularly open locations with access to the universe. These Gates are situated at Mount Shasta in California, Glastonbury in England, the Temple in Jerusalem, the Cheops Pyramid in Egypt, the Chinese Wall, the Kedarnath Temple in the Himalayas in India, the Black Mountains in the USA, Ayers Rock in Australia, Kathmandu in Nepal, Nazca in Peru, Montségur in France and Kilimanjaro in Africa.'

He became silent and looked as if he lacked the right words.

'What is their function and who found these Earth Gates?'

'They constitute particularly open locations where the energies from the universe may flow freely. And the heart meridian which connects these gates constitutes in itself a force which not only has the effect that the various gates influence each other, but also that they have an influence on the universe itself. I do not know who located the other Earth Gates, but it was a Dutch biologist and professor who formed a team of psychics who, years ago, were given the task of finding the gate that is now situated here at Les Contes. I do not know who gave them the task and I do not think that Mar or Leny know.

'It is, however, a fact that after months of intense work they found that this place was the right one. You'll be able to see it tomorrow. It is hidden at the lower end of the garden. It is a construction built to precise measurements. A rather large piece of quartz is hanging in the middle of it. Mar and Leny tell us that the energy from the gate is too much for some people while others are attracted to it from far away without knowing the cause of it. Frequently, people who are just travelling through, suddenly find themselves turning off the main road and coming here because they are drawn by a force they cannot explain.'

Roderick got up and went to the big bookshelf at the end wall. He came back shortly after and placed a thin, pale yellow pamphlet on the table in front of me. The letters on the front practically radiated up at me:

The Path of Mary Magdalene and the Cathars (Earthgate expedition, Pyrenees, 1997).

There, below the title, was a picture of the stele commemorating the Cathars on the Montségur mountain.

I opened the pamphlet and looked at the first page. I couldn't help smiling. I was looking at a photo of the part of the altar in the church in Rennes-le-Château where Mary Magdalene is kneeling in a grotto in front of a book and a human skull.

A book and a skull!

The caption below the picture read: 'Mary Magdalene with the *Book of Love* and the *Crystal Skull*.'

The Book of Love and the Crystal Skull!

A bell with a fine, crisp, ethereal tone that spread in a field around me, cleansed the room of the heavy mood that had threatened to take over. I knew that this was a breakthrough in my search and that it was an important step in the right direction.

The three of us sat staring into the fire. Each of us had something to think about. I tucked the pamphlet under my arm, said good-night and took my leave.

I found a torch in Leny's kitchen. I couldn't possibly go to bed before taking a look at the twelfth Earth Gate. Outside a storm was brewing. I turned up the collar of my coat and shivered as I followed the invisible trail in the darkness. It was further than I remembered. The soil became soft and at places even muddy before I reached the park. When I turned on the torch the cone of light caught a small gnome jumping behind a mound on which an angel was sitting cautioning the visitor to be quiet. I just stood there for a moment. From all around there was the sound of water streaming down from the mountain. On the other side I could hear the Les Contes river rushing by on its way to the estuary where it flowed into the sea far away, reminding me of the journey of man. What was going on here? There was a lively commotion among the gnomes and elves which were apparently celebrating something. It was as if the grass, the bushes and the trees were being garlanded with unconditional, spontaneous and rare festoons of happiness. It was the kind of happiness that took me by the hand and led me between the bushes towards the cosmic gate. I let the cone of light inspect the sculpture that marked the location of the gate. It looked as if it was made to specific measurements. An enormous quartz hung in the middle. I switched off the torch and stood still until my eyes adjusted to the darkness. I felt the power of the place after a few minutes. The Gate radiated faintly like a large ethereal heart beating slowly while it connected the sky and earth.

When I got to my room I felt immediately that I had a visitor. I couldn't see anyone but there was no doubt. The stranger, who by now was quite familiar, was present.

I lay down on the bed and leafed through the yellow pamphlet reading here and there. It seemed to consist of a series of readings made by the team of psychics mentioned earlier, during their journey to France. Some of it seemed to be a clutter of well-known theories and unclear, occult allegories that said nothing new.

The Book of Love and the Crystal Skull, however, touched on something that I hoped the pamphlet could explain.

But I must have fallen asleep because suddenly I find myself on a beach covered with big rocks. In between the rocks are stretches of white sand and black seaweed.

I spot a boat on the horizon, which is slowly getting closer to the beach.

I can taste the air, salty from the waves beating hard against the coast.

A carpet of clouds rolls itself out in front of me.

In the same instant, I see the true face of my earlier life revealing itself in the abandoned track from the travels of my soul.

The window of time is open, the curtain of my memory is waving in the wind and everything is blue and white and green.

Now the boat, without sail or oars, touches the beach.

In the boat a black woman. At her feet a book.

The air is filled with salamanders.

Filled with fire.

Fire!

She is speaking through the fire:

'My name is Neith. The Queen of Heaven.

'I am everything that was, everything that is, and everything which is to come. I am the abyss of the Universe from where the

sun rose for the first time at the dawn of time. No mortal has yet been able to break through my veil. The crown I wear is red and is called Net. I am dark as the nocturnal, star-filled sky, and on its distended arch I am the gate between life and death. I am the isogynic, self-reproducing virgin creating life in all the worlds. With my boat I weave the destinies of all people and all the universes. I am the goddess of magic and the incarnated, eternal, feminine principle.'

7

The rain beat against the windows when I woke up in St Francis of Assisi's room at Les Contes. I woke up with the feeling that the night had brought some kind of understanding. There was no doubt that I had reached a crossroads and I had to take stock.

My journey had not taken me to the dragon, the princess or the Holy Grail. Instead, I was left with a handful of clues, which I couldn't fit together.

Perhaps it was time to go back to Denmark?

Although I clearly felt the presence of Sylvia I still needed to sit opposite her so that I could ask the questions which had been building up in the wake of my journey.

'You want to come?' I asked the being standing in the corner watching me.

No answer.

I got up and showered.

Afterwards, when I was putting away my notes, a folded piece of paper fell on to the floor.

I picked it up and read it:

'Marie Périllos – Belo Bar.'

I remembered the waitress at the café where I had experienced the uncanny déjà-vu. Was this yet another coincidence, that I happened to stumble on the note, which then reminded me of her? Hardly that.

I said goodbye to Leny and Mar after breakfast.

'Do come back soon,' they shouted as I drove out of the driveway. This was the only thing I was certain of. I wanted to come back to this moving place very soon.

I enjoyed sitting in the car letting one beautiful landscape after the other pass me by and driving through the small villages situated like pearls on a string all the way to Perpignan. Driving through Estagel I noticed a sign saying 'Brocante' – 'Bric-a-Brac'

I have passed hundreds of shops like this without stopping. However, something made me park the car and visit exactly this one.

'Well, what are you up to now?' I whispered to my invisible travelling companion.

I stepped into a large hall filled with all kinds of things, from old pieces of furniture, magazines, sculptures, paintings, flower pots, coins and stamps to junk that couldn't possibly have any sale value. I strolled slowly along among this explosion of things until I stopped in front of an old chest of drawers. A picture frame was leaning against the end of the chest of drawers, with the picture on the other side. As if my hand was being guided, I leaned forward and turned it around.

I couldn't believe my own eyes.

In this woven picture she was kneeling in deep prayer, in a

Joan of Arc

coat-of-mail and holding a banner, which, it is said, she never let out of her sight.

Joan of Arc!

On the banner was written: 'Jhesus-Marie.'

Yeshua Mary. As if it was one name. Just by pronouncing the name, a power which seemed as if it could move mountains manifested itself immediately. Was this the power Joan of Arc had invoked and to which she had subjected herself?

I drove into Narbonne early in the afternoon. After a couple of attempts, I soon found the small square with the Belo Bar. I parked the car and went in. An elderly man was standing at the bar serving customers. I waited patiently. Then, finally, it was my turn:

'Excuse me, does Marie Périllos work here?'

The man looked at me, perplexed, as if he did not understand what I was saying.

'Sorry,' he said, 'Who are you looking for?'

'Marie Périllos,' I answered.

'Sorry, you must have misunderstood something, she doesn't work here.'

He turned around in order to make a cup of coffee on a machine.

His answer took me completely by surprise.

'She is tall, with dark hair and about twenty-five years old.'

He shook his head while knocking the coffee-grounds out of the filter.

'I'm sorry, I don't know her.'

Before I managed to say anything else he disappeared into a back room. I was confused. I gave up and left the Belo Bar. Was I going crazy?

'Please help me,' I whispered to my invisible friend, but there was no answer.

When I got back to Denmark I went directly to Charlotten-lund to see Sylvia. Opening the door, she smiled, and I couldn't help thinking that she had known all the time how things would turn out. I simply felt like a very young soul in her presence. I really was in the company of a very mature lady.

'Come in, Lars, good to see you again.'

'Just my words,' I said, hanging my coat on a hook in the hallway. I felt a sense of relief standing there in her living room and looking into her gentle eyes. It was like looking into an eternity of time, past as well as not yet seen; it was like looking into the teasing and unpredictable mind of a little girl, like looking into the innermost and deepest reservoir of wisdom.

I had come home.

Her golden laughter activated the ethereal game of glass-pearls, and I imagined hearing Salome's laughter the way Magdalene heard her so often then, two thousand years ago. She immediately followed me. Her attention lifted me. She saw me the way I was. She saw right through all my barricades.

'Let's get to work. It looks as if I'm only kept alive in order to finish my business with you, so let's not waste any time.'

She motioned for me to sit down.

'Have you had a good time?'

It was one of those rhetorical questions to which she knew very well the answer beforehand. It was more like a strange kind of politeness she felt compelled to show me in order to make me feel at home. I therefore waited with my answer, and anyway what could I say? She sensed my awkwardness and laughed:

'I know what you mean, but let me hear about your journey.'

I told her about the Voice and my invisible friend, about my nocturnal visit to the lake, about Les Contes and my night in the Cave of Bethlehem. When I had finished my story she smiled and I sensed a kind of approval in her look.

'Do you know about the mysterious birth?'

'You mean the Christian one?'

'Bethlehem symbolizes something deeper. Directly translated, Bethlehem means *The House of Bread*. What is meant here is bread or food in a divine sense. Bethlehem, then, is to be understood allegorically and may be translated as *The Location for Divine Food*. The cave where Yeshua was born became a holy place at the moment of birth. No matter where this cave was situated, geographically, at the moment of birth it became Bethlehem. A location where the influx of a higher consciousness has maximum concentration. This happens at a symbolic level each time a person comes to understand his higher Self. When the old one dies and a new one is born. When you laid down on the stone altar in the Cave of Bethlehem it was an expression of your willingness to give up the lower for the higher. It is a ritual known since the beginning of time. They knew about it in the old religion of Zarathustra and in ancient Egypt. The three wise men, the three magi who found Yeshua in the cave, came from Babylon in Persia. The three wise men represent the tripartite principle of Unity. The question now is whether or not you were visited by three magi during the ritual?'

Her gaze was both lengthy and intensely focused. It was quite clear that she wanted to guide my attention to my experiences in the cave in order to make me see them once more. I told her about Sarangarel and Oyugun. I told her about the Voice and the strange being I sensed most of the time, that had been closest on the morning I woke up in the Cave of Bethlehem. But I had no recollection of three wise men.

112

We sat quietly for a moment. Then she continued:

'Pay attention to the archetype of the magus. The three magi or wise men may also be three wise female magi, or three qualities in yourself. When do you leave again?'

This, however, was a question, which took me by surprise. What did she mean? I had just come back. Again she continued before I had time to think about her question:

'You see, you must find the answers to the questions you seek in yourself. But the prerequisite for that is that you go back to Montségur and find the hidden cave in the mountain.'

'The hidden cave?'

I was dumbfounded.

'Up until now you and the Seer have only moved about on the "outside" of the mystery. You have climbed the mountain, you have found the outer point of the Grail in the courtyard itself. You might say that you have conquered the masculine side of Montségur. You have to find the feminine side *inside* the mountain.'

I was about to fall off my chair, that's how dumbfounded I felt. During the six years of working with the Seer on Montségur I had never heard about a hidden cave inside the mountain.

'How do you know about this cave?'

She smiled secretively but didn't answer my question directly.

'I am asking you to go on a quest.'

'Where on the mountain is it situated?'

'You'll find out. But there is an opening leading into the mountain itself. Remember the legend of the Grail about Esclarmonde who opened the mountain during the siege by the Inquisition and threw the Grail into it. Although, of course, this must be understood symbolically, a great truth is hidden here. You really ought to be able to find this truth right

113

now and right here, but with the risk of understanding only a small part of what I'm trying to pass on to you. Your past as a magus demands that you still need the physical journey and the physical ritual, in spite of your growing abilities as an astral traveller. That is why you must go down and find the mystery yourself. Your experience in the Bethlehem cave was not just a preliminary exercise. The cave in the Montségur mountain is quite different. Do you want more coffee?'

She poured before I had time to answer.

'Then there is also another person I would like to talk to you about: Joan of Arc. Do you know her well?'

This was almost too much. I could hardly believe my own ears. When I had recovered I told her about my experiences with Joan of Arc. It didn't seem to jolt her at all. She just smiled and continued:

'There are a few things I must tell you so that you may understand the mystery of Joan of Arc. You know the Sophia aspect, the old wisdom aspect, which through the ages has been carried by various historical persons and various feminine archetypes? The sisters of Sophia, if one can put it that way, have had many names. To repeat it once more: there are two Sophia aspects, a higher and a lower one. The lower one has its foundations in the instincts while the higher one has its foundations on the purely spiritual level. The instincts are of course also tied to the spiritual level in a subtle way, however, at a level with a lower vibration, so to speak. There are no words to cover this or names that are sufficiently precise. That is why any attempt to explain this may seem vague and unclear. It may nevertheless be possible to get an idea of them.'

She looked at me as if to make sure I could follow her.

'You may read all the basic stuff about Sophia. I just want to underscore the fact that the higher aspect of Sophia has

114

a name, which may not be enunciated yet. That is why you must find it yourself, which shouldn't be too difficult for you if you just follow your intuition. You neither can nor should avoid sexuality, however, as this fantastic force may be transformed. In one way you might say that the sexual force is the curse of man because it is and has always been used to create ties and to maintain the power. It is the energy that keeps people in slavery with the strongest possible power, creating dependence, depression and pain. But it is also one which offers fantastic potential. In this day and age, tantra has undergone a renaissance. Unfortunately, it often doesn't go much further than being a refined way of expressing your sexuality in the name of spirituality: a welcome spice with which to pep up a stagnated sex life and sexual pleasures as such. Most people must live their sexuality in good as well as in bad times, while a few people seem to have transformed it as early as the time of their birth. These are the so-called *Venus people*. They do not have to transform their sexuality but can function as sexual healers, to put it one way. This is what some of the so-called prostitute Moon priestesses were trained to be in the old Ishtar and Isis temples. These women sacrificed themselves in order to lift man out of darkness, out of the jaws of death, in order to put him in the sky as the sun he is meant to be. As the representatives of the moon they always reflected the sun. They knew about the two shrines, the earthly vagina and the heavenly vagina. Both these shrines are protected by seven veils, each of which represents a step leading deeper and deeper into the mysteries.'

She stopped once more in order to see if I was following her. She laughed at the sight of me. Probably because I looked totally enraptured.

'Practically all mystery traditions talk about these seven veils or steps. There are really fourteen: seven lower and

115

seven higher ones. The understanding of these things is the quest you are now going on. You cannot avoid your sexuality, but remember that it is only a necessary step on the way to the higher Sophia.'

My head was filled with questions I wanted answered, but I didn't know where to begin. But it didn't really matter since Sylvia so easily seemed to catch the thread I was trying to find.

'I'm sure you have noticed that Mary Magdalene is depicted with a human skull at the altar in the church at Rennes-le-Château, just like all the other altars to her in the Languedoc area. I'm sure you have been contemplating the meaning of this.'

I nodded eagerly. She got up and disappeared into the next room. It took a while before she returned due to her reduced mobility. She placed a picture in front of me. It showed a man pouring water from a big pitcher. To the right behind him a small figure was stepping through a gigantic skull. At the bottom of the picture seven lotus flowers were depicted.

'As you may have seen, it is a woman walking through the mouth of the skull. The mouth symbolizes the heavenly vagina. She is walking through the throat-chakra. The man is the Water Carrier. And the seven lotus flowers symbolize the seven veils, energy centres or steps of initiation. It is the birth of spiritual love. In this connection the thymus gland behind the heart plays an important role. We are talking about transformation all the way to the hormonal level. It is the birth of the divine fire in the fifth chamber of the heart. The lower and higher Sophia are represented by eros and agape. On the external level you might say that Mount Carmel symbolizes the higher sphere while the mount of Venus symbolizes the lower one. Do you know anything about Carmel consciousness?'

'Only through my travels in Israel in 1969 and 1979 as well as the spirituality which is partly communicated through the teaching of the Essenes and partly through Teresa of Avila and John of the Teaching of the Cross which ended in the founding of the order of the Carmelites in the Middle Ages.'

'Good. Remember that there are three women who have played a major role in the European esoteric tradition, and who, each in her own way, is connected to Carmel. They are Joan of Arc, Teresa of Avila and Elizabeth I of England. In the tradition in which I was initiated, *Anyahitha* is the great world mother, the embodiment of the basic principle, the unity of all things. She was the first one to postulate true monism. She is the motherly creating principle of nature. She acknowledged the fertilizing principle of the spirit of the time in the fatherhood of spirit. Progress and development is only possible through the intimate connection of both these principles, the total union of matter and spirit. What is new in our day is the unity of water and fire. The old Veda of India represents the water while the Avesta writings of Persia represent the fire. The Avesta grew out of the Veda. Out of Avesta grew the Sufi, Jewish and Christian traditions.'

She spread out her arms.

'I'm sorry if I'm skipping from this to that, but you must keep your ears open. There is so much to pass on.'

'What was this about Joan of Arc?'

'Right, we mustn't forget her. *Jehanne* of the Arc, the Girl from Orléans, or just the Virgin. This was the traditional name for a priestess in a cult that communicated with nature spirits, fairies, elves and the like. Joan herself, during her trial, told that she had received her first visions at the 'Tree of Fairies'. This was a gathering place for a Diana cult in her home town of Domrémy. She received a major part of her visions from St Catherine of Alexandria and St Margaret. The name Catherine has its origin in the Greek *cathar* – 'pure', which certainly had some influence on the Cathars later on, who celebrated this saint as one of their own. The cult of Diana had spread far into Europe when Christianity started spreading. And the Christians, especially, considered Diana to be their major competitor. They degraded her from being "the Queen of Heaven" to "the Queen of witches". In the Acts of the Apostles the total destruction of the temple of the great Goddess Diana is ordered. In the course of time, all the temples of Diana thus became the temples of Mary. The Inquisition considered Diana to be the goddess of the heathens with whom witches danced at night, and church dignitaries called her the devil herself. In spite of this, they actually worshipped her until the time of Joan of Arc when she was considered the Moon Goddess. There were even places where she was worshipped in the local churches. Even today she is honoured at some places as the protector of hunters. So you see, the great feminine power cannot so easily be destroyed. It always finds a way. St Margaret incarnated Aphrodite Marina, Pelagia and was called "the Pearl of the Sea". "The Pearly Gate" of Aphrodite was a metaphor for a woman's sex, like the Gate of Paradise. Her name is connected to Marga, which in Sanskrit means "the Way" or "the Gate" through ritual sexuality to Paradise for tantric male and female yogis.'

'But how could it at all be possible that a young girl, overnight, seventeen years of age, suddenly found herself at the head of the French army?'

'Well, it really didn't happen overnight. Someone had prepared her for the task.'

'Who?'

She was contemplating how much to tell me.

'You'll probably find a good explanation when you revisit Rennes-le-Château and Montségur. And when you are in the village, you ought also to visit the church. It may hold some of the answers. Have you seen that?'

I hadn't. The church in Montségur was always locked when I was there. However, I had never had the thought that I should or could visit the church. By now, I recognized the ill-concealed challenge in Sylvia's voice so easily that I knew, although it was toned down, that it was her way of planting a clue in my consciousness. There was, however, one question I had to ask:

'You said at one time that where the dragon is that is where the princess is and vice versa. You said that a virgin was waiting for me somewhere out there. What did you mean by that?'

She could hardly avoid laughing. She kept me waiting for a long time before giving in:

'Don't spend too much time thinking about that. I'm sure that the Board of Directors will send you a virgin when the time is ripe.'

'Send me a virgin?' I looked at her, questioningly.

She nodded:

'Well, that is how it happened for me when I was at your stage. I really thought that I was done with my sexuality, but I was wrong. My teacher, van der Stok, drew my attention to the fact that I still had something in me, which had to be transformed. One day there was a knock on my door and a handsome young man was standing on my doorstep, and he thought that he and I had some work to do in the tantric department.'

Her laughter practically opened the room so that every closed heart or stagnated mind had to surrender. When she had regained her composure, she continued:

119

Aquarius

'Well anyway, what I wanted to say is this. The ability to think is not the greatest of man's abilities. The ability to think is simply a product of objectivity contaminated by emotions. Thinking is noise. A Thought, however, is silence, because it is being certain, freed from superficial emotions. Thinking is limited by the thinker. Man is himself a divine form of thought. And when man rests here, thinking is not needed in the way we understand it. What is my point here? Well, surrender to the Thought of which you are an expression. Each and every person is a Thought from God. Each and every individual must learn how to be in it and how to fulfil the mission, which is hidden in the current form of thought. It is fine to ask questions, but it is better to be able to stay quiet and to listen. This is the only way in which to get the true answers. In this state of mind we even receive answers which are not the result of a question, because the knowledge or the certainty here is in itself a part of the individual's foundation based on his specific incarnation. We are so busy trying to get it all, and in pursuit of this we so easily miss the essential. Our lives are built on gossip, judgement and avarice. The time has come when it is no longer enough just to talk about fighting these evils, we now have to do something. If man wasn't so concerned about the physical reality he would understand that the legends and myths of the past are part and parcel of each individual's innermost being and not necessarily historical facts. Each and every individual is affected by one or more archetypes in their current incarnation. The archetypes each provide a matrix for the various qualities in man. We must let ourselves be guided by these archetypes in our own lives, live their dramas but also remember to continue to build on to them. We carry the responsibility of our own personal mythology. This may be one of the most important reasons for our existence.'

'Does this mean that everything is predestined?'

'Only to a certain extent. Man has got his free will because he is of the world we live in, which is written in many places. But nothing is written which may not be corrected. You must understand that there is a meaning to the fact that we have been reincarnated into exactly this universe. There are many other universes into which we might have been reincarnated, but we are here on earth because each of us has something that must be transformed here. A part of us, our higher being, is also present in other universes at the same time where we are expressed through totally different shapes, identities and personalities. We are all basically a part of the divine thought form. Each and every one of us represents a spark from the divine fire. Remember that. The brilliant thing about myths is that they always offer wisdom, which will open that which is closed and expand the understanding of the mysteries to those initiated. And as long as the myths are passed on, their secrets are kept by those who have ears with which to hear and eyes with which to see. Intellectual figments of the imagination speak to the brain; the myths speak to the heart. Dreams are personal myths. Myths are collective dreams.'

She leaned back. Once more, she had transformed the room into a holy sphere in the universe.

'Well, you're something else, you are,' she said smiling and shaking her head. 'I had prepared to go home, and then you show up here and disturb me. Why did you do that?'

In spite of the sound of reproach in her voice she didn't look at all as if she blamed me for anything. On the contrary, I clearly felt that the cheeky meddling of destiny and the Board of Directors really suited her very well.

'Be prepared that now you'll be confronted with your past. That means that people with whom you have had close relations in the past will come and try to balance the old scores. If I'm not wrong, there'll be quite a few women coming into your life. Well, this may be difficult. Be gentle but firm.'

She stressed the last few words.

'Do not get stuck in personal stuff. The images manifesting themselves for you have something to do with you but shouldn't be interpreted on a strictly personal level. Don't get caught up in the past. Your own history is only important in so far as it serves in transforming your lower self and the collective part. Forget about punishment, guilt and shame. Look at the archetypes in the collective light. Look at the overall picture.'

She stopped talking. We sat for a long time. Far too long for my liking. There had been a change. The light mood which had been prevalent had now disappeared. I could see in her face that something was brewing. Something which worried her. She leaned towards me and said:

'Lars, I don't quite know how to say this, because I want to be certain that you understand the seriousness of it.'

She took her time. The sudden change made me nervous. She put her hand on mine:

'Are you really aware of what it is you have agreed to do?'

There was something almost momentous in her voice.

I felt deep down that I could answer her question with a decisive yes, but just at that moment I hesitated.

'What you have undertaken involves leaving everything if that is what it takes.'

I nodded.

'Believe me, I know more than most people what you are going through right now. Your "lapses", your nocturnal journeys, The Voice, the slightly too-well-timed coincidences and your peeks into the ethereal level. But what would you say if I told you that all this is nothing compared to what you may expect?'

It is hard to explain, but somehow I felt relieved that she finally opened the floodgates. Although it was quite frightening on one level, at another it seemed like only the natural continuation of the journey I was on. Her words did not take me by surprise. I felt that I could say yes. Also with this little part of me still feeling insecure. Perhaps it was simply the seriousness of the moment creating this feeling.

'Are you ready to surrender to what is coming? Are you ready to let yourself be surged by energies, which might kill you if you are not well prepared? Can you say that you are ready with all your heart? Look at me and you'll see someone who has experienced more than one transformation. I lost my sight, my hearing and the use of my limbs for a week a few years after my initiation at Montségur. I was lost in the deepest darkness, shut off from the world and other people. If anything may be called *the dark night of the soul*, I assure you, that this was it. This was not for beginners. I simply dissolved and was put together again. You cannot explain something like that. But would you be able to say yes to that?'

A new kind of attention showed itself. Her story had awakened something in me. It was a totally different being sitting opposite me than the Sylvia who moments ago had been pouring coffee and taught me about yet another step on my road. This was a 180-degree change. This was the naked existence talking. She once more got up with difficulty and went into the next room. This time it didn't take long before she was sitting opposite me again.

'I'm going to give you this picture in order to remind you of what is coming.' She handed me an old picture from the sixties. A woman with eyes looking as if they would be able to see through anything, sitting in a contemporary setting.

There was something totally surreal about this picture. Something sinister. The woman was clearly in a state of mind in which everything that may be contained in a human being, everything light and everything dark, is on its way to the surface. It was a being who was not only human but also something else that couldn't be explained.

'This was taken one week before I caved in. As you can see, the process was already well on its way when the picture was taken. This is what a person looks like when the self is leaving them. What you see in these eyes is the same process as Yeshua went through in Gethsemane. It is the quintessence of "Thy will be done."'

She leaned back in her chair but without taking her eyes off me.

I was staring intently at the picture but couldn't recognize her. They were really two different people.

'What other options do I have?'

'Well, that is a good question. That's also what I said. When you are exactly at this point you have no choice. You think you do, but in reality you don't. Because you know very well what a "no" would mean. Knowing that, you can only say yes. On the other hand, I understand very well when someone is signing off. There are people doing that each minute of every day all year round.'

'What is going to happen?'

'You are going to be taught in a way which is quite different from the teaching you have had until now. It will take you much further away from normal reality. It will be more difficult for you to relate to your everyday life and its activities. But it is a challenge to do just that.'

Our meeting was about to end.

'But there is so much I would like to talk to you about. When can we meet again?'

'Remember what I told you. We are in contact telepathically. If you can let go of the little control freak, your intellectual self, and I believe you are on the way to doing just that, then leave the rest to God. Faith, faith, faith, and then more than anything else, patience.'

'Can't you give me just a single clue?'

She hesitated. Then she whispered:

'*The Queen of Sheba.*'

'The Queen of Sheba? Give me just one more clue.'

She laughed heartily. Then she became serious again:

'Hm. All right, I'll tell you this time. But it may have far-reaching and powerful consequences because it doesn't just call for a little, it calls for *everything* in order to obtain this piece of knowledge. You have asked me and the answer is "*Venus*".'

We said our goodbyes in the hallway. I kissed her on the cheek. The crystal above her head radiated with a golden light like a crown of live fire. In the eternity of the blue in her eyes I saw her unconditional love and acceptance radiating out towards me, and I felt how it found its way into every cell of my body, cleaning all my energy field.

'Hurry up,' she said as I stepped out of her door, 'I know you can do it.'

She waved at me from the balcony. I waved back.

PART II

SHEKHINAH

8

Dear reader, I ask not for your patience nor your understanding. I cannot take responsibility for you. If you haven't put the book aside by now perhaps it is time to do so now. It is your choice.

What I'm going to tell you is really a pipe dream in so far as there are no words, which can describe it. And why make the attempt, you may well ask?

Because it was a task assigned to me.

What I'm going to tell you may seem confused; however, confusion is not the purpose.

Seen from our small hiding place there isn't much time. From the point of view of Heaven there is only eternity. This is the paradox of man.

The written word may seem dull. And although words may open something in us, something which gives us hope of other options, their scope is still limited.

Are we prepared to put aside all our regular interpretations of everything? Are we at all able to imagine an endless space in which our ideas and our measures are too small and where they do not fit in? Are we able to imagine a reality where we do not define ourselves in dualistic terms?

A person might be what we normally call clever, intelligent, even a genius, and, however, be totally confused when faced with such a reality. What do we understand by the concept of 'serving God'? We do not know anything. We are not capable of understanding anything at all.

The word 'God' makes us clam up, and after that we do not hear anything.

When we leave language as we know it and let ourselves be dissolved by the concept 'To know and to serve God', it then takes something else and something more than a learning ability and intelligence.

Even the agile intellect does not understand anything when its well-known instruments of navigation are removed from it. Instead, it immediately takes hold of the first available prejudice. The first prerequisite for approaching endlessness is the understanding that we do not understand anything. No judgement. No preconceived ideas. No damnation. No opposites.

Where are we then?

Who are we then?

I am not black because you are white. I am not happy because you are sad. I am not violent because you are a pacifist. I am not a social democrat because you are a conservative. I am not spiritual because you are not. I am not a Hindu because you are a Christian, not a Muslim because you are an atheist. I see no far-reaching difference between us any more. You are carrying a seed that is identical to mine. You may have come here from Sirius and I from Aarhus, but we both arrived here together and both of us came from the stars. We are made from the same matter. The Universe is just a small fraction in a much larger equation. The equation has been solved long ago but it is constantly in motion. You see, there were never any opposites. *Opposites are only to be found in the separated mind. And the separated mind is a result of free will which did not have the courage to be free.* Thus the eternal conflict. Man has reserved the right to be doubtful. Then he got frightened. And now, he is paralysed by fear and caught in his own trap.

Each time we let another carry the shadow we ourselves cannot contain, another dark chapter is added to the cosmic memory. When one of us self-righteously promotes himself and only sees his own version of the truth, yet another limitation and another wound is added to the world. When a whole population is burdened by the shadow of another nation, the effects are always catastrophic. If you cannot contain your shadows and thus your whole being, you are apt to create and to maintain images of enemies. If you deny the so-called dark sides of existence you accumulate even more darkness. This is the challenge that we, the so-called spiritual people, have to face each and every day. Only by integrating our hidden aspects may we transform darkness and be able to see that it is just another side of the light. Any healing of a torn world begins with the acceptance by each one of us of responsibility for our own mess. This takes courage and insight because you are not often able to change anything if you do not know it.

Man is a higher being. However, we may still learn a lot from the animals. We say: the animals are not as fully developed as we are. That is why we treat them any way we like. The animal within our own being, however, is out of control.

So, Sylvia was right. My life never again became what it once was. The breaking down of the old sum total, which once was christened Lars, began the day when, for the first time, I dared leave my bewildered mind in the hands of eternity. For a fraction of a second only, later slightly more – but even a little is not to be sneezed at, exactly because the ideas of 'little' or 'more' have no say in the open field of consciousness. It is only here in this world, in this mental hospital, that we need the little language.

Man and woman are seen as opposites. Man goes out and woman goes in. And still they are created for each other. The out-turned fits into the in-turned. When the two unite all opposites are cancelled out. The need to express oneself in the one is counterbalanced by the need to be quiet in the other.

Willpower and the need for knowledge are the prerequisites for the possibility of having a say in the old world. In the new world I only know one single thing, which is that I know nothing.

Is that wisdom?

I don't know.

Sex and religion have for long been irreconcilable elements. When they are put together noise is usually the outcome.

The word *religion* comes from the Latin word *religio* which again comes from *religare* – tying together, uniting, gathering.

Lust is to take something.

Love is to give something.

What is the problem?

That we cannot control lust?

The Church says that Yeshua is the one begotten son. But Yeshua himself said that we are all children of God. Is the Church right and Yeshua wrong?

Does it really matter? Well yes, but only as far as it concerns the question of maintaining worldly power in the hands of the Church.

If we are all the children of God, do we need the Church for anything? Well, yes, but only if the Church understands the deeper meaning of the words of Yeshua: the Temple is in the heart.

Where the heart is that is where the Temple and its treasures are!

The Kingdom of God is in you and all around you!

Yeshua loved/loves Mariam Magdal. He often kissed/kisses her on her mouth. How can we know this when the word 'mouth' is not to be seen in *The Gospel of Philip* because there is a hole in the manuscript at this place? We know because this is how the initiated greeted each other at the time of Yeshua.

Who was/is Mariam?

I am the first and the last,

I am the honoured one and the damned one,

I am the whore and the holy one.

Are these statements expressions of any kind of opposites?

No, on the contrary, they express the exact identity of the one with the One, and of that which no more *is* the opposite of that *which doesn't exist*. In these three sentences Mariam embraces the universe. She is *whole* and thus *holy*.

Magdal means *the elevated one* or *the one from the temple tower*. The Temple in Jerusalem had three towers. Yeshua had three Marys around him: Miriam, Mari and Mariam. The mother, the sister and the beloved one. They were three and yet they were only one.

According to the gospels, Yeshua cast out seven evil spirits from Mariam but the gospels have forgotten or left out that Mariam also opened seven gates in Yeshua.

On a Babylonian stone tablet the following inscription is to be seen: 'In the depth of the sea they are seven. In the light of Heaven they are seven. From the sea (Mari) they are rising from the hidden quietness.'

Would this be the two Sophia aspects that Sylvia was talking about?

What is revealing itself here?

One allegory after the other. And allegories were the language of the initiated ones at the time of Yeshua and Mariam. And some of those who mastered this language were the Therapists of Lake Mareotis at Alexandria.

There is a room – a secret recess of the soul – the innermost room in every human being where we hide and tend to the most vulnerable aspects of ourselves, where we hide the deepest sorrow and loneliness, where we fall to our knees and cry out in the desert.

This is where I have found Yeshua and Mariam. This is where they live in me. They have always lived there, though under different names.

Dear reader! You who are struggling with your own shadows! You who have no meaning in your life! You who feel Yeshua and Mariam so close. And you who do not. Here is a prayer:

Sit, stand or lie down with a straight back.

Feel your breath.

Go into the recesses of your soul. Go to your most intimate room. Place your left hand on the centre of your heart (at the middle of your breastbone).

Place your right hand on top of the left one.

Now, pull light through the palms of your hands, into your heart and out again while you silently say 'I am', breathing in and 'love', breathing out.

'I am love.'

Stay in this vibration, sitting or lying down as long as you can or want to. That is how you get healing hands. Use them lovingly. If you are not using your hands you may use this prayer anywhere and at any time. All day long if you like.

It happened just as Sylvia had predicted. Women with whom I had had some kind of past began turning up in my consulting room and at my talks, knowing or not knowing what was really going on.

Young Muslim girls began coming to my consulting room who, independently of each other, had been sent to me by a Sudanese Sufi master living in Denmark, whom I had never heard about. These girls related to the female power and they were very eager to be able to express themselves freely about deep spiritual subjects which they could no longer neglect. They were struggling with a sense of modesty, which on the one hand was beautiful and pure, but on the other had such a limiting effect on them that I sensed that it had taken great effort to seek my help. It is one thing to visit a male stranger, but a non-Muslim one at that. That must have caused them a great deal of trouble. One of the girls was very psychic without knowing how to apply her ability. She was exceptionally beautiful. Dark with big, black, radiant and almond-shaped eyes that looked right through you. Although she was dark you could easily see the dark shadows under her eyes telling a tale of many problems, but also emphasizing the intensity of her eyes. It was during a session with her when she was presenting her situation that I saw the very being of her soul and its years of tribulations.

She had neglected herself in one lifetime after the other for the benefit of others. I saw her with the men to whom she had subjected herself as well as all her incarnations as a slave and a servant. I saw the incarnation we had shared in Syria. She had been a servant at a palace belonging to a rich merchant and I a priest at a nearby temple. She was also very beautiful during this incarnation. I managed to arrange her freedom in exchange for her giving herself to me.

I saw her working in a temple in another incarnation, not in Babylon, Jerusalem, Heliopolis or Alexandria, but in Ethiopia.

Another image, which kept coming back to me was the boat without oars, with the Black Madonna and the book on board. The waves were beating against the beach, and I could hear the old Sufi master's sound of *no coast*. I saw the shape of her in the fog, wrapped in a turquoise cloak, standing upright in the boat while it slowly floated into the bay of Marseilles. Her name was Sarah.

Black Sarah. Sarah the Seer!

Another moving encounter was a meeting with Sarangarel, the singing shaman, who in this incarnation, apart from being one of the best sound-healers of our day and age, also turned out to be a dear friend whom I had known for years. We now got the explanation of the mutual attraction between us, which made it easier to contain the feelings and to accept the fact that in the present incarnation she is happily married with two lovely children. Instead, we may work together with sound and healing.

Other women I met had been my subordinates as nuns in convents in one of my incarnations as a prelate in France while others were connected to various incarnations in Lemuria, Atlantis, China, India, Egypt, Persia, the Middle East, Spain and Germany. Women of all ages whom I have met again and with whom I have been able to form friendly and professional relationships.

Over a period of two years, more than thirty women came to me claiming to be incarnations of Mary Magdalene. How could that be? Perhaps it was just a sign of the power of the new feminine archetype. It simply incarnated into more than one woman. Actually, it even incarnated into men.

A female artist came to me in order to show me a locket she had found at the bottom of a river in Cathar country. On one side, Magdalene's image of a six-pointed star with the heart-cross in the middle as well as alchemical symbols surrounding it. On the other side, the image of a five-pointed star engraved with star writing and uniting the elements of fire, water, earth, air and ether.

While I was signing books in a bookshop, another female artist gave me some postcards with two of her paintings. One was called 'The Female Seer', and the other, 'Blue Angel'. And this happened just as I was writing this book, dear reader, the one you are holding in your hand.

In an old film a journalist is asking the old sage Carl Gustav Jung whether or not he believes in God. There is a long sequence of total silence while the camera dwells on an almost trance-like Jung smoking his pipe. After a length of time which on the TV of today would be considered light-years Jung lifts his head and says:

'No . . . I do not believe in God.'

Another long pause:

'I know!'

One cannot imagine a more definite yes to the great mystery. Here is no insecurity, no dogma, no self-righteousness or self-congratulation. Here is the simple wondering, certainty and emotion.

But the *yes* of Jung, nevertheless, has its limitation. He was not able to lift it out of the field of psychology. He did not think that man was able to understand something metaphysically, only psychologically. Through his depth psychology Jung gave us a language in which to get closer to the archetypal and the subconscious. However, in the field without a language he had to keep silent.

This is where man is today: facing the wall behind which self-development, traditional astrology and depth psychology do not have any part and are unable to help man further towards transcendence. On the other side of this wall you have to empty the cup of all acquired learning. All the usual concepts and ideas must be dissolved. We are talking more or less about self-liquidation. What is left then is the essence of the centre of the soul, the word, or the sound which was at the beginning and which is forever – the great silence. It is the decisive farewell to any kind of materialism. The personal ego or *the little self* is an extremely cunning and stubborn state of mind, which does not refrain from the use of fast, prayer and charity as a way of maintaining the image of itself as an enlightened and holy person. An ego sitting on a pillow meditating for twenty years is still an ego sitting on a pillow meditating for twenty years. Nothing else. You are not Christian, Muslim, Buddhist, Hindu or spiritually enlightened just because you say that you are.

My situation was constantly changing. However, it was always, at any given time, dependent on the degree of availability I could muster towards the powers with which I was in contact. Every day I had to start all over again searching within myself for the causes of my actions. Nothing is easier than falling prey to delusions and becoming inflated. In a weak moment one may easily misunderstand one's own position and be tempted by the dream of being important. It is only human. However, in connection with spirituality, it is the mark of an infantile level. On the other hand, I also realized that not being willing to fulfil your role is just as blasphemous as wanting to overplay it. Behind this false modesty often lies a latent megalomania. It was more than merely a question of finding the balance between the principle of 'just who do you think you are?' and hubris. This was a totally new, ethical challenge. Perhaps it is necessary to get lost in the ego's maze in order to come face to face with your own self-righteousness, judgements and hypocrisy? You either flee back on to your pink spiritual cloud forgetting what you have seen, or you open your heart to the cleansing humour, which is able to look at the touching but also totally ridiculous betrayal of the little self.

My need for silence grew concurrently with the growing demand for my talks, consultations and courses. Signs of a kind of inflation became obvious from the fact that the borders between my private space and the public one became more and more invisible. What kind of situation was I getting into here? I sensed that I was getting in over my head. Was I losing my grip on my life or did it all result from the fact that control of my life was being taken away from me?

Each time I tried to control something I had to recognize that the outcome turned out accordingly: the result of that limitation, which follows its own mind and acts upon it. When, instead, I let go of my worries and stepped into the flow of things, everything happened in the best possible way. It was a question of faith and trusting in certainty. But then I also received all the help I could possibly imagine. And that at all levels.

Concurrent with all this, my sense of dissolution and spaciousness became more intense, interrupted only by the feeling that I was walking a tightrope across an abyss of memories, longing and emotional wounds which didn't really matter any more when seen from a new perspective.

Had I come to my hour of Gethsemane?

'The figure 10 symbolizes the consciousness we are approaching,' Sylvia said when I spoke to her on the phone about it.

'The figure 1 is the masculine and 0 the feminine. The figure 1 is the individual and 0 the dissolution of the individual and the unification with the Father, the move from being to non-being. The figure 1 is the point at the centre while 0 is the periphery.'

I slowly lifted my head and looked around. My pilgrim's staff was still lying outside the circle around me. What happened? I sat up. What span of time had passed? I looked at my watch but it didn't give me a clue since I didn't know at what time I had arrived at the castle. The sun had clouded over and it looked like rain. It had to be late in the afternoon because the cold came creeping out from all the gaps in the old castle walls.

I felt totally present and was vibrating like clear crystal. A faint note vibrated as it came out from the ethereal level:
mmmmmmmmmmmmmmmmmmmmmmmmmmmmmmmmmm
mmmmmmmmmmmmmmmmmmmmmmmmmmmmmmmmmm
mmmmmmmmmmmmmmmmmmmmmmmmmmmmmmmmmm
I closed my eyes and let it come.

It felt like a string being tightened to its utmost point. As if the soul itself was being tuned. The note vibrated through everything. It would last for ever, for the simple reason that it had always been and would never disappear.

This note is the red thread connecting everything, that is alive. It connects the past and the future to the present, friend with enemy, woman with man, man with God. It flows through each and every human being; however, only those who have ears with which to hear may hear it, and only those who have eyes with which to see may see.

There was much to transform. A lot of old abuse based on fear. So much that at one time it seemed boundless. There was nothing else to do but step into the circle under construction. The great subject was forgiveness. And it was during this period that I really started to understand the scope and the depth of prayer at a totally new level. All the old symptoms, the dizziness, the pain in my stomach and the back of my neck almost disappeared on that day when, undivided, I could lay a prayer in my heart. This didn't mean that I got free of physical pain, not at all, but the old pattern, which had driven me into a corner again and again, didn't exist anymore.

But there was more to come, much more . . .

9

The rumour had spread like wild-fire. They talked about it all over Damascus, among princes and paupers.

They had a new Babylonian prostitute at the Ishtar temple. Ish-a-tar.

But Ish-a-tar was not like all the others of her calling. She was fair. Fair skin and fair hair. And then she could dance with such ecstasy, they said, that no one had seen anything like it. Rumour had it that in spite of the fact that she was only nineteen years of age she was an expert in her trade. Some were offended. Others felt that she was God-sent. In reality, very few had actually seen her dance.

Hashem Ben Nari shook his head. Could this be true? But the news struck a chord deep inside him. However, he waited a few days before sending someone off to find out. In matters like these it was not appropriate for a man of his standing to show too much interest. Although he had plenty of gold to buy all the prostitutes of Syria and Babylon it wouldn't do to challenge the priests.

The messenger was sent off and he couldn't wait to have his curiosity and his lust satisfied.

But there was no reply.

He waited for two more days. Still no answer. This had never happened before.

On the third day Hashem Ben Nari went to the high priest of the temple, Sadosh.

'You must understand that Ish-a-tar is a free prostitute. She cannot be bought against her own will,' Sadosh told Ben Nari, 'and I have no power over her. The few men who have made her acquaintance would give everything they own for just ten minutes in the company of this divine creature.'

If Ben Nari hadn't been turned on before he certainly was when he heard the words of the high priest.

'I've got to see her,' he said. 'What is she like?'

Sadosh shook his head.

'How should I know? Even I haven't been allowed to see the performance of Ish-a-tar. I have just seen her shadow. You see, she's got her own bodyguard. But those who have visited her during the two weeks she has been here have more than doubled the income of the temple. So what can I say?'

Ben Nari felt faint, and the words of Sadosh only made it worse.

'What kind of power is it they ascribe to this woman. How do you know that she isn't the brood of vipers?'

The eyes of Sadosh flashed:

'She is God-sent,' he growled as if he was manifesting a curse.

'I suppose you mean that she has come *as if* she was sent by God?'

The two men stood facing each other. Sadosh realized that Ben Nari was challenging his credibility. This was a question of honour.

'Very well, I'll arrange for you to meet her and you may see for yourself.'

Seven days later Ben Nari finally received an invitation and he immediately sent a messenger with the required down-payment. His whole body vibrated in expectation when in the evening he was on his way to the temple. From the entrance hall he was led through several minor rooms where about fifteen men, most of them elderly like Ben Nari himself but also a few young men, were drinking mint tea while apparently they were waiting to be let into the Holy of Holies where Ish-a-tar was about to dance.

Time seemed to have stopped. Ben Nari sweated profusely and to him the waiting seemed like eternity. Finally, after quite a while, something seemed to happen. A curtain was drawn aside and two temple servants came in. One of them had a sheet of papyrus in his hand, a list from which he began reading in a slow voice:

'Yakob Ben David; Salek Shalem; Melchior Zantor; Yohannan Ben Yokim.'

The waiter looked up from his list and let his gaze move around from one to the other of the men gathered here as if he were looking for someone. The men whose names he had just called out were already on their feet eager like young men who enter a brothel for the first time. Ben Nari tried to catch the attention of the temple servant.

'I'm here. Ben Nari. Right here!' he said lifting his hand in the air.

The waiter, however, looked right through him.

'Paltu Nazami!'

Before Ben Nari had time to react the five men mentioned disappeared behind the curtain, which closed behind them, and a guard took up his position in front of it. All happened as if in a dream. What was this? Ben Nari had never experienced anything like it. He was not a man to whom anyone denied anything. His influence and his riches were too great for that. He just sat there, with the ten other disqualified men, feeling like a cuckold, rejected by the loved one.

Some of the men couldn't hide their disappointment. One of them felt so dismayed and cried out in such a loud voice that the temple guards came in and cleared the room. Ben Nari, however, succeeded in hiding in the shadows in a corridor where he stayed until the disturbance had died down. He could hear the enchanting music far away and he tried to imagine Ish-a-tar and her enticing dance, which could drive any man to madness. But he could not imagine the fair skin and hair of this creature. How far would she go? How daring would she be?

He disappeared into his own thoughts and slipped into a hot cave of pumping blood, which made his heart pound away to the limit of bursting. He came to at the sound of a familiar voice:

'What are you doing here?'

It was Sadosh, the high priest.

'I was passed over,' Ben Nari answered, as if it were all a nightmare from which he couldn't wake up 'I don't understand, I was passed over.'

Sadosh looked at him thoughtfully as if he didn't understand it either.

'No one knows the ways of Ish-a-tar. No one can say what she is going to do next. With her, gold is just ordinary trivia.

This is not something for which she yearns. She goes by other criteria.'

'Which criteria?'

Ben Nari was desperate:

'Tell me what her criteria are and I shall do my utmost to fulfil them.'

Sadosh looked at Ben Nari with some compassion and tried to find a solution. After all, Ben Nari was one of the most stable supporters of the temple. He had paid large sums of money over the years. He looked intently at Ben Nari:

'Do you remember this Yeshua Ben Yoasaph of whom so many stories were told a few years ago? You know the one the Romans crucified with the help of the Sanhedrin in Jerusalem?'

Ben Nari nodded. He himself had seen this Yeshua and heard him talk during a business trip to Jerusalem.

'Do you also remember that this Yeshua always had a woman at his side, Mariam, the one they call Magdal?'

Ben Nari nodded, and this time eagerly.

'Of course, I remember her clearly. She was very beautiful. What is it about her?'

'I know that Ish-a-tar has talked quite a lot about her. She wants to meet her. Actually, she talks about nothing else. But no one knows where she is to be found. It looks as if she disappeared completely at the same time as Yeshua.'

Sadosh looked at him cunningly:

'I wouldn't be surprised if you could come before Ish-a-tar if you could help her in this matter. You with your many connections, you ought to be able to do something.'

Ben Nari looked into empty space. He already saw a solution.

'Yes, I can help her. Right now and right here. Let me see her now. I have the information she wants.'

'Are you sure?'

Sadosh looked doubtful. Ben Nari smiled broadly.

'Quite sure.'

Two hours later Ben Nari was led through the corridors of the temple to a guarded door. The door opened shortly after and Ben Nari almost floated into a dimly lit room where he could barely see a figure sitting comfortably in a richly decorated easy chair. There was a heavy scent of expensive oils and perfumes with obvious aphrodisiac powers.

'Come forward you of whom they say that you may bring me the only gift I really want.'

The voice of the woman was hoarse and broken as if it had been used too much. Ben Nari stood rooted to the spot.

'You may sit down,' the woman said.

He took a step forward and sat down on the pillows which the temple servant pushed under him. The voice of Ish-a-tar sounded impatient:

'You wanted to see me. And you have something for me as well.'

Ben Nari felt faint. In front of him sat the most beautiful creature he had ever seen. He had never seen a woman with such long limbs and so fair. Her breasts were bare as if this was the most natural thing. Ben Nari couldn't take his eyes from this intriguing sight. She only wore a very thin, transparent garment, which hardly covered her hips and her sex. She wore her hair down and she was warm and sweating after the dance that she had just finished. She was sitting on her throne with her legs slightly apart looking inquisitively at him.

Ben Nari pulled himself together.

'Quite right, quite right,' he stammered with a smirk, 'What is it you want to know?'

Ish-a-tar pulled a scarf up around her breasts.

'I understand that you are able to take me to the Seer, Mariam Magdal. That is all I want. What do you say. Can you do that or can't you?'

'Perhaps, it depends . . . '

'It depends on what?'

'Whether or not you and I may come to some agreement.'

'And what do you want in return?'

'I want to see you dance.'

There was a short break. Then she laughed tiredly and threw back her head.

'You are like all the others. Like a sheep running after the shepherdess. By Ishtar, if your member isn't sticking out right now like that of a young man. By Isis, I'm certain there's only one thing on your mind right now.'

She was watching him as he sat twisting and turning on the pillows.

'Very well, give me your word and I shall show you something you'll only see once in a lifetime. I don't want to dance for you now, because I'm tired. You are not allowed to lie with me since I do not lie with men any more. However, I shall grant you something which only very few have seen.'

Ben Nari looked both disappointed and excited. He was bewildered, since he didn't know what this creature was planning for him.'

'I give you my word. If what you are talking about does live up to my expectations, tomorrow morning I shall take you to the brother who knows for certain where you may find Mariam Magdal.'

As was the custom, he placed his left hand over his heart while giving her his word. Ish-a-tar laughed at him indulgently.

'So much wealth. Such a great man and yet such a small spirit. Everything in your world is divided into exact portions.

Each person you meet is nothing but a weight on your scale, a figure in your accounts. You do not believe in anything or anyone and least of all yourself. That is why your world is so small and that is why you will not understand the scope of the gift I'm about to give you. You only live in the external world. For you, the power of sight is what you see, and the more you look the less you understand. But enough talk.'

She looked at him with even more indulgence. But he didn't understand anything. He only thought about her body and what he might expect to see.

'You must promise not to touch me. You may get as close as you like, but don't touch me. Do you promise that?'

He nodded eagerly.

'Give me your word.'

Once more he placed his left hand over his heart and gave his word.

She waved him closer and he stepped so close to her that she could smell his heavy garlic-infected breath.

She then leaned back into her chair while she slowly took off the transparent garment. He got very short-winded as her breasts leaped out towards him and he had to concentrate in order not to touch them. Thousands of secret scents floated towards him from her body and he was not certain that he could keep his promise. He started dribbling when she showed him her firm stomach and her hips. And it got worse when she moved her garment aside to reveal a little of her shaved sex. She held her legs together so that he only saw very little of her crack. She could hear his heart's heavy beating and she could see that he was about to lose his senses. She then opened her legs and lifted her exposed sex towards him. Her labia were red and swollen as if she had just made love. His breathing was now so heavy that she feared he might have a heart attack. But she was determined to keep her part

149

of the bargain and show him what she had promised him. She parted her labia with her fingers and exposed her pearl of love, which was hard and purple.

'This is what I can give you,' she whispered.

Her eyes caught his for a moment as if to make sure that he had seen what he was supposed to see. She then put her legs together and wrapped the garment around her. He wanted to protest but she was already on her feet and had called the guard.

'Tomorrow it is your turn to keep your part of the bargain. I'll be ready to leave at dawn.'

Ish-a-tar disappeared like a shadow into an adjacent room.

Ben Nari was unable to speak and he hardly noticed that he was taken to the exit of the temple. He hadn't regained his senses as the heavy gate closed behind him.

The small caravan left Damascus the following morning. Ben Nari was silent and morose. In spite of many requests from Ish-a-tar to tell her the name of the brother dressed in white who had served Mariam Magdal, he remained silent. The experience of the previous night had turned everything upside down. He had been given a sight, which no man before him had been allowed to see. But his lust had been met by a strange, gentle and yet dispassionate attitude, which excited him but which he didn't understand. It was as if she had revealed the innermost despairing darkness of his soul with the bare nakedness of her body. As if by her act she wanted to show him how pathetic he was, and that the external world, which was his only focal point, was nothing but a poor reflection of the inner world. Not in order to hurt him, but in order to show him that another reality existed. He couldn't say that this is how it was; however, this was what he felt. And in spite of the apparent apathy that this experience had made him feel, lust still burned unabated in his big body.

Ish-a-tar sat behind her veil rocking on her camel in the cool shade of the canvas. She too was silent as she looked into the horizon.

Each time Ben Nari motioned to stop she motioned for them to continue. They got to Jerusalem in the evening of the following day and they immediately rode to the Gate of the Essenes.

They found lodgings at the caravanserai outside Jerusalem. Neither Ben Nari nor Ish-a-tar would be welcome at the house of the Essenes situated inside the walls.

Ben Nari immediately sent a message to the Brotherhood.

'We'll get an answer tomorrow at the earliest,' he said to Ish-a-tar, who was sitting at a small fire outside the caravanserai. However, she pretended not to hear him. He was watching this unreal being whose skin radiated as he could only imagine an angel could radiate.

'Goodnight,' he said and contemplated for a moment asking her to join him. But he kept his tongue, seeing that apparently she was somewhere else.

Her coarse voice suddenly cut through the night:

'If I sleep with you tonight would you tell me the name of the one who can get me closer to that which I am looking for?'

Her question struck him like lightning. But before he could react her voice changed:

'Do you think you would be satisfied with that? I wonder what you would desire after that?'

Ben Nari stood like an animal that had just caught the scent of a hunter and was now looking for an escape route. He didn't answer. Without knowing it he had already been hit.

'No matter how many times I gave my body to you, you would never be able to possess me. You would repeat an act with your genitals as if you were possessed or like a dog mating. Your senses would rejoice for a moment. Then you would want to start all over again, just like you do when you are scratching an open sore that itches and keeps itching as long you are scratching it.'

She was aiming directly at him. Her words were aimed at his heart:

'Think about how many whores you have had. Think about how many times you have performed this act, which long ago changed you into a dog. You claim to be a great and important person. Nevertheless, you are nothing but a simple slave driver, more wretched than the lowest of your own servants. You are a slave to your own desires. A slave to your loveless lust.'

She was silent for a few moments. Her voice was filled with pity when in a low voice she gave him the coup-de-grâce:

'You are the poorest and loneliest soul in this God-forsaken desert.'

Tears were rolling down Ben Nari's cheeks. Her words had laid his hardened heart bare and he stood in front of her, naked and unarmed like a little child. For the first time since they had met Ish-a-tar seemed to be able to see the shadow of a human being in the crying man who in his despair had thrown himself to the ground.

'I shall give you what you want,' he sobbed, 'the name of the man who may help you is Lamu . . . are you happy now?'

He practically shouted the last words as if he might thus obtain absolution from an invisible god. Then he added in a low voice:

'If he isn't in Jerusalem the Brothers can tell you where you may find him.'

Ish-a-tar got up. She moved towards the kneeling man like a gazelle. He lay there with his eyes closed. She placed a hand on his forehead:

'Blessed be you, Ben Nari. Be you blessed among sinners. May the Power have mercy on you.'

Then she disappeared into the night.

The scent of incense and newly baked bread as well as the sound of bells and the shouting of shepherds filled the narrow streets as the sun sent its first rays across the roofs of Jerusalem. Ish-a-tar was standing in a passage outside the house of the Essenes waiting for a sign as the door finally opened like a miracle. A young Brother dressed in white appeared carrying a jar of oil. When he spotted Ish-a-tar he quickly crossed himself. Standing there, pale and transparent, she looked most of all like a ghost from another world.

'Who are you and what are you doing here,' he said trying to regain his composure.

For a moment she considered the idea of giving another name than her own but came to the conclusion that it wouldn't make any difference to the Brother dressed in white.

'I am Ish-a-tar,' she said in an almost inaudible voice, 'I'm looking for a Brother by the name of Lamu.'

The man dressed in white looked at her questioningly. In a split second Ish-a-tar thought she noticed a slight vibration at the mouth of the Brother dressed in white and took this to mean that he knew the person in question. Apparently, however, he had no intention of helping her.

'Be gone, you brood of Satan!' he said harshly and tried to kick her, though he only managed to kick some sand into the air. Then a deep soft voice was heard from the forecourt of the house:

'Why all the commotion?'

An elderly Brother appeared in the doorway. When the younger Brother began explaining, the older one put his finger to his lips and shushed him.

'Go in peace Brother, you have chores to do. But remember: do not welcome a new day with your anger.'

He turned to Ish-a-tar and said:

'What can I do for you my child?'

The kindness of this man embraced her in a way she had never been embraced by any man. He did not want anything from her. He didn't want any quid pro quo for his helpfulness. She slowly relaxed and surrendered to this person who no doubt only wanted the best for her.

'I'm looking for a Brother called Lamu,' she said.

The man smiled.

'They say that he may lead me to the holy Mariam Magdal.'

The elderly brother's smile disappeared and he became serious. He seemed to look for a suitable answer for this young woman. But Ish-a-tar already knew that she was on the right track. And he knew that she was aware of that.

'What makes you think that this Mariam Magdal is holy?'

'But isn't she?'

Ish-a-tar didn't understand why he tried to dodge the question since it was obvious that he knew. Then it struck her that perhaps he knew her but didn't consider her to be holy. He didn't answer her question. Instead he said:

'What makes you think that you may find Lamu here?'

'But isn't he a Brother?'

'Yes, but not here with us. He was brought up by the Brothers at Mount Carmel but he belongs to the Nazarene Brotherhood now. You must go to their house in the Syrian quarter and ask for him there. Tell them that you were sent by Yohannan the Essene. This will make it easier for you. But you ought to be more careful. Your beauty may lead even the most dedicated Brother astray and cause many problems. Go in peace.'

The smile was back on his face as he turned around and closed the door behind him.

The pain was excruciating when the stone hit Ish-a-tar on the shoulder.

'It is the white whore from Babylon!' a shrill voice shouted.

She looked around in bewilderment and saw a drunken man at a spice stand pointing at her with an accusing finger. Before anyone had time to react she pulled the shawl around her shoulders and let herself be swallowed up by the crowd and disappeared into the bazaar. She tried to make herself invisible, creeping along the walls, but it was as if a devilish power had thrown its revealing light on her.

'It is the white whore!' another voice shouted. But she didn't turn around to see who it was.

'The white whore!'

'Where?'

'There. Right there!'

She was running now. Faster and faster. A stone missed its target and hit the wall behind her, bouncing back in the direction of the one who had thrown it. She now heard someone running behind her. Her breath was out of control and the blood was pumping around in her body. She gave up holding on to her shawl and let it slip to the ground.

'Look, the whore is already getting ready!' someone shouted.

The cacophony of voices got closer. She turned a corner and ran through a dark and empty passage. Thoughts were whirling around in her head. Right or left?

No time to waste. She chose the passage to the left. Too late she saw that it was a cul-de-sac. She was like an animal forced into a corner.

'There she is!'

'She is right here!'

She pressed herself against the wall in a desperate last attempt to disappear into the darkness. But it was too late. She closed her eyes as she felt strange hands all over her body.

10

They pulled her through the passageways and into one of the squares in the Syrian quarter. Around her the men were gathering stones for a quick execution. Ish-a-tar saw everything through a veiled, unreal haze. Then she was lifted up, up – and up above the square from where she could see the men beginning to throw stones at a huddled figure in the middle of the square below her. She was lifted up above the roofs of Jerusalem, higher and higher, until she could see a large part of the landscape. Up among the clouds where she floated – happy and free while the sound of fire rushed through her ethereal being:

'Forgive them, for they do not know what they are doing. Forgive them, for they do not know what they are doing.'

But what was it she was supposed to forgive? She did not feel that there was anything to forgive. On the contrary, they had just freed her from slavery. They had taken a yoke off her shoulders, which she could not explain at all. She was about to let go of the last thought about the insanity going on below her when the sound of another being made the stream flowing through her change its direction:

'Your time has not come yet. You have not yet done what you came to do.'

A radiating being appeared:

'Here is the power which once you were too proud to accept but which is rightfully yours. You must take the responsibility upon you and use it wisely.'

A blue light floated down and united with her ethereal being. Then she was pulled back at an enormous speed, down into the figure in the square in the Syrian quarter where the men were quenching their lecherous feelings and their blood thirst.

The moment Ish-a-tar was back in her body the stones fell to the ground like wounded birds shot in mid-air. The men stared with disbelief at the white whore who miraculously now stood in front of them, partly naked and with blood running from the wounds the stones had torn. But she was surrounded by a light so powerful that they were forced back.

A tall man in a white coat stepped into the square and stood next to Ish-a-tar.

She was still in a dream-like state of mind. He took her by the arm and led her away from the square, through the passageways and towards the eastern gate. They seemed to float along.

'Who are you?' she asked when they found themselves safely in a small closed courtyard in front of a tall narrow house.

He didn't answer but pushed her into the arms of a woman standing in the doorway who looked about the same age as Ish-a-tar:

'Take care of this woman. Dress her wounds and give her water from the holy well. Find her a place with the women where she may rest.'

He then said to Ish-a-tar:

'Tomorrow we'll talk.'

He began walking back towards the exit. He then turned around and smiled:

'My name is Lamu. Welcome to the house of the Nazarenes.'

Then he stepped out into the light.

Ish-a-tar woke up at the sound of voices chanting a hymn, which seemed strangely familiar. She wanted to get up from the cot but was immediately stopped by a hand gently pushing her back. She hadn't noticed the sister who had taken care of her before and who was now sitting at her bed.

Ish-a-tar uttered a protest:

'I must speak to Brother Lamu. It is my only chance.'

The woman shook her head as if she already knew about Ish-a-tar's willpower.

'Hush. You must rest. We have given you a herbal mixture which demands that you stay calm and quiet. Brother Lamu doesn't return till this evening so you might as well rest.'

Ish-a-tar realized that the sister was right, she closed her eyes and let go.

When she opened her eyes again she had no sense of how much time had passed, but she felt good and rested.

'Brother Lamu is waiting for you in the library.'

The sister helped her out of bed and supported her until she found her balance. She then gave the stranger a cup with holy water.

Ish-a-tar was shown into a big room where the only source of light was two oil lamps on a large table where Lamu sat reading a scroll.

'Well, you have finally returned from the dead,' he said as Ish-a-tar stepped into the room. He looked her up and down as if she was a surprise to him. However, there was no judgement in his look the way she was used to when other men looked at her.

Instead, she was looking at him with the same kind of interest, as if she couldn't believe that this was the man who had been so close to the holy Mariam.

'Where can I find Sister Mariam?' She blurted out.

Lamu smiled.

'You are in a hurry. What do you want from her?'

'I thought that would be obvious considering the fact that you know her and also know all about the wonderful things she is doing. Perhaps it isn't true what they are saying about her?'

'But what do they say about her?'

'That she is a great Prophet who raises the dead and initiates people into eternal life.'

Lamu sat staring into the distance at Ish-a-tar's words. Then he looked once more at the woman in front of him. He had asked other people about her and knew of her background. But it was not a prostitute he saw in the semi-darkness but a seeker, naked in more than one sense. There was a radiance around her which he had only seen once before. She reminded him of the first time he had seen Sister Mariam, when he had been sent off to accompany her from the Therapists in Alexandria.

'Sister Mariam is far away,' he said in order to gain some time.

'Wherever she is, I'm ready to go there.'

Lamu couldn't hold back his laughter any longer. Her eagerness was so appealing to him that he couldn't help being moved by it.

'What are you laughing at?' she asked feeling offended, believing that he was deliberately making fun of her.

He pulled himself together:

'It is not you but your stubbornness and eagerness I'm laughing at. There is no doubt that you mean what you say. Unfortunately, your wish is not that easy to fulfil. Apart from the fact that Sister Mariam is living in a strange country far away she has also withdrawn from public life. Not everyone may come before her.'

'I am not everyone,' Ish-a-tar answered.

'Well no, I can both see and hear that.'

They stared at each other as if it was a duel to the death. He was the first to give way.

'All right, I give in. On one condition, however.'

She stared at him coldly. She had heard this sentence so often that it immediately made her push her hips forward in a certain way indicating that the condition mentioned was of a particular kind.

'Tell me. I'm ready!' she said in a seductive tone of voice.

He looked at her with a surprised look on his face and then made a dismissive gesture with his hand.

'No, no, not that.'

He got up from the table and went over to her. She didn't turn away when he placed his hands on her shoulders. She immediately felt the change caused by his being. It was in all his movements. In the sound of his words. There was no sensible explanation for it. It was just the way it was.

161

'If you really want to meet Sister Mariam you must let go of the old world.'

He wanted to say more than this, but, while he stood face to face with this strange woman and looked deep into her eyes, he saw the shadow of another being totally free and unblemished, and at that moment he was seized by an inexplicable urge to embrace her. He also realized that any kind of moral preaching would be blasphemy regarding this soul which in one sense stood naked in front of him but which had been so close to re-entering the body of the prostitute. He could see both the prostitute and the pure soul. This was what made him uneasy. Before he was able to collect his thoughts, something in him made up his mind for him. It was his longing that spoke. It was his need once more to see the holy sister and, perhaps, his longing for that unknown place within himself, all of which was centred in the prostitute, who was freedom itself standing right there in front of him.

'I shall go with you and show you the way,' he said quietly. 'However, first we must go to Alexandria in order to make the necessary preparations.'

She took hold of his hand even before he had stopped talking and pressed it against her mouth kissing it. Her action made him perplexed and he lost his composure.

'It is written,' he said, 'it is written.'

*

I was packing my suitcase in order to go to Montségur on the quest on which Sylvia had sent me when the phone rang. I considered letting it ring but for some reason or other I decided against it and responded. Call it destiny or whatever. It doesn't make any difference.

'Hello,' I said into the receiver and was met by an indefinable mixture of white noise and a mysteriously sparkling and endless universe.

'Hello!' I practically yelled. It was a call from another reality. I stood for a long time trying to sense what this both distant and very close consciousness tried to communicate to me. No such luck. Either because I was unable to understand that specific 'language', or because it was a matter of two different frequencies.

To my own great surprise I heard myself saying, 'No matter who you are or where you are, – I'm on my way.' Instead of trying to shout my way through, I tried to listen and adjust my own voice to the pitch of the unknown one. Apparently, my efforts made a difference. The strange, white noise continued but the voice went silent, which gave me the impression that someone was listening at the other end. After about half a minute or maybe a full minute the voice was activated once more. It now moved on to another pitch with a different, rhythmic stress pattern and I realized that contact had been established. However, no matter how much I tried, I didn't succeed in getting any meaning out of the sounds. Not until the voice gave up trying to 'speak' and began 'singing' did I give up trying to find an intellectual explanation for this phenomenon. Instead, I now opened up to the voice which then split up into several voices participating in a song which grew from a drone in a medium pitch, followed by seconds and augmented fourths and fifths in inexplicable riffs which would be heard by normal ears as dissonance. It continued like this for a few minutes. The sound was so disturbing that I had to hold the receiver away from my ear. When the voices joined in a series of pure fifths I was again able to put the receiver close to my ear. But suddenly and without warning the connection was cut and

I only got the usual beep-beep-beep sound you hear when someone hangs up on you.

Here I was with my limited faculties and perception not knowing what to make of this experience. This was something new. In spite of all my nocturnal escapades into the astral sphere as well as my growing penetration into the ethereal one, this was totally new to me.

I boarded the train in Aarhus late in the afternoon and got out again at the station in Foix on the following day. I had made this journey so often that by now I knew it better than the personnel at the DSB Travel Agency and the changing crew on the train.

There was a drizzle but the weather was warm when I stepped onto the platform in the town of Esclarmonde and walked to the car hire office on the outskirts of the town.

Foix is in itself a fairy tale. Above the town looms the castle where Esclarmonde lived until she became dedicated to the plight of the Cathars. The situation of the town, on the river, surrounded by mountains, limits its potential for external growth. Nevertheless it is a little power centre for an area that for many years was one of the poorest in France and is still considered by many to belong to the stagnant periphery. Instead, the population has developed another kind of inner power. It lies hidden in the old Cathar families and the mysterious spirit that rests on this Shangri-La. Then again, there is quite a different aura around the people of the Pyrenees than around most other people. The ethereal Akasha is much more open and accessible to me here in this area than the ethereal aura is around the descendants of the Cathars, which is much more closed. Perhaps this is because of the terrible destiny which befell them during the Inquisition?

I signed the rental agreement and threw my bags on to the rear seat of the Renault Clio I had hired. Shortly after I was on my way to Les Contes along roads I knew as well as the back of my hand. As taught by the Seer, who always carried a small supply of wine, gin and canned beer as presents for hosts, which were meant to break the ice and renew old friendships, I bought a supply at the local supermarket. This was a tradition which I did not quite understand but which I soon learned to appreciate. These presents were simple expressions of respect and gratitude, which were direct without causing any kind of embarrassment.

I passed the Montségur mountain half an hour later and drove through the four hairpin turns down to the village where I parked outside number nineteen, the by now legendary house where the Seer and I had stayed so often that I dare to call it my second home. I knocked on the door at the end of the house leading into René's workshop. René Briol is the owner of the house and a descendant of an old Cathar family. This is not only visible in his features but is also expressed in his views, the Cathar symbols in the house and the subjects that he paints.

'Ah, Monsieur Lars, bonsoir!' he said as I stepped into his small studio. I had brought two cans of beer.

While we drank to each other and talked about this and that, he showed me his latest paintings. René paints in a very intuitive style, obtaining an almost surrealistic effect through his use of manneristic shadows. The subject invariably is the same, the mountain and the village.

Paintings of the mountain and the village, spring, summer, autumn and winter. All kinds of perspectives. Close up and far away. From above and from below. However, always from the outside. Never from the inside. At least this was not the feeling I got looking at them.

'You cannot paint the innermost heart of Montségur,' he always said.

And I knew he was right. Any description of the holy mountain, be it in pictures or in words, will always be exactly that, pictures and words.

When we had talked for a while I plucked up enough courage to put the question to him, which I had come to ask:

'Do you know how to find the secret cave in the mountain?'

He was replacing a painting, which he had just been showing to me and looked as if he was looking for another one to show me. He didn't answer and since I took it to mean that he hadn't heard my question I therefore repeated it. Another length of time without any reaction. Then he got up and showed me yet another small painting of the village covered in snow.

'René!'

'Oui.' he answered and deliberately looked more absent-minded than usual.

'Do you know anything about the secret cave which some people claim is to be found in the mountain?'

He laughed awkwardly and then shook his head:

'Well, it's the usual nonsense. You know, for some people reality isn't exciting enough and they therefore invent these kinds of figments of the mind. If you repeat such a tale often enough it soon finds its way into travel guides to the Pyrenees and before you know it, it is a historical fact.'

'Come on, René, my information comes from a reliable source.'

'That's what I'm saying. When you repeat it often enough there is no limit to the reliability of the sources and how far they'll go in order to make reality and fairy tales meet. I have lived here all my life. I know that this mountain is endless, but I promise you, if anyone knows this mountain it is me and I have never, repeat *never*, seen the shadow of an internal cave or heard about anyone who has. Sorry.'

He placed the winter landscape in front of me like a trump to end the game.

We drank up and while René continued his presentation of his paintings I was thinking that maybe it was Sylvia who had got it all wrong. After all, it was years ago that her experiences had taken place here. Of course, it was also possible that René didn't want to take me into his confidence. I knew that these old Cathars could be quite reticent about the secrets in which the area is so rich.

I left René and took a stroll in the village in order to investigate the matter further. At the Hôtel Costes, Gilbert and Maurisette were preparing supper. Their daughter was helping. The idea was that she and her husband were supposed to take over the hotel during the following year. The husband, Jean-Luc, also had a café in an alley across from the hotel and rumour had it that he was an expert on all the myths and legends of Montségur.

After having met Gilbert and Maurisette I found Jean-Luc in the café. I only knew him superficially but he was aware that I knew his parents-in-law quite well and that I had mentioned them in *The Seer*. I ordered a cappuccino and sat down at a table on the terrace from where I had the most wonderful view over the valley. When he brought me my coffee I decided to phrase my question differently:

'How do I find the secret cave in the Montségur mountain?'

I noticed his small twitch as he placed the cup in front of me. But the question didn't seem to shake him.

'You don't' he said with a big smile, 'for the simple reason that it doesn't exist.'

167

I also smiled. Either the story about the secret cave in the mountain was one big joke or it wasn't something about which they wanted to inform strangers.

'Ah,' I said, indicating that I had no intention of following up on this question.

I didn't want him to think that I was desperate. Apparently this was the right tactic since he continued where he had stopped:

'Many adventurers have searched for the Holy Grail which, according to one of the many legends of the Grail, is supposed to rest in the mountain. Well, some even claim that they have been there. The marvellous reports tell about a gigantic hall and a maze of passages where you may walk for hours and eventually lose your life if you go astray. Some even say that they have seen the Grail in there.'

He laughed mockingly and had an expression on his face that clearly showed his contempt for this kind of adventurer.

'Do you also believe in this kind of fairy tale?' he asked me.

I shook my head.

'No, I'm only interested in the myths, that's all.'

He nodded and looked as if he had regained his confidence in me.

'Do you want more coffee,' he asked pointing to the cup, which I had just emptied.

'No thanks, I'd better get on my way. Thank you.'

I paid and got up, but then I thought about something:

'How come the church in the village is always locked?'

'Oh, the church. Religion is a sensitive subject here. Remember that old Cathars and former inquisitors live next to each other in the village, actually, some of them even under the same roof. If you want to go to Mass you have to go to Bélesta.'

'Is it possible to borrow the key if I would like to see the church?'

'Try the tourist office,' he said, wiping the table from which I had just got up.

They didn't know anything about a cave at the tourist office but I could probably get the key at the mayor's office.

When, shortly after, I knocked on the door to the mayor's office I got the same message. No cave, and the key was probably kept at the museum.

This was turning into a farce. A farce that was enhanced when shortly after the person in charge of the museum sent me on to the tourist office. Before that he had given my dreams of a cave in the Montségur mountain the final coup-de-grâce:

'It's a ridiculous myth, invented by dreamers!'

It is very strange. But the more assurances and proof you get that something is impossible, the more you want to find it. Perhaps this is what I felt and perhaps I felt this way because I had the feeling that there was more to this story than pure imagination. Those people spoke against their better judgement. Or did they?

I backed out of the car park, turned around and drove slowly down the hill towards the valley. At the bottom I noticed a figure walking up the hill. A couple came from a side street and began walking in the same direction.

I passed the lonely wanderer shortly after. It was a young, dark-haired woman who seemed familiar. I slowed down and looked in my rear-view mirror. She was tall and wore a flowered dress. Then it struck me that I really had seen this woman before. Wasn't it Marie Périllos, the young waitress from Narbonne I had met the last time I was here and whom I had agreed to meet again?

I braked and put it in reverse. The gearbox complained loudly because I got too eager. I backed all the way up the hill but when I got to the top the woman had gone. I got out of the car to look for her. But she had disappeared.

What was going on?

'Do not lose yourself in the external journey of the Grail.'

Those were Sylvia's words. On the other hand, she was the one who sent me off on this quest. Was it all an illusion or was this the way Sylvia was teaching me? Letting me run around in circles in the old myths, which had nothing to do with form or any kind of reality? Perhaps the cave didn't exist at all. Perhaps it was Sylvia's way of telling me that the cave was within me and not in a mountain that some obscure myths happened to have named 'The Mountain of the Grail'?

And what about the girl? Could I still trust my own senses? I was fed up with everything. Astral journeys, ethereal sights and voices speaking, God knows from where. Perhaps from my own strained imagination, or perhaps it was all just another construction or a colourful compensation for a normality which was both grey, sad and hopeless.

I got into the car and bowled along down the hill toward Les Contes.

Mar and Leny were sitting on the bench outside as I drove up in front of the beautiful old building. They were sitting with their common golden aura hovering around them and confirming their unity. I was again shown to the room of 'St Francis of Assisi', which apparently was 'my room'. The guests from last time had been exchanged for new ones. Roderick and his mother had also left.

I sat next to Mar at suppertime. I hadn't really planned to waste any more time on this obscure cave but something or other had other ideas. I heard my own voice, tired and dispassionate, asking:

'I realize that this is probably a foolish question but do you know anything about a hidden cave inside the Montségur mountain?'

I was lucky that I was already sitting down because his answer would otherwise have made me do it since it took me totally by surprise:

'Yes, I do.'

11

Lamu and Ish-a-tar followed the route along the coast through Gaza, Raphia, Ostracine, Pelusium and further through the Nile delta to Alexandria. They rode directly to the society of the Therapists at Lake Mareotis situated some distance from the town. The news of their arrival had gone before them and they were met by a small group of women dressed in white. For the first time since they had left Jerusalem Lamu saw a smile in the eyes of Ish-a-tar. The closed, worried look had disappeared.

'How fair everything is here,' she said to Lamu as if he already knew what she was talking about.

He nodded. He had also come home.

They were taken to the water tank where they washed the dust away. Then they got something to eat in the big common hall in the middle of the cluster of houses which made up this unique society where men and women worked together for the glory of God.

'What is going to happen here? Is Sister Mariam here?' Ish-a-tar asked while they were eating.

'We are here to prepare ourselves. This is the society of the Therapists where sister Mariam was initiated. When we have received the necessary education we shall continue our journey and I hope get the opportunity to meet Sister Mariam.'

They continued to eat in silence, then he said:

'Sister Mariam's personal teacher still lives here. She is a very holy woman.'

'What is her name? Take me to her at once!'

Ish-a-tar put her bread down and was about to stand up when a woman's voice interrupted her:

'Mariam Salome, my child. Do not trouble yourself. I'm right here.'

The voice was like balm on their hearts, a healing balm, which removed every shadow but at the same time awakened everything which had been lying about unused for far too long.

'Here, I am called by my initiation name, Salome.'

Although the woman was getting old she was still beautiful with a straight and dignified bearing. She moved gracefully and almost hovered across the floor as she stepped into the room.

Ish-a-tar got to her feet and Lamu followed her example. Lamu folded his hands in front of his chest and bowed:

'I greet you, holy one.' he said.

'Isn't this Lamu, the young man who was sent here long ago in order to take Sister Mariam to the Celestial City?'

She also folded her hands and greeted him. Lamu nodded his assent. He was too moved to speak. The whole scene also seemed to move Ish-a-tar. She was, if anything, even more pale than usual, but it simply made her still more strange-looking and radiant.

'And you must be Ish-a-tar,' Salome said, 'I have heard much about you. I'm glad you decided to come. But rest now. Tomorrow is another day and we shall start your education.'

She greeted them once more.

'May peace be with you.'

Then she was gone.

After the meal they were taken to the guest-house where they were each given their own room.

'Tomorrow we part,' Lamu said, 'you'll be staying with your teacher and I with mine. We'll meet every seven days when men and women meet at the forum. Sleep well, I hope you'll get what you want.'

Ish-a-tar looked at him. For the first time she saw his innermost being. Perhaps because she was so moved that she didn't know what was up or down.

'Sister Salome is also called Mariam. I noticed that several of the women who received us are also called by that name. What does it mean?'

'You see, when you are initiated here you are given your true name. Until then, you have lived with the name you received at birth but this is only your worldly name. After the initiation you are given your heavenly name. The name Mariam signifies that the one bearing it has been accepted into the society of the Therapists. 'Mari' means sea. Mariam means the sea from which the spirit of the peace of God has risen. After her final initiation, Sister Mariam got the name Magdal, 'The Exalted One'. Sister Salome is also called Mariam. This way the initiated ones know that one bears the same rank as the others with this name. Her heavenly initiation name is Salome, which means 'The Perfect One'. She is the daughter of God, the soul, dressed in sound, unity, love and peace.'

174

'Thank you,' Ish-a-tar said quietly, 'thank you for bringing me here.'

He smiled. He was beginning to realize that something in her being had touched his heart.

'Goodnight.'

*

'Yes,' Mar said, 'I know the cave very well. I was there about five years ago with a professional guide and two friends of mine.'

'But are you certain that it was inside the Montségur mountain itself?' I asked holding my breath. My tiredness had gone completely.

'Absolutely. But it is very difficult to get there. In order to get there, among other things, you must climb a very steep cliff wall. The cave itself is so well hidden that I wouldn't be able to find it again. The local people who know its whereabouts cover the entrance so that it is practically impossible to find.'

'You were inside it?'

'Of course.'

'What did you see?'

'Not that much. You first enter an antechamber. From there on you must crawl four to five metres through a channel, which is not for people suffering from claustrophobia. The channel opens into a large cave from which a very intricate system of passages branches out. We didn't stay for a long time since we didn't bring a proper torch. But it was a very special experience.'

'How big is the inner cave?'

'It is hard to say. So big, however, that it wasn't possible for us, with our poor light, to see where it started and where

175

it ended. But from the sound itself we were able to perceive that it has a very high ceiling. The experience, however, made me ill. I felt faint when we got out of the cave and were on our way back. After a few days I went to the doctor and he advised me to get a thorough check-up. However, the doctors couldn't find out what was wrong with me and it stayed with me for about a year when finally it subsided and then disappeared completely.'

'What were the symptoms?'

He was contemplating his answer.

'I had difficulty breathing and my whole body ached. I myself wondered about the cause of it but finally arrived at the conclusion that there must have been some stale air in the narrow channel which, according to the guide book, may be the case in caves where people and animals seldom go. I was the first one to go through it and may have inhaled the stale air which found its way into my blood through the respiratory passage.'

I couldn't help thinking that it reminded me of the theories that scientists have come up with in connection with the opening of the Tomb of Tutankhamun in Egypt when quite a few people also became ill. Or it actually *was* a matter of a curse to protect the place from unwelcome visitors. No matter what, Mar's story was good news to me.

'Do you know anyone who could show me the cave?'

'Well yes, I do actually. He is Dutch and has the necessary licence allowing him to work as a guide in the mountains for payment. I don't know if he is around at the moment but I'll find out by tomorrow.'

It was a long night. Just as had happened on my first visit to Les Contes, I woke up to the sound of a child crying, and once more had to light a candle and say a prayer for the souls which still seemed to be held back by the place and the events which happened here. I lay for a long time and let my thoughts roam. I floated along above desolate and rugged landscapes. Then a voice announced:

'The Mountain of the Grail is the Mount of Olives!'

I let go of my resistance and felt a buoyancy in a smooth upward glide. The words were directed at me and had something to do with my quest.

'But the Mount of Olives is situated in Jerusalem in the Holy Land,' I answered, 'what has that got to do with the Pyrenees?'

'Jerusalem and the Holy Land will always be where man is able to see that the ethereal openings are wherever the energies are centred.'

That was it. Apparently the Voice had nothing more to say and I slowly floated back to my room. I was wide awake.

The Mount of Olives!

What was it the Voice had tried to tell me?

The Mount of Olives was the place where Yeshua ascended into Heaven. This was where they expected his second coming.

Oil! Mariam anointed Yeshua with oil.

Oil equalled initiation.

I switched on the light and found a map of the area. It was a pure intuition. I didn't know what I was doing and reacted strictly from this intuition.

It was Michelin map '344 Local – Aude, Pyrénées-Orientales'. I was looking for my pendulum when a glance at the map, which by now was spread out on the bed, made my eyes catch the name *Mont de Grail*.

The Mountain of the Grail! I could hardly believe my eyes. I immediately got down on my knees and studied the area more closely. Then I spotted it.

I looked at the name for a long time. All kinds of doubts went through me, however, another second and all doubt disappeared.

OLBIÉR!

Apparently, it didn't mean anything in French. It sounded more like German. But I had no doubt that there had to be a connection to the Mount of Olives on which the Voice wanted me to focus. I couldn't find any better explanation to this phenomenon, I can only tell it the way I experienced it.

Olbiér is not far from Tarascon. You pass the Church of Notre-Dame-de-Sabart in front of which Mariam and Yeshua stand side by side greeting visitors. Then you continue to Vicdessos. And Olbiér is right next to it.

Not much sleep that night. Instead, I meditated and waited for the sun to rise.

*

They parted the next morning. Ish-a-tar just had time to wave to Lamu and then a woman took her to the house of Salome.

'I'll personally take care of you and your education,' Salome said when Ish-a-tar sat in front of her, 'and there is no time to waste.'

She started learning the same day. Like Mariam before her, Ish-a-tar was taken through the initial lessons, day by day. She was very keen and it didn't take Salome long to find out that Ish-a-tar was made of sterner stuff. Sometimes it struck Salome how much she really resembled Mariam. But there were differences. Sometimes Salome wondered whether or not Ish-a-tar was aware what these differences would mean to her. She was poised to talk to her about it a few times but when she saw the eagerness and enthusiasm with which her student dedicated herself to the work, she postponed it indefinitely.

Ish-a-tar had to go through all the initiating steps preparing her for the real task. They were as follows:

1. Continue to repeat the name of God and become aware of the eternal Being.
2. Give up any kind of egotism and sing the praise of God.
3. Do no harm to others. Do not speak ill of others.
4. Live continuously in awareness of the Divinity in you.
5. Abandon lust, hate and greed. Do not envy the happiness of others.
6. Be true, be compassionate and practise forgiveness.
7. Abandon your doubts. Seek God, know your own true Self and see God in everything.

Ish-a-tar learned about the cycles of women. When their moon time came the women went into seclusion. Not because they were unclean but because they had opportunities during that period which were not possible otherwise.

When her holy period came Ish-a-tar spent seven days in a cave from where she had a view of the Lake of Mareotis. Her only food was drinking water, crushed sesame seeds and ripe figs. She gathered the moon blood in a pan made for the purpose. The blood was later used as a life-giving mixture, which strengthened the earth and made it holy as well as creating ethereal powers around the medicinal herbs in the garden of the brother and sisterhood.

For the first two days the moon woman had to concentrate on and invoke the archangels Uri-El, Micha-El, Gabri-El and Rapha-El.

Pain and other disturbances were, in fact, entrances to the state of mind one wanted. The practised moon woman would have eliminated any kind of unpleasantness and was able, by way of the invocations. gradually to create contact to the ethereal field, which was necessary in order to see and hear the messages and visions awaiting her.

'*The holy one finds the truth by abandoning delusional lust. She lets her thoughts unite with SHM, the holy sound, forming the stream of life – the word, which is given her by her teacher. For two days she intones that sound until she and SHM are one. She will receive her true name in a vision but she does not voice it. Mind and body are still and the fire of lust is refined until it is finally pure. This is her true bridal gown. There is one light. It shines in everyone. Honour all living beings. This is the true marriage vow of the bride. Accept that that which man calls "death" is, in truth, the door to the bridal chamber. "Die" before you die! Forget the past and abandon your dreams about the future. Become dust and come to Me.*'

Ish-a-tar learned that the Therapists worked with metaphors and allegories and that the more refined the language the more precisely they would be able to communicate with the Heavenly level. The sounding and the stressing of the words were important if rapport was to be achieved. Everything had more than one meaning and all beings consisted of more than one body, and each of them was in contact with various levels of the hierarchy of the angels.

The Seraphim, the snake-fire of love, was the first order of angels. It was under the direction of Micha-El and this angel also played a leading role in some of the other angel choirs. Micha-El was the angel in the burning bush who had spoken to Moses in the desert.

Micha-El was the ruler of the fire and the blue-purple flame, which could be seen reflected on the sky in the star formation of Aldebaran or Oculus Tauri.

Micha-El was an isogynic angel-like being whose name meant '*One Who is like God.*' Micha-El had his origin in *Tifferet* on the Tree of Life. The traits of *Tifferet* are compassion, beauty and divine strength.

The appellation '*El*' simply meant '*shining or sparkling*', which was seen as one of God's qualities. Micha-El thus was an extension of God Himself, a power running through the spheres, internal as well as external, when needed and invoked. The traits of Micha-El were divine inspiration and the power that might overcome any resistance and barrier. In other traditions they compared Micha-El with the Greek Hermes, the Egyptian Toth and the Roman Mercury. When this angel was invoked with a pure heart there was no limit to what one might do with its help.

The Therapists began their day with prayers. They turned to the east welcoming the sun, their hands and eyes turned heavenward praying that the day might be light and clear and their visions pure and true. The sun was an allegory. It symbolized the divine light behind the physical sun. The morning prayer and ritual were repeated at sunset.

The number seven played a special role for the Therapists. Seven was a holy number. Apart from keeping the seventh day holy they also celebrated the evening of the 49th day, which meant that the 50th day was especially holy.

One morning after prayers, Salome introduced Ish-a-tar to the secret of numbers:

'Fifty is the most holy of numbers. That is what Pythagoras taught us. Fifty is the most natural of numbers and it represents the power of the right-angled triangle: $(3 \times 3) + (4 \times 4) + (5 \times 5) = 50$.'

Salome paused in order to let her student take it all in. Then she continued:

'Here are the three most holy numbers following fifty. Seven is the basis of any form and any quality. It first and foremost represents purity and virginity.'

She paused once more.

'The Pythagoreans called 7 Lucifer's number. However, contrary to the priests of Jerusalem the Pythagoreans realized that Lucifer was the angel who brought the light into the world and gave it an ethereal form. Only the opponents of light do not understand this and thus demonize Lucifer.'

She made another rhetorical pause so that Ish-a-tar had time to let the words sink in.

'It is important that you ponder these thoughts until they rest in your being. The statements about these figures have more than one meaning.'

This time she paused in order to make way for new lessons:

'Now, listen well. This is a meditation, which does not ask for any questions, only reflection. You see?'

Ish-a-tar nodded.

'Good. Notice carefully what I'm telling you now. It concerns the transcendence of the three holy numbers, 7, 9 and 12.'

THE TEACHINGS OF THE HOLY FIGURES

'When 7 becomes one, it is 8 at a higher level. Eight is the number of infinity and of Isis.'

It was completely quiet in the room.

'The human body has 9 gates, 2 eyes, 2 ears, 2 nostrils, 1 mouth and 2 exits in the lower region. These 9 gates in the physical body have 9 parallel gates in the heavenly body. 9 +9 = 18. 1 + 8 = 9. When 9 becomes one, it is 10 at a higher level. 1 is man and 0 is the universe. 1 is the masculine, 0 the feminine. 1 is the centre, 0 the periphery.'

A long pause.

'The twelfth depth is the Truth from which all truths originate. This is the image of the Source (Father-Mother). This is the mirror of Creation. This is the Source of all aeons. This is *the Monad*, the One who is unknown. The Spotless One in whom all the virtues are. This is the eternal Source the incomprehensible and the unthinkable. The saving principle, *Messiah*, was born from the first thought of God (the Source), which was feminine. The feminine principle brought the son into the world and gave him the birthright of the first-born.

She gave him the power over angels and archangels. She gave him twelve qualities to serve him. And she gave him a habit, clothed in which he could achieve everything. In this were all the bodies of the spheres: a body of fire, a body of air, a body of earth and a body of water. A body for each of the angel choirs: the Seraphs, the Cherubs, the Thrones, the Rulers, the Powers, the Authorities, the Princes of Power and the Magnificent Seven.'

Salome made a long pause before continuing:

'The figure twelve means: $1 + 2 = 3$ which is the uppermost triad, *Kether, Hokhmah* and *Binah* at the Tree of Life.'

'When 12 becomes one it is 13 at a higher level. Thirteen is the figure of the initiated one. And $1 + 3 = 4$. Four is for the four corners of the world as well as the four elements which in this way are contained in the 13.'

Another long pause.

'When you add up the three transcendent figures $(8 + 10 + 13)$ you get 31. When 31 becomes one you get 32 at a higher level.'

Salome stood up and went to the window and looked out across the lake giving Ish-a-tar time to take the secret of the numbers into her being. Then she returned to the table and picked up a scroll from which she began reading:

'*The female dancer is the daughter of light in whom the proud clarity of kings is resting, and the sight of her is wonderful because happiness and beauty radiate from her. Her gown is like the flowers of spring: a bouquet of seducing scents. And from the crown of her forehead the king is consolidated who nourishes those who are founded in him with his divine elixir. Truth is in her head and her feet dance with joy only. And her mouth is open and it does her good. Thirty-two are those who sing her praise.*'

Salome looked up from the scroll. Ish-a-tar sat as though enchanted.

EIN SOF

CROWN
Will

KETHER

UNDERSTANDING
Palace
Circle

WISDOM
Beginning
Point

DIVINE
KNOWLEDGE

BINAH

DAAT
METATRON

HOKHMAH

POWER

BEAUTY
Compassion, Harmony
Blessed, Holy One, King

GRACE

GEVURAH
♂

HESED
♃

SPLENDOR
Prophecy

TIFFERET
MICHA-EL
☉

ETERNITY
Prophecy

HOD
RAPHA-EL
☿

FOUNDATION
Righteous One
Covenant, Phallus

NETZACH
URI-EL
♀

YESOD
GABRI-EL
☽

PRESENCE (MALKOOT)
Kingdom, Queen, Communion of Israel
Apple Orchard, Vagina

SHEKHINAH
⊕

185

'Remember there are 22 paths in her gown, 22 paths connecting the 10 sapphires on the Tree of Life. And 10 + 22 = 32. When you add up 3 and 2 you get 5. The feminine power rests in the pentagon. When 5 becomes one you get 6, which is the sun, and you get *Tifferet* on the Tree of Life. The hexagram, the six-pointed star, symbolizes the melting together of the terrestrial and the celestial, the masculine and the feminine, the lower and the higher. When 6 becomes one we have returned to 7 which has further transcended to a totally new level where the cycle may begin all over again, however, now with far more refined qualities.'

Ish-a-tar sat for a long time and contemplated Salome's speech. After a while she said:

'"And her mouth is open and it does her good," what does that mean?'

Salome looked surprised at Ish-a-tar as if she hadn't expected such a question from her.

'That is a very relevant question. It tells us that the creative principle is revealed through the gate in the neck. This is a prerequisite for receiving visions and passing on prophecies. It all corresponds with the various sapphires on the Tree of Life. And the powers, which have to be activated in order to open up into these kingdoms, are the archangels.'

THE TEACHINGS OF THE ARCHANGELS

'Micha-El represents the 6th point on the tree, *Tifferet*; while Uri-El represents the 7th point, *Netzach*, the eternal; Rapha-El represents the 8th point, *Hod*, refulgence; and Gabri-El the 9th point, *Yesod*, the foundation stone.'

Salome went silent. Then she laughed and danced around in the room singing:

'Everyone must become one with *Shekhinah*. She is the one getting these qualities to the level of the earth and makes sure that they get to the places where they are needed the most.'

'*Shekhinah?*'

Ish-a-tar looked somewhat confused. Salome danced in front of her, took her hands and pulled her into the dance:

'Yes, *Shekhinah* is the 10th point, *Malkoot*, on the Tree of Life. This is the point closest to the physical world. This is where you find the "fallen" *Shekhinah*. The wisdom that voluntarily floated down to the visible world in order to enlighten us and free us from our prison.'

They whirled about in Salome's room.

'Don't let your speculations stand in the way of true knowledge – wisdom. Wisdom is the world of *Shekhinah*. However, she has a sister who is known by few people only, because she rarely comes down from the higher worlds and lets herself be known. Her name is secret and may only be pronounced by the one who has the key to the Holy of Holies in her temple.'

During the following weeks Salome taught her student about the power of the archangels.

Rapha-El (God has healed) as the name indicates, was the carrier of the healing power of God. The angel was reflected in Regulus or Cor Leonis. Rapha-El ruled the air and the green flame.

Gabri-El (God is my strength) was the angel of compassion who ruled the waters and the mother-of-pearl-white flame. Gabri-El was reflected in Fomalhaut.

Uri-El (the light of God) was the angel of peace who ruled the earth and the golden flame. Uri-El was reflected in Antares or Cor Scorpio.

Ragu-El (the friend of God) was the angel guarding the other angels.

Remi-El (the mercy of God) is the angel who helped the souls to the resurrection. He is also called 'the angel of judgement'.

Razi-El (the secret of God) was the angel who guarded over the mysteries.

'You see, Ish-a-tar, these powers are part of you. They live in you as they live in all people. However, only a few people are aware of it, and only a few people know how they relate to these powers. Study the qualities of these powers very closely. Not with your intellect but with your visionary force. "And her mouth is open and it does her good," you see? Empty yourself of the thoughts that will always try to keep you within the old limitations until you realize that your thinking does not take you anywhere. Instead, unite with these powers. Make them your servants. This is the only way to serve God.'

They walked side by side while Salome took Ish-a-tar to the hill outside the town of the Therapists.

'When you understand all this I shall teach you about the greatest one of them all, the angel waiting for you.'

They were looking across the desert as the sun set behind the horizon.

*

When the sun was rising behind heavy black clouds I was already dressed and helping Mar in the kitchen.

'Have you heard about the Mountain of the Grail at Olbiér?' I asked him while Mar put a bowl with eggs in front of me.

'No, what do you mean? The general opinion is that it is Montségur which is the Mountain of the Grail that the various legends are talking about.'

I took the bowl and placed it on a tray together with cheese and butter.

'The town is called Olbiér. Do you know it?'

'No. Can you tell me more about it?'

'No, not really,' I said and carried the tray into the dining room.

We were having our coffee before the guests came down from their rooms.

'About that,' Mar said, 'I have talked to the guide who can take you to the hidden cave at Montségur. But not until tomorrow. His name is Bart. I wrote his address down and you yourself must go and make the arrangements with him.'

He handed me a slip of paper. I folded it without looking at it.

I packed a light bag after breakfast and took off in order to find the Mountain of the Grail at Olbiér. It was pouring down. I drove to Tarascon and turned off at Notre-Dame-de-Sabart and drove towards Vicdessos. I was contemplating what might be in store for me when out of the corner of my eye I spotted a human shape standing under the branches of an old oak tree, seeking shelter from the rain. It was not until I had passed this human shape that I realized that I had seen the person before.

Marie Périllos!

The young waitress I had met at the Belo Bar in Narbonne.

I stepped lightly on the brake and looked in the rear-view mirror where I could see a dark-haired woman in a flowered dress retreating in my field of vision. I then stopped the car completely and looked after her. She looked real all right. But for how long? I slowly rolled backwards towards this woman standing at the roadside waiting with one hand resting challengingly on her hip.

12

The air was still and Lake Mareotis was bathed in a red light from the setting sun. It was the evening of the 49th day, the holy evening, and the beginning of the 50th day when the brothers and sisters and the novices gathered in the big common room.

The women went in first and were seated to the right. A priestess lit the incense in the large thuribles at each side of the altar, then got up and began chanting:

'Holy, holy, holy – *Marmariotha* – come, come, come out of the four winds of the Kingdom, rise from the four corners of the world, come *Rukha d'koodsha*, come Holy Spirit, You who are in the deep as on high, to the right and to the left, You who ride the chariot of the breath of God. Unite the chaos of separation and tie up the dragon and all its shapes. Come *Shekhinah*, and protect your beings of light, whose gates are open and habitations are many.'

Shortly after they began to sing:

AAAAAAAAAEEEEEEEEIIIIIIIIOOOOOOOOOOUU
UUUUUUUOOOOOOOOIIIIIIIEEEEEEEEAAAAAAA.

While the women were singing the men stepped into the procession and took their positions to the left.

It disturbed Ish-a-tar that she felt a stab of longing in her heart at the sight of Lamu. A priest placed himself in front of the men. The women kept singing, in subdued voices, however, in order to let the chanting voice of the priest be heard:

'Let Micha-El stand to my right, Gabri-El to my left, let Uri-El's trumpet sound in my mind, let Rapha-El rest in my heart, let Ragu-El crown my head, let Asu-El give me strength and mercy, and let Saraphu-El bless me. I call you today. Heavenly Source, Heavenly Source, Heavenly Source, Heavenly Source, Heavenly Source, Heavenly Source, Heavenly Source, Sanctus, Sanctus, Sanctus, Sanctus, Sanctus, Sanctus, Sanctus, Holy, Holy, Holy, Holy, Holy, Holy, Holy, You who rest in the holy place. You the merciful God, the invisible One and the incomprehensible One, *Marmaroulach, Christos.* Receive our children. Receive our song. And let us enter Your Kingdom.'

Then the men sang:

'SABAOTH SABA AO, SABAOTH SABA AO, SABAOTH SABA AO.'

When they had all finished they got up and carried the benches to the side of the hall. Three temple virgins came in, each with their basket of twelve unleavened loaves of bread, which they carefully placed in three rows at the altar at the end of the hall, four in each row. They were followed by three young male novices carrying a large cask with unfermented wine.

Salome held the communion. A sister and then a brother would take turns and walk by the altar where they would share a piece of the bread and the wine in remembrance of *Marmariotha*, the Heavenly Source, *Rukha d'koodsha*, the Holy Spirit and *Shekhinah*, the Wisdom.

When everybody had received their communion the brothers and the sisters gathered in the middle of the hall where they quietly intoned:

Mmmmmmmmmmmmmmmmmmmmmmmmmmmmmmm mmmmmmm mmmmmmmmmmmmmmmmmmmmmmmm mmmmmmmmmmmmm.

This went on for such a long time that Ish-a-tar lost all sense of time. Suddenly the closed sound dissolved into a more open one:

AAAAAAA   EEEEEEE   IIIIIII   OOOOOOO
UUUUUUU   OOOOOOO   IIIIIII   EEEEEEE

AAAAAAAAAEEEEEEEEEIIIIIIIIOOOOOOOOO
UUUUUUUU   IIIIIIIEEEEEEEEAAAAAAAA.

The song got more and more intense and ecstatic. Without knowing how it happened Ish-a-tar slipped into a deep and meditative state of mind where the sound was everywhere, within as well as without. When she opened her eyes she saw the most surprising sight. Around her several men and women had started turning and turning while they kept singing the holy sounds. Others were in a trance-like state of mind standing or sitting on the floor while they were swaying back and forth, still singing. She closed her eyes again and travelled along on the sound, which caught her, lifted her up, up and up until she stopped feeling her body. She was pure energy on her way into a new and foreign world.

*

My thoughts were swirling in my head as I was reversing the car in the direction of the woman at the side of the road. When I got to her I reached across the passenger seat and opened the door. She leaned towards me and smiled. It was as if I was following an invisible manuscript. The problem, however, was that it wasn't Marie Périllos, the waitress from the Belo Bar in Narbonne as I had expected. This woman was blond and seemed taller. She looked in her middle twenties. The sight of her confused me totally. I had no doubt at all that a moment ago I had seen Marie Périllos in a flowered dress standing at the side of the road. Now, suddenly, she was wearing a pair of jeans and a short, red-striped sweater. Where did this woman come from, who was she and what had happened to Marie?

'Are you going to Vicdessos?' she asked.

It sounded more like a statement than a question.

'Well yes,' I answered more confused than ever.

She was soaked and was already entering the car.

'Can I have a lift?'

'Well of course,' I said moving the maps on the passenger seat.

'You can put your bag on the rear seat.'

I stepped on the clutch and put it into first gear while watching her out of the corner of my eye. I was caught between my interest in looking at her more closely and my modesty, which, however, was limited by the age difference between us. Most of all I wanted to ask her directly what was going on, but at the same time I realized that she couldn't

193

possibly know how to answer such a question. I therefore held my tongue, trying to sort out my own thoughts until she broke the silence:

'Are you going to Montréal-de-Sos?'

I took the opportunity of looking at her face. She was transparently pale with fine features, which almost disappeared into the light surrounding her.

'Watch out!'

I was pulled abruptly back to reality as she took hold of the steering wheel with one hand, almost making me go into the ditch.

'You'd better concentrate on the road,' she said with a smile.

'Sorry, I lost my concentration there for a minute,' I said and focused on my driving, 'I was on my way to Olbiér.'

'Good, then we are going the same way.'

I sat for a while trying to find something to say. Then I began with the most obvious thing to say:

'My name is Lars.'

'Just call me Ba-Bé.'

'Is that your name?'

She shook her head:

'You wouldn't be able to pronounce my name anyway.'

'Try me,' I said flippantly.

'I don't think so,' she said in a tone of voice, which put a lid on the subject. It took about twenty minutes to get to Vicdessos. We then continued towards Olbiér. The road narrowed and wound its way through the mountains surrounded by trees and dense thicket.

'This is it,' she said as we turned a corner and saw the fantastic view in front of us. She pointed to the mountain lying like an island in the valley in front of us. Miraculously, the rain suddenly stopped and the sun came out behind its veil.

'Montréal-de-Sos. The Mountain of the Grail.'

'Is this the Mountain of the Grail?' I asked surprised.

'Yes,' she replied surprised, 'didn't you know?'

'Not really, I . . .'

I gave up trying to explain. It was all so certain anyway. No reason to ask any more stupid questions. What was going on? I was utterly lost and fought to regain my centre. I slowed down considerably and shortly after we drove along a very narrow street towards Olbiér.

I parked the car outside the church. We started walking into the village. Apparently she knew the way. It all seemed so paradoxical and yet quite natural. Like the air around us, she was cool and fresh and yet inexplicably present. No superfluous words. Just this wonderful presence.

We passed what must have been the smallest town square of any town. There was only room enough for two benches. Further ahead a sign pointed to the right towards Montréal-de-Sos. A narrow passage ended in the path we were going to follow.

I followed her closely. The climb was not particularly difficult and the path was not very long. The path continued into a grotto from a ledge.

'This is the birth-canal,' Ba-Bé said matter-of-factly and stepped through a mandorla-shaped opening, which most of all looked like a woman's vagina, but it was high enough for a man to stand upright in. It got darker and darker and the ceiling got lower and lower the further we went into the cave. About twenty metres ahead we could see a small hole where the light was very concentrated.

'There is the exit, you don't have to worry,' she said.

It suddenly struck me that she was talking to me like a kind of midwife, a maternity helper, and that in this case it was not the mother but the child, the person to be, she was trying to calm down.

And then it opened up:

A small self is floating about in an impenetrable darkness. A kind of umbilical cord is connecting it to another sphere outside, filled with light. The small self knows nothing about the radiating reality and nothing about all the other small selves surrounding it in the sphere of darkness. This small self, that is my personal identity, is recognized by a consciousness looking at the unity of darkness and light from a neutral position which may be the Great Nothingness. And the consciousness of this Great Nothingness is seen and recognized by a consciousness in another dimension, which has no name as far as we know. This consciousness sees the consciousness looking at the consciousness, which recognizes the small self fumbling about in the sphere of darkness. And all of it is gathered in a single opening at the moment of birth, when consciousness is on its way through The Shaft of the Soul.

Suddenly I'm back in the cave. A drop of water has hit me in the exact middle of my forehead. Right between the eyes. It feels as if it is continuing through the chakra of my forehead, creating its own birth-canal there. At that moment I understand that the consciousness seeing the consciousness which is seeing the small self really are one and the same, and that there has been no other separation than the one the small self has created with its separated and separating mind. At the same time I do recognize that the sphere of darkness is the sphere of possibilities and that each time a person gets a glimpse into the sphere of light it may change something in the weightier department, the known world where man is situated at this moment.

Ba-Bé supported me when I had to bend over in order to get through the stone mouth of the birth-canal.

'Welcome to the women's mountain. Or should I say *the Mount of Venus*.'

Ba-Bé had flung one of her arms out while she continued towards another grotto.

I could hardly believe what I heard: *the Mount of Venus*. This was the exact name that Sylvia had used about one of the two initiation mountains. She had called the other one Mount Carmel.

Ba-Bé went into the grotto and disappeared into the darkness. I followed her, trying to get my thoughts in order. What kind of being was she, where did she come from and what was going to be the outcome of this meeting? She wasn't particularly feminine, however, not the opposite either. She was more an example of isogynic man. She wasn't at all my type of woman. Nevertheless, she had ignited something within me to which I hadn't paid much attention for a very long time.

While I was fumbling along in the darkness, following the figure in front of me, I was contemplating the question that she had accessed. There was nothing sexual in our meeting. Or was there? In that case it was a totally different kind of sexuality than I had known before.

The grotto was not as long as the previous one and before I knew it we were out in the open again walking along a narrow path towards the remainder of the old Castle of the Grail.

It is difficult to find words to describe the feelings I had, when we were standing side by side at the top of Montréal-de-Sos. A flock of goats were jumping down the side of the mountain when we took the last steps to the top. The sounds from the village below us sounded sharply in the clear air. Ba-Bé pointed towards the long valley cutting through the mountains to the east.

'This was the way the three Cathars from Montségur followed to the mountain carrying the secret treasure of the Cathars. There was no village then, nor any kind of habitation here. It was a desolate place which had been used by various groups of holy people in connection with a cult of the sun and as a place of initiation.'

I was listening to her words but I don't know if I heard everything she said. I was far too occupied by the inexplicable radiation and magnetism surrounding her.

She was standing so close to me that I could feel her energy, which spread to me and made me feel a vibration in the side closest to her. Everything happened in slow motion.

Slowly, slowly she turned around to face me. I closed my eyes and felt her lips very close to mine . . .

*

Salome continued educating Ish-a-tar. During the days following the great festivity Ish-a-tar felt as if she was floating along. She was both confused, happy and slightly

The Shaft of Re-birth

despondent. Salome knew the kind of process her student was going through and felt that the time had come to intensify her education.

'Do not lose heart Ish-a-tar. Your faint-heartedness is only natural, but do not surrender to it. When you learn how to make a holy space and how to maintain it the way you want it to be, then you'll know all that you now only feel. Feelings are usually evasive and changeable. They are rooted in the temporal. Not in eternity. For the queen to live she must have a space in which to manifest herself. And only a palace is worthy of a queen. Your body is not your own, it is the temple of the Great Mother.'

She pointed at Ish-a-tar's heart:

'This is not *your* heart but the altar of the Great Mother. Do you understand that?'

Ish-a-tar nodded her assent. She was relieved to start working so that her thoughts had other things to do than just roam back and forth between giving up and having her most desired dream come true.

'When even the worldly embrace is a mystery it is quite clear that the embrace in which the hidden unity between man and woman is incarnated must be of another world. It is not only a reality of the flesh because the embrace about which we are talking contains a quietness, which has not been known until now. It does not originate in impulses or lust but is solely a conscious act of will. It is not darkness, it is not light. Imagine that you are embracing your own innermost being. The name of this being is *Shekhinah*. It is the holy name for the middle column of the Tree of Life. That which I may tell you in words is only a pale reflection of the certainty that you yourself must acquire through experience. *Shekhinah* is the soul of the world giving a little of itself to each and every person, male or female. At the same time she is the essence resting at the foot of the Tree of Life. *Shekhinah* is resting in her Palace while her wooers are passing by hoping to get a glimpse of the beloved one. But she only dances without veils for the one who deserves it.'

Salome smiled at the sight of the concentration of her student. She continued:

'*Shekhinah* is the being with which you must consciously unite in order to receive initiation. But *Shekhinah* is not a static state of mind. She is always on the move and therefore set rules for the initiation into her spheres may not be given. Each man or woman must find the exact gate most suitable to him or her. One thing only may be given which is the same for everyone: the true *Shekhinah* hides behind seven veils.'

'What are those veils?'

'The seven veils of the worldly *Shekhinah* are connected to the seven secrets of her sex, while the veils of the heavenly *Shekhinah* are woven into the seven lower sapphires of the Tree of Life. It is valid for both that the seven departments of the temple are metaphors for and represent both sides of the seven veils. The Ark of the Covenant is an allegory about the mystery. When we celebrate the seventh day and the seven by seven days, it symbolizes the cycle with which we are working. The 50th day thus is the beginning of a new cycle. After that we have the moon cycle of women, the four by seven days giving 28 days. This is the time it takes for the moon to go through its phases. Women have always been subjected to this cycle, however, just as with breathing it is a matter of being consciously present in this cycle. And breathing is also part of it. Well actually, everything in the visible world is subjected to the great heavenly cycle.'

Ish-a-tar was totally fascinated by the teaching of Salome and she couldn't keep silent when it looked as if Salome had ended the teaching of the day.

'When shall I be initiated into these secrets?' she asked, holding her breath.

Salome looked at her intensely. Then she said:

'Now, at this very moment.'

She rolled up one of her sleeves, took a tablet and a piece of chalk and started to draw the shape of a vagina.

THE TEACHINGS ABOUT THE INCARNATED SHEKHINAH

'*Malkoot* represents the very incarnation of *Shekhinah* into the world of man and is symbolized by the anus. *Yesod* is the foundation stone and is symbolized by the perineum. *Hod* is the refulgence of *Shekhinah* and is symbolized by the clitoris. *Netzah* is eternity that is symbolized by the entrance to the vagina. *Tifferet* is beauty expressed through compassion and is here symbolized by the antechamber of women (the g-spot in the front wall of the vagina). *Gevurah* is strength and power symbolized by the yard of Israel (the a-spot in the back wall of the vagina and slightly higher placed than the g-spot). *Hesed* is mercy symbolized by the altar in the yard of the priests and the priestesses (the cervix). These are the seven veils covering the Holy of Holies: *Kether*, the divine will, *Hokhmah*, the divine wisdom, and *Binah*, the divine acknowledgement, symbolized by the Ark of the Covenant (the uterus). Do you understand this allegory?'

Ish-a-tar nodded:

'Does this mean that there is also acknowledgement through intercourse with a man when both are aware of these levels?'

'Yes, this is the way of the incarnated *Shekhinah*. For the higher *Shekhinah* this may be compared with a fall through the spheres into the visible world. Behind each of the levels curses are hiding which must be dissolved and transformed. Darkness hides behind *Malkoot* as an expression of the physical world. When you dwell and meditate at this point you get into harmony with the incarnations. This is the world of animal instincts, which is tied to the lust-filled world of pain and pleasure. *Yesod* is the level at which man must make a foundation of rightful being. A part of man's lower nature is hiding here. It is the level that corresponds to the lower realm of angels (the lower astral level). By dwelling here we get the opportunity to accept the Will of God within us (the great Self) instead of staying in our own limited being (the small self). Our ignorance and intellectual resistance is hiding behind *Hod*, which tells about our limited mental state precisely because we are still caught up in the world of desires. Dwelling here and surrendering to the radiance from the clitoris may change the ignorance so that we may experience the unlimited freedom of wisdom. Here your own will is dissolved and intuition is born. The envy of death is hiding behind *Netzah*, limiting any access to eternity. Dwelling here dissolves all the negative aspects connected with jealousy. Behind *Tifferet* hides the state of being caught in the body believing that it is the only reality of man. Dwell here, and all the animal-like qualities are transformed into humanity through acts of compassion. Behind *Gevurah* any kind of worldly knowledge hides. Dwell here and place the higher intuition before the written word. The poisoned wisdom hides behind *Hesed*. Dwell here, and transform all the falsity, which pretends to be the correct teaching. These three points all belong to the world of the individual which at the moment of man and woman melting together in loving certainty, may be lifted into the heavenly spheres.'

She stopped in order to give her student the opportunity to take in her words. She continued after a while:

'All levels are also contained in the four letters of the holy name YHVH. Yod-He-Vav-He (Yehova). Y = the Father (the masculine Origin), He = the Mother (the feminine Origin), Vav = the Son (the Incarnations), He = the Daughter (the Bride).' Salome stopped and put the tablet down. Ish-a-tar looked at her fascinated.

'What about the heavenly *Shekhinah*?' she asked, eager to continue her education. Salome laughed and all the ethereal aspects danced around them. Then she took Ish-a-tar's hands, swinging them back and forth.

'You'll have to wait a while before you meet the heavenly *Shekhinah*. But I suppose the words that I have given you will suffice for now. Take them along into the night and into your next moon time. Here you may get a glimpse of what is waiting for you.'

She leaned forward and kissed Ish-a-tar on her forehead.

'But when?' Ish-a-tar whispered, 'when?'

*

I could feel her lips very close to mine.

'A heart has two sides to it.'

The words of Ba-Bé practically embraced me. My field of energy united with hers and I saw with my inner sight how a new field of energy came to life above us. It was almost like two people deciding to have a child. Everything, conception, pregnancy and birth, happens instantaneously in a perfect and unconditional closeness.

This pure closeness of thought form slowly floated upwards, reproducing itself again and again until it formed a circle around the mountain. I then felt her lips on my forehead. At that moment a light flashed through my third eye, this time deeper than the drop of water had done in the grotto. What once I had experienced as glimpses of a distant and intangible world now opened itself and took the shape of a mandorla in which all distant and intangible things suddenly become present. It was like standing on the banks of a river tearing past at an incredible speed, but instead of water it was simply floating and radiating energy. Ba-Bé's voice seemed to come from that radiating river:

'This is the fountain of wisdom and foolishness, *the Akasha* where all the thoughts, words and acts of man are stored. Look closely at it. Here is your past, your future and the eternal now.'

I saw in that moment how my own thoughts, almost before I had them, disappeared like drops into the river, which then slowed down. This then revealed a large amount of cinder-like matter mixing with the light.

'As you can see, here is both wisdom and foolishness in total turmoil. When the speed is increased all the cinders are thrown towards each other and dissolved in the light. However, it takes more than the efforts of one individual if all this field is to be cleansed and be of eternal help in the future. Concurrent with the one-sided tension accumulating because of man's present lack of empathy and ethical understanding, the river moves so slowly that the cinders, instead of dissolving, become more compact and limiting to man's exchange with light.'

The mandorla folded into itself and grew smaller and smaller and slowly disappeared totally. I opened my eyes. The sight and the experience had been so moving that I simply stood there trying not to cry.

I looked around bewildered. Ba-Bé was not to be seen. I suddenly had the thought that she didn't exist in the visible world and that she was either a result of my own imagination or spoke to me from another level.

'This way!'

I turned towards the sound. Her head appeared from the ledge below me.

'Come here, I want to show you something.'

She disappeared under the ledge and I started walking along the path that led to her. When I stepped on to the ledge I just saw her golden locks of hair as she disappeared around a corner further ahead.

She waited for me outside a grotto, which had a grating in front of one of its openings, apparently for safety. Her eyes glittered like diamonds. She pointed towards the grated opening:

'Do you see the cave painting on the cliff wall behind the grate?'

I moved closer while I concentrated on seeing the phenomenon to which she was referring. It took a short while before I saw a few reddish lines. I stepped even closer and now clearly saw two rows of six crosses on each side of a square decorated with smaller, equilateral crosses surrounding five drop-shaped symbols and five equilateral crosses. Above the square a circle and a sword could be seen. Above the circle and the sword there was another cross next to a bell-like symbol resting on a long stem that leant against the upper right corner of the square. The whole painting did not make sense at first glance. It might be a map of positions in a landscape, which someone had wanted to pass on, perhaps a treasure map. Or it might be a kind of code containing a secret, which wasn't meant for everybody.

'Look closely at it because it is a symbolic image of the old knowledge of the Grail and isogynic man brought here by the three Cathars who got away from Montségur.

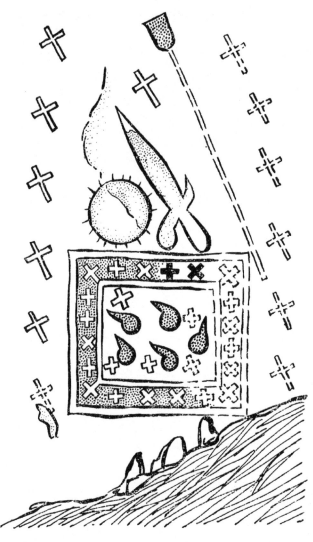

Cave painting at Montréal-de-Sos. The secret of the Grail, possibly painted by the three Cathars who escaped the stake at Montségur in 1244. (Rozekruis Pers Haalem)

Before surrendering to their destiny they hid their precious knowledge in this painting.'

'But how ... '

'Shush!'

She put a finger to her lips.

'No questions. Give your intellect a rest. Look, listen and learn.'

Thousands of years of memory whispered their oracle answers in the wind, like a mystical choir of timeless voices singing their message about eternal creation, the expansion of the great breath followed by the contraction, expansion, contraction in one eternal now.

I do not know for how long we stayed like this. However, when I got back to the grotto and the cave painting I was alone again. I started walking back along the path. Ba-Bé was not to be seen. I wanted to call out to her but didn't.

I saw her when I got free of the church. She was leaning against the radiator of the car, waiting for me.

'Well, here you are,' she said in a neutral voice.

We drove in silence back towards Sabart. It was very strange. It seemed totally wrong having to say goodbye to her now. Nevertheless, it would be the most natural thing to do, considering the situation. But somehow I realized that there was nothing natural about this in the normal sense of the word. It nevertheless took me by surprise when she quietly stated:

'We have a common past as magicians.'

13

As the tests grew harder and harder the days seemed longer and longer. At one point Ish-a-tar was losing her grip on all the knowledge Salome poured into her.

'What I'm telling you is not directed at your intellect but solely at the most elevated part of your soul. You shouldn't trouble your brain with knowledge; it is the wisdom of the heart that matters. When you understand that, the knowledge about the numbers, the letters and the holy sounds becomes manifest in your being of light as superior symbols because it is the language of angels. When your soul becomes the master of this, you'll be able to contact the heavenly powers as you see fit. Remember that all the heavenly qualities are mirrored in you. You must trust the highest level in yourself. Have faith in the fact that your heart knows what is best for you. Know also your obligations. You gave a promise before entering this incarnation. I have read the course of your life in the Book of Life, and I'm not the one to judge that to which you have bound yourself. There are things that even I do not understand. Your road has been a hard one. I have heard about the hard life in the Babylonian temples. Looking at you now it is difficult to imagine what you have been through. I shall have to leave you in a short while. Until now you have danced in the temples and slept with men as a prostitute. Now you must take the road of the temple virgins and the temple prostitutes, and I'm neither authorized nor do I want to witness this part of the honouring of your pledge.'

Suddenly Salome looked into the distance and Ish-a-tar didn't quite understand what was behind her words.

'What does it mean to be a temple virgin or a temple prostitute?' she asked hesitatingly.

'First of all that you're not allowed to marry.'

'But you are not married then?' Ish-a-tar asked.

Salome didn't answer and went over to the window and looked at Lake Mareotis, the surface of which was completely calm. She stood for a long time like this before she continued:

'The difference between being a simple prostitute and a temple virgin or temple prostitute is that you now bring both your open and your goal-oriented consciousness along into your new position. Being a temple virgin is *a state of mind*. As a virgin you do not need the acceptance of others but are an independent person who is no longer dependent upon external circumstances. The virgin is independent. Taking the next step, becoming a temple prostitute, she brings this independence with her into the temple so that she may work with total freedom, without any ties at all.'

'But I don't want to go back to the temples. I have had enough of the lechery,' Ish-a-tar almost shouted.

Salome couldn't help smiling at the violent temper of her student.

'I know. But you are going to teach at a higher level in the future. As a Moon Priestess you are going to help the man, who has such aspirations, out of the darkness and put him in the sky as the sun he is destined to be. You must be ready to reflect this sun to a certain degree until he finds a woman whom he can marry and who can take over this part of the matter. Contrary to the prostitute, as a Moon Priestess you are in equilibrium. The prostitute only has an identity through the erotic power she has over men. Beyond that she is nothing. The temple virgin, however, is a being of equilibrium. During your time as a dancer it was the unconscious side of you, the coldness of the moon and your wish for power, which was the generating force. You were able to lure and tease, but you didn't know true lovemaking. Love in the real sense of the word you didn't know at all. You reflected the innermost part of man in your own way, his unrealized bride. Your task now is to help him acknowledge this divine bride within himself by giving him unconditional love and without the desire for power. When the Moon Priestess sets sail on her moon-boat and steers towards the sun she is uniting the feminine and the masculine aspects.'

Ish-a-tar was also standing now and she ran to Salome at the window.

'But my destiny is different. I must find Sister Mariam. There are more important things in me than performing the trivialities of the temple.'

'Some have come to do one thing and others another. Everyone must take upon them what is theirs to do. Until now you have followed the direction taking you here. As I said, it has been a hard road to travel, but you have learnt everything about a man's way of thinking, about his needs, his dreams and his desires. You know about each and every nook and cranny of his brain and mind. It is in your power to wake him up and take him exactly where you want him to go. In your own words: you can take the animal to the trough. And here the animal will eat whatever you set before it. Up until now, however, you have done that by giving the animal nothing but the blessings of your body. But these gifts do not last forever. One day not one single man will turn around to look at you, because the only means of power you possessed was the beauty of your body. Now, however, you have other things to offer. And this is your future task. The trough has now been filled with wisdom. You were created for this one purpose and you have made a promise in confirmation of it.'

'When?' Ish-a-tar quietly asked.

'Soon.'

*

'We have a common past as magicians!'

Her words were vibrating in the air.

'What do you mean?'

'In ancient Syria and Alexandria,' she replied.

She pushed the passenger seat back enabling her to place her long legs on the dashboard. Her whole being had something unspoiled, obvious, carefree and nonchalant about it. Similarly, however, I also sensed something deep and dark below this apparently carefree nature. But I also knew that this was what made her so attractive – and so dangerous.

She was surrounded by an indefinable, protective sphere, which invalidated the most natural questions about her own person. But I felt so confused that I decided to confront her with the most obvious question of all:

'Where do you come from?'

She was looking out of the side window, which became misty from her warm breath. She drew a heart with her finger. Then another one upside-down, linked with the first one. They ended in a star of Mariam in the middle while at the same time the two hearts themselves formed one. She took her time before answering:

'You need a woman to help you get to the heart of your quest. And here I am!'

I was again struck by the obviousness with which she concluded and ended the matter. All doubts were ruled out beforehand.

I refrained from any further questions and we drove on in silence. What did Ba-Bé know about my quest? Could she be the princess that Sylvia had predicted that I would meet? I could practically hear her admonitions to me before I left: 'Find the princess and you have found the dragon. And where the dragon is there the Grail also is.' Had I finally found the princess? I couldn't help laughing within myself since she was really the one who had found me. I realized, however, that, no matter what, I had to see where the encounter with her would take me.

We drove into Foix half an hour later. I parked the car in the large square, which was filled with stalls since it was market day. We walked between the tents. She stopped at a stall selling bric-a-brac. A table was filled with all kinds of things. My eyes had just caught a small, tarnished silver heart when she picked it up and handed it to me. Something was engraved on it. Holding it into the light I could read the word 'Jesus' on it.

'Try turning it over,' she said.

I turned the heart over. Another name was engraved on the other side: 'Marie'.

'A heart always has two sides to it,' she laughed.

I paid the three euros that was the price and attached it to my necklace. We continued to the end of the square and walked into one of the narrow passages. I walked along lost in my own thoughts when suddenly I felt her arm in mine.

Shortly after, we were in a square at the other end of town, just outside the church. She pushed me gently into the nave and I heard the door slam behind us. It was quite dark in the church. She let go of my arm and started walking down past the side altars in the aisle to the right. I followed her when she called out to me. She squatted in front of an old altar.

'Look,' she said pointing to a relief where the paint was partly peeled off. It was a scene from the Last Supper. However, in this painting there was no doubt that the person next to Yeshua was a woman. In contrast to most of paintings of this subject, the one by Leonardo da Vinci being the best-known, in this one Mariam sat to Yeshua's left instead of to his right which is usually the case. In this painting in the church of Foix she is looking devotedly at her partner. Everyone apart from Mariam, of course, is depicted with a beard.

'It may very well be,' Ba-Bé said, 'that the Catholic Church in general has had its problems with Mary Magdalene. However, this does not seem to be the case here in the south of France.'

When we got back to the square it was cloudy and the day was fading. I then remembered the note with the address of the guide given to me by Mar in the morning. I found it in order to see where this Bart lived, the one who apparently knew about the hidden cave at Montségur.

He lived in Roquefixade, the town with the castle, which the Seer had 'given' to me as an initiation gift a few years earlier. Apparently, it was now time to visit it once more.

'Do you want to come?' I asked Ba-Bé and told her about it.

'What are we waiting for?' she replied.

Roquefixade is situated about halfway between Foix and Montségur and it took us twenty minutes to get there. We had to ask for directions a couple of times before finding Bart's house slightly below the town. In the meantime the sky had changed into a taut canopy filled with rain and thunder that was about to burst.

It was Bart himself who opened the door when we finally got there. He was a tall, broad-shouldered man with a weather-beaten face. Apparently, Mar had told him about my plans and he asked us in right away and we were soon seated around a refectory table drinking tea in the kitchen. He went straight to the heart of the matter:

'When do you want to go to the mountain?'

I was just going to answer when Ba-Bé said:

'There'll be two of us.'

Bart looked questioningly at her and then at me. He then said to me:

'Do you think that is wise? This is no picnic like walking the straight path up the mountain. It can be quite rough.'

I don't know why but I heard myself saying:

'This is fine. There are two of us and unless you're dead against it we would both like to go.'

'All right. So when do you want to go?'

Once more it was Ba-Bé who answered:

'How about now?'

At that moment lightning flashed outside followed by an ear-splitting peal.

'I'm afraid that is out of the question,' Bart said.

'Tomorrow then,' I said.

'Fine. If the weather clears we'll meet here tomorrow at ten.'

Bart got up and went over to the window.

'We are rebuilding our house and I'm afraid we cannot offer you any accommodation for the night, but I'm sure you can get a room at Maris's place.'

He pointed through the window:

'He is the mayor of the town and also has a B & B. He lives in the small castle up there, you can just see the outline of it.'

We said our goodbyes and ran through the rain to the car. The thunderstorm was right above us now and the flashes came more frequently and it wasn't difficult at all to see the small castle just mentioned by Bart.

The castle was really a large villa with a tower giving it a certain air of aristocracy. A narrow, steep avenue led up to a beautiful square in front of the house.

We ran as fast as we could in order to get out of the rain, which by now was pouring down with a force you only see in the Pyrenees. There was a light on the first floor. We went under the porch supported by a few symbolically decorated pillars, which formed an impressive entrance. While we were shaking the water off Ba-Bé laughingly pointed to one of the arches above us:

'Take a look at this.'

A beautifully shaped, flying phallus was caught in mid air.

'And there.'

She pointed to a star of Mariam hanging on a pillar next to us.

'And by God – here as well.'

'Who?' I asked forgetting all about the rain and the thunder.

'Yeshua and Magdalene!'

Sure enough and here they were, one on each side of the same pillar, just the way she had said: Yeshua and Mariam. Apparently this mayor, Maris de Roquefixade, was no ordinary man.

I pressed a button but the thunder made it impossible to hear whether or not it was connected to a bell in the house. We waited for quite a while and were about to give up when finally the light went on in the hall. Then the door opened and a man about my own age, tall, lean with a bald patch and long hair at the back of his neck, looked at us through a pair of round, thick-lensed glasses.

'Sorry about the late hour, but we are looking for lodgings and have been told you have rooms to let.'

He sized us up. Then he seemed to take pity on us and stepped back:

'I see.'

We went inside. The house was furnished in a classic style but I immediately noticed the books covering most of the walls. I spotted a book with an occult subject. Between the books the walls were decorated with esoteric symbols and there was no doubt that Maris de Roquefixade had an interest in this kind of thing.

'How many nights?' he asked while he still looked closely at us.

'Just one,' I said.

'Double or single?' he asked.

I couldn't say why but his question disturbed me. Ba-Bé beat me to it:

'A double.'

'I see.'

He turned about and walked down a dark passage. We followed him. He opened a door at the end indicating with one arm that this was our room:

'At what time would you like your breakfast?'

'At nine, please,' I answered.

'I see. Goodnight.'

I heard his footsteps disappearing and then it was totally quiet. We stood in silence. My thoughts whirled in my head. What now? What was on her mind? Then she broke the silence by throwing herself on the double bed. She sat up and bumped up and down the way you do when you want to make sure that the bed is useful for something other than sleeping...

*

Lamu could hardly wait for the seventh day when men and women were to meet and sing together. However, it was quite a different song burning in his heart. The song was called Ish-a-tar.

When the day came and the men were getting close to the common room he got so impatient that he could hardly stay in his place. From inside the temple they could hear the song of the women the way the ritual demanded it. His heart was about to burst. The procession moved along very slowly and when finally they got to the room his eyes immediately looked for the beloved one. She wasn't there. He looked around bewildered. What was going on? Another woman had taken Ish-a-tar's place. This was totally unthinkable. Something must have happened. She might be ill? His heart missed a beat and he felt faint. He then pulled himself together and dismissed the thought. Meanwhile, the men took their positions. The priest had started chanting. Lamu could not concentrate. His eyes roamed from one woman to another. He spotted the tall figure of Salome. She stood there with her eyes closed, apparently already lost in prayer.

Shortly after, the rotation around the altar with the wine and the bread started. He walked trancelike, as if in a fog where he registered everything without really being present.

It was not until he passed the altar with a strange woman, with whom he received communion, that he woke from the dream and realized the painful truth that Ish-a-tar was not present.

He didn't think at all when contrary to all rules he turned to the woman at his side and asked her:

'Where is Sister Ish-a-tar?'

The woman looked at him terrified. They kept their places and continued the rotation. The seriousness in his voice must have convinced her since she whispered to him:

'In the temple of the Moon Goddess.'

Then he started running.

Excited voices were calling after him. He clearly heard one of them which was the voice of a woman:

'Let him go. It is written.'

It was the voice of Salome.

He was running for love. Or was it lust or both?

He was running for his life. He ran until he lay at the foot of the stairs of the shining temple of Aphrodite in the middle of Alexandria, more dead than alive. He lay there surrounded by busy men who had more than enough to think about with their own affairs: the necessary visit to the chosen daughters of the great goddess.

His lungs hurt and his legs shook under him as he climbed the stairs. Not until a temple guard brutally pushed him down the stairs again did he regain the use of his senses. He got up and bowed apologetically. The guards laughed at him and let him pass. What did a brother dressed in white want in the house of Aphrodite?

Lamu didn't notice them, just as he didn't notice that he was wearing the gown of the Therapists. He was only focused on one thing: finding Ish-a-tar before it was too late.

He followed the crowd of men and ended up in one of three queues outside three gates. He could hear from the dialects spoken that there were men from all parts of the kingdom. However, he didn't notice what they were talking about, only the excitement and the pressure towards one of the gates, which suddenly opened and embraced him like a pair of caring wings.

They were guided into a hall and one by one they passed the women who sat there in their enticing costumes, each in her own cubicle. He felt faint. There were women of all shapes. Young and old, lean and fat, tall and small, but all were overdressed to a degree that made most of them look like unreal beings or demons from another world. He saw their bare breasts and he saw the humiliation. There were women among them whose beauty was obvious and they wouldn't stay there for long. However, Ish-a-tar was not to be seen.

Before he could react he was taken to the exit where a temple guard pushed him into a blinding light.

'Better luck next time.' the guard laughed laconically.

As soon as he found himself outside the building he ran to the entrance once more and this time he ran up the stairs. The guards shouted mockingly after him but let him pass. The second time he made sure that he was in the group at the middle gate. Here, however, he also only found the same grotesque exhibition of women who tried to get their temple duties over with as fast as possible. And Ish-a-tar wasn't here either.

When he walked up the stairs for the third time he felt panic seizing him. What if she wasn't in the temple at all? Then he suddenly froze hearing a few words, which struck him like lightning, 'The White Whore from Babylon'. He couldn't see which one of the passers-by had spoken these words. Desperately he reached out at random and took hold of a man who was on his way into the sanctuary. The man tried to tear himself away but Lamu held on to his cloak.

'What do you know about the White Whore from Babylon?'

The man looked at Lamu, frightened, surprised at the violence in his voice. Then he regained his composure:

'Take it easy brother. There are prostitutes enough for everybody. The one you are looking for you probably cannot afford anyway.'

The man freed himself from Lamu's grip and continued into the darkness. But Lamu didn't let him go that easily. He ran after him and caught him again:

'Where?'

Apparently the seriousness of the situation slowly dawned on the victim because he pointed into the darkness towards an almost hidden door leading to a side chamber.

'There,' he growled.

There were no guards at the door. Lamu went in. A long passage lay in darkness. Lamu stood still listening, hoping to get an indication of which way to go. He couldn't separate the sounds, which all seemed to emanate from the entrance hall from where he had just come. He touched the wall with one hand until he gradually regained his sight. He saw another door at the end of the passage and slowly approached it.

The door was ajar.

Lamu slowly pushed it open.

The dust was dancing in a ray of light coming from a small opening in the ceiling. Lamu stepped into a beautifully decorated but empty room. There was a door in each of the four walls. Standing in the middle of the room he noticed that all the worldly sounds had disappeared as if by magic. He stood still, listening intently, but there was only this silence, the sound of a present containing the sounds of everything from the past. And for a moment he was struck by the feeling of a time gone by or perhaps a new time rushing through his consciousness. Before he could identify with it the feeling was gone, but he felt that something within him had fallen. He felt vulnerable and unprotected in a strange way that worried him. In this strange feeling, the decision to make a choice was hiding, a decision he knew he had to make without knowing why. The door through which he had come led back to the entrance hall of the temple. The access to

Ish-a-tar was behind one of the three remaining doors in the empty room, he had no doubt about that. He heard a voice from far away. As it became clearer he realized that it came from within himself. This was also something that rushed through his consciousness like a whirlwind in an inexplicable way. He was totally concentrated and tense at the moment the voice rolled up towards the surface of his consciousness and left its ephemeral imprint before disappearing into the ethereal level:

'The door is on the inside!'

He was standing in the middle of the hall looking indecisively at the three possibilities. A set of invisible rules stemming from an unacknowledged fear told him he had one chance only. His mind was in turmoil. 'The door is on the inside.' What kind of statement was that? How was that to be understood?

He was looking for a solution in his mind. But his thoughts were like a hundred wild horses running in all directions. He tried to hold on to one of them but in vain. He didn't get any further than a desperate attempt to try to understand the devious mind behind this fiendish game. Which door was supposed to misguide him? Which one called for him especially? If he could find that one then there would only be two from which to choose.

But no matter how he twisted and turned the matter, another possibility always presented itself with another hidden explanation more diabolical than the previous one.

'The door is on the inside!'

Then suddenly it was as if the cone of light from above was pointing at him. He couldn't decide whether the light was an external or an internal one. But he knew that all that had been fluttering about around him moments ago suddenly gathered and found its way back to its starting point in his heart. Everything he had learned but which he had been on the point of losing: certainty, wisdom, confidence and faith.

He slowly sank to the floor and into a lotus position.

'The door is on the inside!'

Of course it is, he thought and gave up his fear and his thoughts' insane spinning around.

He didn't know how long he sat like this. But he stayed in this position until the door appeared in his mind and then opened and revealed a radiating room where Ish-a-tar sat smiling and waiting for him. He then got up from his place in the hall and walked towards the middle door. He opened it slowly. A sea of secret scents met him as he went inside.

Ish-a-tar lay on a richly decorated bed, waiting for him. He approached the bed as in a dream. Getting closer, he noticed that she was naked under the transparent material. He did not notice how he got out of his own clothes; all he saw was her warm and inviting smile. He slipped into bed and embraced her tenderly. They kissed as only lovers kiss. Then she whispered in his ear:

'I knew you would pass the test.'

But at that moment it was very difficult for him to recognize her.

'Who are you?' he asked in the way a child might talk to an angel.

'I am *Shekhinah,*' she said while slowly she let herself slide down upon him, anointing him.

Then they slowly moved into the Holy of Holies of the temple, uniting and becoming one light.

*

Ba-Bé went to the bathroom to get ready for the night. I was slightly embarrassed and didn't quite know what to do about the situation. In an attempt to act naturally I sat down in a chair in a corner of the room and waited. It was a poignant moment but I was so full of resistance and had so many reservations that I was neither able to hear nor see what was going to happen or understand any part of the situation. Instead, I saw only seduction with all its trimmings. In a desperate attempt to create a kind of light suitable for the sleazy atmosphere, which my unconscious, hurt sexuality was arranging, I put out the light in the room except a small lamp above the bed which barely managed to give the room a faint, pale hue.

I heard the tap in the bathroom being turned off and took this as an indication that she had almost finished.

And so it was. Shortly after the door opened and she stepped into the room, naked, placing herself against the light from the bathroom behind her. I was paralysed, gasping for air at the sight of her lithe body. Then she turned off the light in the bathroom and stood in the semi-darkness of the room. I could only hear the thumping of my heart beating so loudly that I was convinced that this was all she as well could hear. Time stood still. And suddenly all the sleaziness dissolved. Like a soap bubble seeking toward the surface and exploding at the confrontation with reality, my old feelings of guilt faded like morning dew.

Then something happened which is very difficult to explain. Small vibrations manifested themselves around her body. Those vibrations most of all reminded me of butterflies dancing and being filled with light at the same time. I was so surprised at the sight of these radiating butterflies that I didn't immediately see that the light came from her. The sight of her filled me with such an inexplicable and deep sense of joy and gratitude that I cannot find words to describe it.

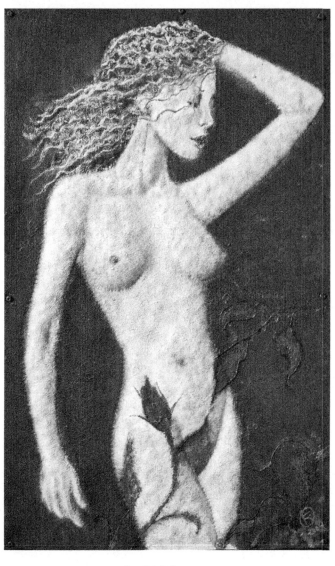

Ba-Bé/Ish-a-tar
(Painting by Francis Andreasen Østerfelt)

227

She was standing in the opening of the door. The chair in which I was sitting was situated at the other end of the room. It was therefore so much more surprising to see how small, radiating butterflies, like the ones coming from her, were now also dancing around me.

The current around me seemed to get stronger and stronger as if there was a simultaneous charging of both my ethereal body and the butterflies. But before I could put my feelings into words I realized that the butterflies *were* my star-body like the butterflies around Ba-Bé's body were *her* star-body, which however, vibrated so fast that they became visible in this wonderful way.

She stood in front of me, totally enlightened. The butterflies were suddenly sucked into the middle of the room, and at that moment I saw her true being and origin.

This being had no face and no personality. It was nothing but pure light.

My own true being and my own true origin were also reflected in this light. This faceless being of light sending its breath into eternity was an expression of the condition that may only be expressed by the concept so maltreated by man:

Love.

PART III
SALAMANDALA

14

A faint light crept in between the curtains and fell on my face. I stayed in bed dozing, with my eyes half shut, while I slowly found my bearings. I felt as if I had been on a long journey but I couldn't remember the destination.

Ba-Bé!

I got up and looked around in confusion but she was not to be seen. Was it all a dream or had the meeting with her taken place at another level? The covers on my side were halfway to the floor indicating that she might be more real than I thought. I took the pillow and held it to my nose to see if I could smell her scent. But where was she?

I got up and opened the door to the bathroom but she wasn't there. I pulled the curtains aside and opened the window slightly. It was impossible to mistake her golden laughter. It mixed with a man's voice, which apparently was the cause of the frivolous merriment. I immediately felt a pang of jealousy but shook it off and got dressed.

Walking through the hall, I saw her sitting on the terrace on the other side of an enormous arched window that extended from floor to ceiling. Maris was serving breakfast and Ba-Bé already had a mug between her hands and was sitting flirtatiously with her legs pulled up under her. She was still laughing and it was quite obvious that Maris considered her to be both charming and irresistible. I stood still, watching them and trying to keep my jealousy in check.

Who did I think I was? The experience of the previous evening might be just another one of a series of astral journeys which was the result of the process I was in and which I had been in for a long time. There wasn't really anything going on between us. Or was there? No matter what, the feeling of jealousy was real. I went outside.

'Good morning. Here is the transformed prince,' she laughed patting the empty chair next to her.

Her gesture made me feel like a dog or a frog more than a prince, but I accepted her invitation and sat down. Maris hardly looked at me – his whole attention was riveted on Ba-Bé. He didn't even try to hide his obvious admiration of her. She, for her part, however, was totally natural. But it was exactly this openness that to my mind could so easily be misunderstood and misinterpreted by a Latin like Maris as flirtation. The fact that this was saying more about me than about him or her didn't bother me at the moment. I coughed in order to get Maris's attention. However, it was not until I knocked an eggcup to the floor that I woke him up from his infatuation and he looked at me reluctantly with regret in his eyes:

'Yes!'

'A cup of coffee would do me good,' I said flippantly trying to sound unaffected and natural.

He placed a bowl with strawberry jam in front of Ba-Bé before he turned around and in an exaggerated fashion walked towards the kitchen bent over and dragging his feet. Ba-Bé laughed out loud and when Maris turned around and looked at me with a diabolical smile I realized that his little performance somehow had been an attempt to ridicule me.

He came back shortly after with the coffee and two cups. When he had arranged everything he sat down and poured the coffee. For a moment I was confused. What was he thinking? We, Ba-Bé and I, were the guests and he was the host. But I didn't say anything. Instead, I sat fuming over my coffee and a piece of burned toast listening to their conversation. I felt totally overlooked and didn't hear exactly what they were talking about, only that it was about Maris and his claim to Cathar ancestry and his ideas about them, the fact that he thought they were 'Paulinites', or that they had adopted many of Paul's doctrines in their teaching. Instead of listening properly I tried to convince myself that I could let her go just like that. Then I heard her voice penetrating my defences and I heard say:

'But Lars knows all about that. He also writes books and is interested in the same subjects.'

I looked up from my burned toast, which I tried to hide under a thick layer of jam, and caught the eyes of Maris who now looked at me with a limited amount of interest.

'What do you write about?' he asked without much enthusiasm but more in consideration of Ba-Bé.

I hesitated. How could I answer his question in a few words? I really didn't want to answer it and more than this I didn't want to start a dialogue with him. There was an abyss of resistance between him and me. The answer I finally gave him had only one purpose:

'I write about the secret of the Cathars.'

He reacted promptly like a boxer who has been hit in his most tender spot: his pride.

'What secret?'

The fire was lit now. And as I was about to add fuel to it Ba-Bé pushed me in the side and pointed to the ground between Maris and me. Two salamanders were twisting and twirling in a fight to the death in the dust. It was a merciless battle between lizards. The battle at the same time took place in a very distant past. The sight activated something age-old, deep in my subconscious. I then realized that the duel between Maris and me was the continuation of something with roots further back, perhaps even before the earth existed. I looked up at him but, apparently, he hadn't noticed anything. Then I gave him the coup-de-grâce:

'Well, I cannot tell you, can I? It wouldn't be a secret then, would it?'

The moment I spoke the words I was painfully aware of the primitive direction our confrontation had taken; however, at the same time it was unquestionably the only way in which to solve this old problem. What surprised me the most, though, was the fact that I enjoyed every moment of it.

Ba-Bé broke the spell:

'We must go now. It's a quarter to ten.'

She got up and put her arm in mine. She turned to Maris and said in the most innocent way:

'You see, we are going to have a look at the secret of the Cathars today.'

*

'I hereby give you the initiation name *El-Phatah*, "The opener".'

The priest drew the cup with the holy fire across Lamu's chest from right to left. He took a piece of incense from the cup and made the sign of the cross in front of Lamu's heart as a sign that the eye of God had now been opened. Then he gave Lamu the staff of Mercury, the sceptre of Hermes, as a sign that the power of the man in him had been lifted into the heavenly sphere and that he now had the power to heal and to prophesy.

Finally the priest embraced him and kissed him on the mouth. This was the sign by which the initiated ones greeted and acknowledged each other.

Then Salome stepped in front of the altar. It was now Ish-a-tar's turn to get a new name.

'I hereby give you the blessing of *Shekhinah*. From this day on, your initiation name shall be *Mar-Iona*, 'The White Dove of the Moon-sea'.

Salome lifted the cup with the holy water into the air. She then dipped two fingers into the water and made the sign of the cross in front of Ish-a-tar Mar-Iona's forehead as a sign that the eye of the Goddess had now been opened. Then Salome gave her the Venus ring as a sign that the power of the woman had now been lifted to the heavenly sphere and that she also from this moment on had the power to heal and to prophesy. Salome embraced Ish-a-tar and kissed her on the mouth.

'Remember,' she finally said, 'remember that these names must remain a secret until the day they are either confirmed or exchanged for another. It is all written. But only the one who is able to read the Book of Life shall know when the time has come.'

After the initiation the brothers and the sisters sang in honour of Ish-a-tar and Lamu. The ceremony ended with a common meal after which the newly initiated ones took leave of their two teachers and went out into the world.

The rumour about this holy couple who healed and prophesied spread like wildfire. Ish-a-tar and Lamu could hardly move in Alexandria without having crowds of people following them. They did what they had been trained to do but Ish-a-tar was losing her patience. One day she heard a woman talking about Mariam Magdal and the words reawakened her deep longing to meet this sister about whom so many beautiful stories were told. However, the foreign country where Sister Mariam now lived was far away and to get there, they would have to cross the *Mare Internum.*[*] And in order to do that they had to find passage on a ship.

Summer was coming to a close and soon the first storms of autumn would make any kind of sailing perilous. But it happened that Ish-a-tar heard a name mentioned in the crowd one day when she and Lamu were in the process of healing people. At first she tried to repress it, and that made her sad, but then it struck her that perhaps the name was heaven-sent. Had she really heard it?

She called out over the crowd:

'Who among you has just mentioned the name of the merchant Hashem Ben Nari?'

A murmur was heard in the crowd and a black man stepped forward:

'I did.'

Ish-a-tar walked right up to the man: 'Is Ben Nari here in Alexandria?'

'He is on board one of his ships which is presently berthed in the harbour. I myself am employed on board.'

---

[*] The Mediterranean.

'And where are you going?'

'*Melita*,[*] we set sail tomorrow.'

Ish-a-tar and Lamu looked at each other. This might be the opportunity they had been waiting for.

They finished the treatments and followed the man to the harbour. Shortly after they were walking up the gangplank to board the good ship *Isis* in order to meet Ben Nari. Ish-a-tar couldn't help smiling at the thought.

Isis.

How could it be otherwise?

The great Ben Nari received them in his saloon on the upper deck. He had better things to do than spend his precious time with dubious people who wanted to do business or obtain passage, just like these two Therapists who had come on board. He lay on his couch being massaged by one of his slaves when Lamu and Ish-a-tar were shown in.

'Well, what do you want?' he asked without getting up from the couch.

It was Lamu who answered:

'We are going to *Massilia*[†] in *Narbonensis*[‡] and we are looking for passage.

Ben Nari dismissed it with one of his thick arms:

'We are not going that far. You must look for another opportunity.'

He rolled on to his side with great difficulty while the masseur worked on his shapeless body.

They stood in silence watching the grotesque scene.

Then Ish-a-tar spoke:

---

[*] Malta.

[†] Marseilles.

[‡] At the time a Roman province in the vicinity of Narbonne.

'We have heard that you are going to Melita. It is part of the way and sufficient for us.'

The big man's body jerked. Then he got up on his elbows with great difficulty. There was something in the voice of the woman that sounded familiar.

'You!' he almost shouted when, full of doubt, he saw Ish-a-tar standing in front of him radiating a kind of beauty far above the animal-like sensuality of former days.

With an impatient movement he signalled to the slave that he wanted to get up from the couch. He practically tore the cloak from the slave's hands.

Shortly after he was sitting in a chair huffing and puffing from the exertion so that it took some time before he found his voice. He was looking at Ish-a-tar with a curious eye trying to estimate his chances with her. It was not a coincidence that he was considered to be one of the most cunning merchants in the part of the world from Babylon to Alexandria and back.

Ish-a-tar looked right through him and she must have touched something deep down in the man, which, however insignificant it might be, nevertheless made him meek as a lamb.

Ben Nari laughed self-consciously. But Ish-a-tar knew all too well that the meek lamb was a disguised jackal.

'So, you haven't found your Mariam Magdal,' he smirked. 'Very well, you may join us as far as Melita. From there on you must find other means of transport.'

He pointed to the slave:

'Anglus here can show you around. Go now. I need my rest. Unless of course, you, Ish-a-tar, want to stay and revive old memories?'

His laughter filled the saloon as he invitingly patted the cot with his hand. Ish-a-tar didn't respond at all but turned around and walked towards the door.

238

The hoarse voice of Ben Nari sounded through the wind as they stepped onto the deck:

'We leave at sun up.'

*

As I paid for the B & B I couldn't help noticing the series of crystals, with a reddish-brown hue, hovering around Maris's head. But the crystals were not interactively connected. Instead, each of them constituted its own autonomous thought form which, although it bore witness to great knowledge, also showed that this knowledge was rigid, dry, separating and intellectual.

Suddenly, I felt great sympathy for him, so much so that the scene, which had just been played out between us and was reflected in the battle of the two salamanders, embarrassed me. In a peculiar way, I also sensed that he felt the same thing.

I looked around for Ba-Bé. She was waiting by the car, surrounded by an unreal light. Although the distance between us was too great for me to see the expression on her face with any certainty I had no doubt at all that she was smiling up at us. Perhaps she was the one who had caused the energy between Maris and me to change?

'You are welcome here any time. Just give me a call beforehand,' he said shaking my hand in farewell. I thanked him with a genuine feeling of warmth and started walking down towards Ba-Bé.

There was an abyss between the two realities we had just experienced. Not to mention what had happened the previous evening and night. I had never experienced anything like it. At least not in this life.

It was still cloudy and in spite of the thunderstorm of the night it was foggy and humid. Ba-Bé was standing in her usual pose, hand on hip. And yet something had changed. It was as if I could see two different people in her, or rather two beings: the worldly Ba-Bé with her natural charm, who could seduce any man, and the heavenly Ba-Bé about whom nothing else could be said but that she opened and lifted everything to another sphere with her wonderful, radiating light.

As she stood there leaning against the car it was difficult to decide which one of the two was the more prominent one. But then it dawned on me that she was neither of them; she was yet a third being, a being without a name which didn't claim to have a specific personality, didn't want to claim anything at all for itself or to be treated with any kind of preference. This being simply *was* pure being.

While I was thinking these thoughts a frightening field of nothingness opened inside me. One thought said: this is how it feels when all your well-known references are taken away from you. When you are confronted with reality and you realize that most of our sense of reality, our lives and our safety are tied to false premises and ideas, then the house of cards comes tumbling down. It is all hidden in the small things and the way we judge others or the way we cling to everything. Up until now we thought that what you see is what you get. We thought that we were able to judge the contents by the wrapping.

I was watching Ba-Bé in an attempt to force my way into the mystery. But she just smiled at me. I saw the finest crystals forming a radiating ring around her head, and with a bit of imagination it looked like a crown. I had no doubt at that moment about what had happened the previous night or that she was the virgin Sylvia had talked about who would come when the time was ripe. I felt a burning desire to ask her for her own explanation. However, a strange thought told me that if I did she would disappear as mysteriously as she had come.

And the dragon?

Perhaps this was the salamander within myself, which had battled with the other salamander just like it?

'You took your time,' she said without any reproach in her voice.

We turned out of the driveway and drove down the mountain.

Bart was standing outside his house waiting for us. He had the gear we needed in a stack in front of him. I was somewhat surprised when I saw the small ice-axes, water bottles, a narrow, foldable light-metal ladder and three helmets with torches strapped on to them.

'Say, are we going mountain climbing?'

'Well yes, both outside and inside the mountain,' Bart said with a sound of secrecy in his voice.

We put the gear in the boot of the car and took off.

Twenty minutes later we passed the car park at the Montségur mountain. I was excited to find out from which point we were going to start the ascent, but Bart didn't say anything as I drove through the hairpin bends and into the village.

'Further ahead,' Bart said as I pulled to the side.

We drove down into the valley, around the bends and followed the road out of the village again. Apparently we were going up from the south, the same side I had taken with the Seer, eighteen months earlier when we took the hidden road up there. This time, however, we were to start further down as we had gone through practically all the turns before Serrelounge .

'Here it is,' Bart suddenly said and signalled for me to stop the car.

Bart and I divided the gear between us and packed it in our

backpacks. Bart took the lead, Ba-Bé followed and I brought up the rear.

Bart climbed the high stone wall which stopped the eroded rocks from breaking up and rolling down towards the road.

'Montségur is a living mountain,' Bart concluded.

What looked like a piece of cake for the first five minutes soon turned out to be an almost insurmountable task. It was practically impossible to step on a rock without it immediately rolling away under you.

Although it was still foggy we could feel the warmth of the sun hiding behind the clouds. The humidity was higher than normal. After fifteen minutes of balancing on the slippery rocks I was soaked with sweat. At the same time the mountain started getting steeper and steeper until it felt as if we were climbing a vertical wall. The combination of slippery rocks, the steep incline and the humidity was insufferable. I leaned out to see how my companions were doing. Bart was moving upwards with ease ten metres further ahead and Ba-Bé was following him with just as much ease halfway between him and me. I gritted my teeth and tried to concentrate. This was quite different from my last trip on Montségur when the Seer and I had had minor problems only. However, they were nothing compared to this. I dared not think about what was in store for us. Instead, I tried to find a way to keep focused and found that the best point of focus was Ba-bé's behind moving from side to side above me. To my great surprise I suddenly experienced how my focus shifted between my struggle to keep concentrating on my climb and the struggle to control the lust that the sight of her constantly called forth in me.

We came out of this rolling hell shortly after and into a fairy tale of a low wood of gnarled trees, hazel, boxwood and birch. The surface consisted of a soft moss and it felt as if we were walking on clouds.

We paused in order to recover our breaths.

The sweat was pouring down my body. None of us could talk. We had already slipped into another state of mind.

A vibration went through the underbrush. I thought it was an animal and turned towards the sound and just spotted a small shining being of light disappearing behind a wooden stump.

'Did you see it?' Ba-Bé quietly laughed '– there and there . . .'

She pointed here and there and to my great surprise I saw several beings of light identical to the first one slip behind some trees while I had the feeling that they were watching us the same way as we were watching them. Apparently Bart had not noticed anything since he coughed so loud that the beings disappeared as fast as they had come.

'Wait here. I must reconnoitre the area before we proceed.'

He started climbing and soon disappeared between the trees. Once in a while we heard the crack of a branch breaking and a growl, which could have been a bear. But it was Bart. He was moving about in the wood with the same ease as a bear.

Ba-Bé must have read my mind for she whispered in my ear:

'Bart the bear.'

He was back shortly after:

'This way.'

We continued the climb.

Once in a while we passed a cairn or a *stone-man* as Bart called them. Beacons of stone set by Bart or other guides who knew the area.

We had reached a plateau where the incline wasn't as steep. At the same time I had the feeling that we were moving

243

into a field where only a very thin veil separated the various realities. The radiating net behind everything became more and more visible the deeper we penetrated into the indescribable nothingness.

The plateau levelled out and we now moved between hazel trees only. Bart pointed to a bonfire place in the middle of an opening in the forest:

'This is an ancient site where the charcoal burners made their charcoal 200 years ago. You can still find personal items which they left or forgot in the area.'

We continued to the ruins of the old guard tower on the rock, *Roc de la tour*, where we rested once more. I had long since forgotten how to get here. And it wasn't very important. Instead, another road was showing itself in a totally different dimension.

Soon we were on our way again. It was clear that Bart wanted to stay on the trail, now that he had the feel of it.

'It can be very difficult to find the right way if you get lost and once you have lost sight of the stone-men,' he said.

Not only did we balance on the edge of reality but also virtually on the edge of a ledge, with the abyss an open mouth below us ready to devour anyone who lost his concentration. And just then I felt the mountain move with a deep tremor and come alive just the way Bart had said when we started the climb. Everything was dissolving. I felt dizzy, sweaty and hypnotized by Ba-Bé's sweet behind, which was still enticing me to climb up and up, step by step. My legs felt like lead and I lost my footing once in a while, but I always managed to find something to hold on to. It is still a riddle to me how Ba-Bé could be so unaffected by the rigours of the climb.

The mountain rose up once more and became even steeper. I was just about to announce that I couldn't go on when Bart signalled for another break. Once more he had to make sure that we were on the right track. Every step was agony and every break was paradise.

I sat down on a rock, resting my head in my hands, watching my sweat dripping on to the rock surface. The sun came out behind the clouds and the face of the mountain was like the surface of an anvil. I imagined that I was the heavy, hard material, the steel that had to be softened in the forge in order to be re-formed.

Ba-Bé stood tall and lithe, looking into nothingness. I sat there watching her and wondering what she might be looking at.

It came floating down. It floated in from all sides.

A peace as soothing as a playing fountain on a bright summer's day. A transparent, radiating veil of intervals and breaks, stops and nothingness spreading over us, freeing us from all burdens and any kind of worry.

A moment only.

And this was the exact moment when it reappeared, the unbelievable, vibrating sound – the song of the mountain like a humming, below, over, around and inside of me.

In front of me Ba-Bé had transformed into a totally enlightened field opening out – or was it in?

I got up and took a step toward this vibrating field.

Irresolute. Hesitating.

Then I stepped into it. Through it and out – or was it in?

It doesn't matter now as it didn't then.

I followed the path through the radiating ethereal level with its sparkling air. I walked without any difficulty. To my left a stone-man, to my right a snake. The symbolism was obvious. But by now I was so used to it that I wasn't surprised at all. And although the stone-man wanted to tell me about the antiquated and petrified parts within me, he was still a signpost. The snake was also an age-old part of me but at the same time it was newly born. It had shed its old slough and had risen like a phoenix from the ashes.

The dragon?

A bear stood on the trail in front of me. It was standing on its hind legs, paws in the air and claws showing, blocking my way.

'This way!'

I turned around and walked toward the sound of the voice. Bart stepped out from the brush.

'I have found the cave!'

15

As the good ship *Isis*, after three days sailing, found itself on the open sea and far from land, Ben Nari for the first time put forward his demand. Either Ish-a-tar danced for him and gave herself to him for one night or she and Lamu would be thrown overboard. It was all so predictable and Ish-a-tar just shook her head at this insane requirement. She immediately confronted Ben Nari with the fact that neither she nor Lamu had expected anything else and they both looked forward to their deaths by drowning with pleasure rather than complying with the lecherous desires of a madman.

Ben Nari spent three more days and nights pondering this until he realized that the two Therapists didn't fear death and that he therefore had to find another way to reach the goal of his dreams. Four days later he set forth his new demand;

however, this time with the added ultimatum that, if his orders were not complied with, two innocent slaves would be sacrificed to Neptune.

That made the difference.

Lamu fumed but Ish-a-tar calmed him with a smile:

'There are other ways.'

She kept Ben Nari at bay for ten days with the excuse that she was in the middle of her moon period.

When the long expected evening finally arrived for Ish-a-tar to dance for Ben Nari the great merchant's saloon was decorated like a Roman brothel.

Ben Nari sat heavily on soft cushions eating from all the dishes that his slaves set before him in an endless flow of food. Two Egyptian musicians were readying their instruments, a harp and a few drums, for the event of the evening. Ish-a-tar was preparing herself thoroughly in a small cubicle. From her time as a prostitute she knew exactly what to do in order to emphasize her beauty in the most cunning ways. And especially for this event she didn't hold back but tinted the most intimate parts of her body red. In other places she underlined the shadows with black and brown charcoal. Transparent veils and small, intriguing pieces of material were fastened with thin leather straps, giving the finishing touches to the most hot-blooded and daring harlot the world had ever seen.

She let Ben Nari wait while the music played in order to build up an atmosphere.

Ben Nari turned and twisted impatiently on the pillows. He was already scarlet in the face from lecherousness and excitement.

'When does she come?' he shouted hoarsely to a servant.

The servant immediately ran to Ish-a-tar to check that everything was all right. But Ish-a-tar simply ordered the poor man to go back to his master and inform him that the White Whore wasn't ready yet but that she would soon make her appearance.

When the atmosphere was so tense that Ish-a-tar could feel it all the way to her small cubicle she walked down the passage, pulled the curtains aside and stepped into the dimly lit saloon.

Ben Nari gasped for air. He had imagined all kinds of things but this was more than any man could imagine. A being from another world was standing in front of him radiating such an intense sensuality that he immediately felt his member move. He then pulled himself together and shouted at the servants:

'Out, out. I don't want to be disturbed.'

Only the musicians and the servant who had contacted Ish-a-tar were allowed to stay. His task was to operate the big fan made from palm leaves that would prevent Ben Nari sweating to death.

Slowly Ish-a-tar slipped into the rhythm of the music. The veils whirled around her like butterflies and before long it was she who conducted the rhythm and the music and not vice-versa. She was mistress of this kind of game to perfection and she allowed no one to have any doubts on that score. She hovered across the floor, round and round, so that everyone could see that her movements were worthy of a queen. However, this was just to show where dignity lay: with the dancer not the audience. When Ish-a-tar had demonstrated this impeccably, she took the dance to another level. She found a centre and started dancing around it removing the outer veils. This, combined with the intense turning, started a centripetal force moving inwards and down towards a centre in her body. She let one arm circle towards the ground while the other moved upwards as if she held on to an invisible rope connecting the terrestrial with the divine. She danced faster and faster, round and round, forming a circle totally free from any kind of sensuality. Out of this intense centre a centrifugal and upward-moving force was whirling, which was so powerful that it filled the saloon with a penetrating light. Everything which was untrue was revealed in its intensity. From within this ecstatic dance Ish-a-tar saw the fearful, wry face of the great merchant and his futile attempts to hide himself from the merciless light. The musicians played as in a trance. Never before had they experienced that music and dance were able to enlighten and transform space like this.

However, Ish-a-tar knew all too well that this was just a short respite. Ben Nari would continue with his demands until he got his way.

She stepped out of the whirling enchantment with ease and at that moment the light seemed to dissolve so that the saloon once more was steeped in the sleazy semi-darkness of repressions. Then she started on the last dance, which she danced to perfection. She slowly led the music along into an erotic universe leaving nothing to the imagination. She resembled a bird of prey, which until now had only circled the air, watching its prey, but now dived like lightning in order to plunge its sharp claws into the soul and flesh of the paralysed victim.

She danced back and forth, provocatively and enticingly, in front of Ben Nari, who was now in a state of mind beyond understanding. Ish-a-tar wanted to get this whole charade over and done with and took the dance to its final goal. One veil after the other fell to the ground until she was standing in front of him wearing a short, transparent loincloth only. Ben Nari fell on to his side grunting like a pig as he tried to get on his feet again. His cloak opened and Ish-a-tar saw his enormous erect member like that of a horse. The time had come. She gracefully let herself slide to the floor and took up a position on hands and knees with her bottom in the air luring him to come closer.

'Why don't you help me?' Ben Nari shouted at the servant who was just as caught up in the enticing sight and didn't notice anything else while his master was rolling around on his pillows.

Ish-a-tar knew that she was balancing on a razor's edge.

She lifted her loincloth with one hand making herself totally open and accessible. But somehow, with that gesture, she underlined the fact that it was him, and not her, that had been stripped.

Ben Nari, in the meantime, got to his feet and stood staggering from side to side like a drunkard holding on to his erect member.

'I'm yours,' she whispered leaning her forehead on the floor and looking behind her between her legs. Ben Nari staggered forward with one thing only on his mind.

He wanted to get down on his knees but almost lost his balance. The servant had to support him when he slowly approached the entrance to the holy temple of Ish-a-tar with his swollen member.

The time had come for Ish-a-tar to finish her task. She quickly pulled the energies back, closed her eyes and began chanting:

'Everything that ties in heaven, everything that ties on earth, everything that ties in the air, everything that ties in the firmament, everything that ties the Pleiades, everything that ties the sun, everything that ties the moon, everything that ties the birds, by the holy ring of the Father everything that ties the seven words which Iliseus said over the heads of the holy ones the names of whom are: Psuchou, Chasnai,

Chasna, Ithouni, Anashes, Shourani, Shouranai! Let these ties be transferred to this man's member, its flesh and the soul behind it. Let it dry up like wood and turn it into brushwood which is only good on a fire!'

Then she felt Ben Nari's hands on her hips. He pushed himself against her while he roared like a wild animal. She opened her eyes and looked over her shoulder where she saw his earlier so-potent weapon hanging limp and wrinkled between his fat thighs like a nestling falling out of its nest.

He pushed Ish-a-tar away very forcefully and only because of her agility did she avoid falling over. Before he had time to react she was on her feet wearing her cloak.

'Apparently, he has lost the power of the gods,' she said innocently and with fake compassion to Ben Nari who didn't know what to say. This had never happened to him before. What kind of devilry was this?

'You damned whore!' he said as she withdrew between the curtains and disappeared on to the deck.

From that evening Ben Nari had to stay in bed. He sent for Ish-a-tar every day and begged her to heal him. She, however, simply pretended not to understand. Instead, she offered to dance for him and to spend the night with him, which just made the merchant cringe in despair.

'Can't you take pity on me? Don't you have a heart?' he sobbed.

This lasted until they touched at Valetta at Melita. Here Ish-a-tar for the last time went to Ben Nari in his saloon. As the weeks had passed by the big man had shrunk in size, which made him look like a real human being. At the same time he had totally changed his character and was now so compliant and grateful for any service done to him that no one could believe it.

Ish-a-tar went close to the sickbed and put her left hand on the forehead of Ben Nari.

'I thank you for your hospitality, Ben Nari. From this day on you shall leave your sickbed as a new man. As of today you shall leave all your sins of the past behind. As of this day you shall never again exploit anyone since now you understand what it means to be reliant on the help of others. Do you agree to that?'

'Yes,' he whispered.

'Then be you healed!' she said in a clear voice.

When Lamu and Ish-a-tar went ashore on Melita they walked straight to the holy Hypogeum in order to meet the legendary oracle who lived in the passages below the temple. Innumerable were the stories about this oracle who from the beginning of time had only had male priests but who was now serviced by priestesses. Legend had it that a complicated channel system, which communicated the messages of the oracle, in those early days, only reacted to the voices of male priests. It had been like this for centuries. But one day the unthinkable happened: the oracle went silent. For more than a hundred years the oracle of Hypogeum was silent. Until one day when a holy woman came to the island. This woman had taken the place of the oracle as if it were the most natural thing and had spoken the most amazing prophecies. The woman, however, had to travel on to an unknown place. But before leaving she had taught a few suitable women to carry on the tradition.

Ish-a-tar was impatient and hurried Lamu, who was more occupied with the fact that once more they had their feet on firm ground.

She wasn't satisfied until they stood at the entrance to the holy place. A smell of burned sage and other holy herbs came up from underground. Ish-a-tar immediately began descending the narrow and steep staircase.

'Come on!' she said.

∗

'It's this way,' Bart said and signalled with his hand.

I could hardly believe that we were there. Perhaps I hadn't believed that the cave was really there. The time had come to find out if the dream was real.

Ba-Bé was looking into eternity as usual. We followed Bart closely, balanced sideways on a ledge, around a sharp corner, and then we were surrounded by gnarled trees once more.

'There it is!'

Bart pointed in between the rocks.

I couldn't see anything. There was nothing to be seen.

'Where?' I asked suspiciously.

'Come over here.'

Bart took my hand and helped me keep my balance over a hole surrounded by sharp rocks. Ba-Bé followed without Bart's help.

There it was.

The entrance to the cave.

I noticed immediately that the entrance was shaped like a pyramid and that there was just room for one person to get through at a time. It was a beautiful moment. We stood still watching the entrance until Bart handed me a helmet and broke the silence:

'Do you want to be the first one through?'

I nodded.

Having put on my helmet I approached the holy spot. I squatted outside in order to collect myself. I then took a deep breath and crawled in.

I was met by the characteristic smell of sage. It was an old smell filled with purification and mystery. It was difficult to see anything and I sat down on the floor a metre into the antechamber so that my eyes might get used to the darkness.

I suddenly felt an indefinable hush pass through the cave. There was no doubt. Another being had made its entrance and was now also present here. I looked around. The contours of another opening into a larger cave were just visible and I couldn't help laughing at the sight. This entrance was shaped like a pyramid turned upside down. It was then I noticed that I was sitting between two entrances the shapes of which formed the Star of Mariam.

Of course.

Naturally.

I remembered with affection the sight I had seen a year earlier when the Star of Mariam had manifested itself for the first time while the Seer and I were climbing the mountain. I was enveloped by a deep peace coming towards me from all sides. Then I felt that I was lifted from the floor about twenty centimetres.

An electric current ran through my body with a faint vibration. At first I was frightened but before this feeling really manifested itself it was replaced by a feeling of total surrender, and I felt how everything within me unanimously agreed to what was about to happen.

I don't know whether or not I said it aloud or if it was just something I was thinking, but the question to the being in the cave came out like this:

'Who are you?'

I had hardly finished the sentence or the thought before the answer came:

'Be you greeted. I am one of the Nameless Ones.'

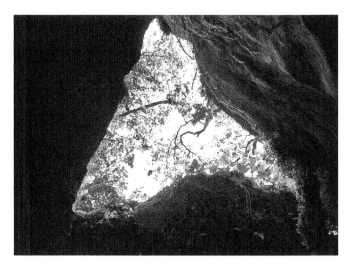

The secret cave entrance seen from inside the first chamber (the Chariot of Fire)

The entrance to the inner chamber seen from the first chamber

The cave was silent. The level of vibration went up a few degrees. Everything went so fast and yet it seemed as if a whole series of options appeared before me. I could choose fear or I could surrender to this being. I chose the latter.

'Where do you come from?'

'I have always been with you. From the beginning of time and until today. However, you yourself have not acknowledged that before.'

Silence.

'You have a question?'

There was something both gentle and matter-of-fact about the being. But there was no time to lose and I seized the opportunity:

'What is happening?'

There was a long break. Or rather, this is how the silence seemed to me. In this great, cosmic thoughtfulness I sensed an equally great sense of humour trying to care for me in a way that suited my level of understanding.

'Up until today, you have followed the way of water. This is the horizontal, forward-moving reality run by the trinity of time, space and matter. You are now to follow the way of fire. This is the vertical, upward-moving reality opening to the fourth and fifth dimensions. Up and until now everything has been conditioned by body, soul and spirit. The fourth dimension is now being opened up: the ethereal reality of the Holy Spirit.'

Silence.

The being continued communicating shortly after:

'You are in the Chariot of Fire. You may travel wherever and whenever you want to.'

'How does this work?' I asked and immediately felt unworthy.

But just as immediately I felt the care of the being:

'Put any kind of limitation and any feeling of inferiority behind you. Think the thought and by it you may move anywhere and at any time, whenever you wish. Try it!'

My thoughts went chaotically through my head. This opened all kinds of possibilities. But something in me collected all the threads and I was immediately aware that I should call on a dear friend who was ill and needed help. As soon as I united with this thought I felt a tickling sensation in my forehead and at once found myself by my friend's sickbed.

He was asleep but smiled at me in his sleep. I quickly put a hand on his heart and blessed him with the words: 'I thank you, I respect you, I love you.' Then I removed my hand and was immediately back in the cave.

I am, of course, quite aware of the fact that such an explanation is insufficient and I shall not tire you, dear reader, in trying to explain or defend myself with words that, naturally, must sound like total nonsense. Nevertheless, my words are quite true to the degree I am in my right mind or in possession of all my faculties.

I sat in an indefinable time-space continuum in a meditative state of mind as the being continued its communication with me:

'As you see, it is not at all difficult in itself to work with fire. The only condition is that you give up every kind of judgement.'

The words of this being made the joy of recognition flow through me, since Sylvia, the Seer and the Voice all had earlier underlined the fact that it is always man's inclination to judge everyone and everything that builds the biggest limitations. How, I wondered, were Sylvia, the Seer, the Voice and this being connected?

Once again, I had hardly had the thought before the answer came:

'Everything is connected. All beings like everything in all the universes are interactively connected. We either get closer to or remove ourselves from each other by way of our thoughts or our actions. Each one must choose. This is the secret behind the freedom of choice. And any conscious choice is an expression of an act of will. Only the one who opens himself to this reality may step actively into it. Man is already in this reality and has always been there but only a few have had the courage to acknowledge it. And this makes all the difference. Man keeps himself away from his most supreme possibilities through his endless judgements.'

Silence.

Shortly after the being added:

'Fear is the refuge of the weak.'

Silence.

'If you have more questions please ask?'

Once more I was seized by panic that time was running out. But once more the being calmed me:

'There is plenty of time.'

There was so much I would like to know but sometimes it happens that you are totally blank when you get an opportunity like this.

'What kind of time is it we live in. What awaits humanity?'

'Chaos!'

I felt a stab in my heart.

'Chaos?'

'Or certainty. But that is the decision of the people. Closing your eyes and leaving responsibility to others leads to chaos. Each person now must take responsibility for him or herself.'

'But doesn't this lead to total egotism?'

'No! Being responsible for your own life means that you understand that you are divine and absolutely necessary for the greater picture. It doesn't mean that man should only look *after himself, his own career and his material comfort. Didn't He say: "Love your neighbour like yourself." This means: "Know yourself." How can the one who knows himself do evil to others? It is impossible. The one who knows himself will gladly take his place in the great, collective transformation. Each person has a role to play. Each person has come into this world with some unique qualities. If they are not put to use chaos will arise, sickness will arise and finally destruction will come.'*

'What does it take for man to avoid chaos, sickness and destruction? Are we to follow the traditional directions of the old religions?'

'Man must take responsibility for himself and avoid comparing himself and his work with that of others and with their work. No one, and I repeat, no one can know the processes other people go through or why people think and act the way they do. Find your way to the truth in yourself. The old directions and guru systems are out of date. All religions have outlived their roles. All hierarchies must fall. Both the secular and the spiritual ones. Religions and hierarchies have been necessary learning aids for man to lean on. Man must now learn to stand upright without any artificial aids. Then he shall be able to perfect himself and to help others.'

'What about Krishna? What about Buddha? Or Jesus? What about Jesus Christ?'

Silence.

'Let them go. The problem with all you human beings is that you always personalize everything. You worship people. We are talking about pure energy. Krishna, Buddha and Christ are cosmic forms of energy and qualities present in human beings.'

'What about God then?'

'Do you want to meet Θ?'

'Θ?'

'Yes, Θ.'

'But is ☉ the same as God?'

'*Well, you might say that. The concept of God covers your limited idea of ☉.*'

'No human being has ever seen God.'

'*Do you, or don't you want to meet ☉?*'

'I certainly do!'

In one flowing movement everything visible was turned inside out. Like something positive becoming negative, or vice versa. In a space between the two poles, positive and negative, a ball of light was burning intensely in all the colours of the rainbow. From all sides millions of rays of light flowed back and forth like a gigantic nerve system of light.

'*Let me introduce you to: God!*'

'Yes, but . . .'

I couldn't say anything.

'*Can you imagine that God is the result of Man's idea of God? If you stay long enough you'll find out that God, apart from being an old man with a long, white beard, also is a black woman, an alcoholic homosexual, a neurotic communist, a blind boy of five years of age, the current President of the USA or whoever you have the ability to imagine.*'

I closed my eyes. This was more, much more, than I could take in. Instead I heard myself saying:

'What is the task of man here on earth?'

'*Man is the link between heaven and earth. Man is the transformer. His task is to transform darkness into light, matter into spirit. Darkness is not evil in itself. Darkness slowly becomes evil if it is not changed into light. Darkness is a series of qualities, which haven't been acknowledged yet. If they stay unacknowledged or unchanged they carry in them the possibility of what you call evil.*'

'How does man transform anything?'

261

'*By exchanging the horizontal way of thinking and acting for vertical understanding and reality. By taking a vertical way of thinking man unites earthly things with heavenly things. This is the task.*'

'Yes, but how?'

'*If you will come to us we will meet you halfway.*'

'Could you be slightly more specific?'

'*Man must lift himself above himself. When this happens we will bow down and lift him up. But it is totally the responsibility of each individual. This is the only way for us to co-operate.*'

A long silence followed. I sat meditatively for a while. The being exclaimed:

'*LOVE IS A HEART WHICH MAY SEE IN THE DARK.*'

Another long silence followed. Then I felt compelled to say:

'But many people need a teacher?'

'*Today's teacher is tomorrow's student. Today's student is tomorrow's teacher. Everybody needs coaching. But people all too often leave the responsibility to charismatic personalities who claim to have the truth. There is not one single teacher on the earth today who knows the true potential of man. Mark my words: not one! Cleverly built hierarchies and systems, seemingly logical and esoteric explanations, theories and theologies are the devilish web barring the sight of the true path. Man loves fantasies.*'

'But what then is the true path?'

Silence. I sensed a quiet, vibrating laughter.

'*It is so simple that no one will believe it.*'

'Why not?'

'*Because you cannot make a personal fortune or an identity through it. The truth is not a career-maker. Wisdom is not for sale and may not be bought.*'

'What and where is the truth then?'

'Truth is a power. It is everywhere. Did He not say that Heaven is within you and everywhere around you? The message about truth sounds the purest in silence. But it is drowned by the noisy messages that are shouted from every rooftop. The political, the materialistic and the spiritual marketplace.'

'But what are people who seek going to do, then, where should they go?'

'THEY SHOULD STOP SEEKING AND LET THEMSELVES BE FOUND BY ☉.'

'But how? What if this ☉ cannot find man?'

'That is why man must come forth from his hiding place. Everything man longs for is, and has always been, within his reach. If he would only acknowledge this there wouldn't be anything else to look for. When this happens man will step out of his self-made prison and into reality.'

Silence.

The level of vibration was now so high that I stopped shivering. Instead, I felt the light of acknowledgement flowing through me.

The being continued:

'Has it not been said that faith can move mountains? When man loses his faith in what is real he places the responsibility in the hands of dubious experts and leaders. And when these leaders only believe in mammon, honour and power, illness arises. Illness within society and within each human being. And illness creates more fear. If money is the highest power and power the highest goal and this goal justifies the means then man has turned his back on SPIRIT. When you deny Spirit you twist everything. It is an evil circle, which can only be broken when you regain your faith in the highest qualities and have the courage to step out of the curse. Hasn't it been said that it isn't possible to solve the problems of the world by the same way of thinking which made them? Those are words of wisdom that many of you

263

may be able to articulate but that not one of you learns from. Positive thoughts that do not turn into actions become negative dead weights instead.'

There was nothing didactic or preaching in the words of the being. They were totally devoid of sentimentality. I had a sudden thought. Perhaps this being didn't have any feelings. As before, the answer came promptly:

'Feelings are an important means of expression. Control them and become realistic or let them control you and stay within your illusions. All emotions have two sides to them. At the other side of joy you'll find malice. Compassion is the heart's answer to sorrow. Without feelings man would not be able to experience empathy towards another human being. Feelings unite people. People are baptized in water. The time has come to baptize with fire. Only what is true will survive the fire. Everything unclean and false shall perish.'

Silence.

'What is the Holy Spirit?' I asked hesitatingly.

'The Doer. The Heavenly Fire. It is the new way of thinking which does not look back.'

'If you are not supposed to look back does that mean, then, that all that history has taught man must be abolished?'

'What has mankind ever learned from history?'

'Did millions of people die in the concentration camps in vain? Are we just to forget that?'

'How could you forget that? It was you who killed each other. It was you who invented the atom bomb and destroyed thousands of brothers and sisters. It will remain a part of you. But it shouldn't be cultivated. It must be recognized and then let go. In this way homicide can never again become a solution for man.'

'And we were the ones who built the pyramids, right? Should we forget all about that? What if there is a totally new kind of knowledge hidden there waiting for man to find?'

'*Do not get taken in by outward circumstances. Everything the pyramids contain, you also contain. Everything – and I repeat: EVERYTHING IS CONTAINED IN MAN!*'

Silence.

'What is the fifth dimension?'

'*You wouldn't be able to understand it yet.*'

'Please, help me to understand it.'

Silence.

'*Compassion.*'

'Compassion?'

'*Compassion is the fifth dimension.*'

'Would you care to explain that a little further?'

'*As I said: you wouldn't be able to understand it yet.*'

'But I really want to understand.'

'*I salute you. We'll meet again.*'

16

'Who gave you permission to enter here?'

Ish-a-tar and Lamu stopped. In front of them they saw a figure wrapped in a cloak – unrecognizable in the semi-darkness. The voice was indefinable. Ish-a-tar spoke:

'We are looking for the Oracle.'

'Who are you?'

'We are two itinerant Therapists from Alexandria on our way to Massilia.'

The figure looked at them and at their white gowns.

'Don't you know that only the chosen ones come here?'

Ish-a-tar's answer came quickly:

'But maybe that's what we are?'

'In that case you're welcome. However, if you do not speak the truth . . . you will die. But tell me now what is the secret word?'

For a moment Ish-a-tar looked in bewilderment at Lamu but he couldn't help her. She then spoke the first words that came into her mind:

'Mariam Magdal!'

The figure was visibly shocked. The sound of heavy breathing filled the room. It was obvious that Ish-a-tar had spoken if not the secret word then at least a name that was not unfamiliar in this place.

The figure's voice suddenly sounded more inviting:

'What do you know about Sister Mariam?'

Now Ish-a-tar dropped all her reserve:

'She's the one we are looking for. My travelling companion here has also been Mariam Magdal's travelling companion. And we are now looking for passage to Narbonensis where she is supposed to be staying.'

A sound of a suppressed surprise was heard from behind the cloak:

'You'd better come with me.'

The figure turned round and started walking back along the passage from which she had come. Arriving at the end of the passage they saw an even steeper staircase than the earlier one leading to a subterranean cave branching out in all directions. Ish-a-tar and Lamu followed the cloaked one closely.

They stepped into a large room illuminated by several oil lamps.

'Wait here.'

The figure pointed to a stone bench and disappeared into a narrow opening in the wall. Ish-a-tar and Lamu sat down.

They sat for a long time. After a while, however, the smell of burnt sage became more and more insistent. A delicate white smoke came up through a grate in the floor below the stone bench on which they were sitting. Shortly after the

267

Oracle started to speak. The voice sounded as if it belonged to God himself. They could not determine where the voice was coming from, but it filled the whole room and was so powerful that Ish-a-tar and Lamu crouched and put their hands over their ears.

'*Step forward vain one and state your business.*'

Ish-a-tar got up and took one step forward. Then she said:

'We're only travelling through, but we thought that . . .'

The oracle cut her short:

'*Step forward!*'

At that moment Ish-a-tar saw a small hole in the wall in front of her. The hole was marked with red dye and she understood that she was supposed to speak into it.

'We're travelling through. We're looking for the renowned Mariam Magdal. Can you tell us where we may find her?'

The oracle hesitated before answering:

'*With the Highest One.*'

The room was now almost filled with smoke. Ish-a-tar did not understand. The answer of the oracle was no answer at all, it sounded as if it was speaking in tongues.

'But where do we find the *Highest One*?'

'*Here, there, everywhere!*'

Ish-a-tar was slowly beginning to understand how the oracle worked. Apparently, it was not possible to get a direct answer from it.

'Does this mean that she's also here?'

This time the oracle did not hesitate:

'*Of course.*'

'How am I to understand that?'

'*Who's saying that you're supposed to understand it?*'

Ish-a-tar was getting tired of this foolish game. It did not lead anywhere. Or did it? She looked towards Lamu for help, but he was totally hidden by the smoke. However, he must have sensed that she was on the point of giving up because he suddenly came out of the smoke and walked up to Ish-a-tar, saying to the oracle:

'I know that sister Mariam has been here, but also that she has left again. Please tell us how she can still be here?'

The oracle kept silent.

Lamu and Ish-a-tar looked knowingly at each other. Then Lamu continued:

'Please tell us what the chances are for us to get a passage to Massilia?'

The echo of Lamu's words reverberated in the silence. They were about to give up hearing more from the oracle when it spoke again:

'You'll have obtained a passage before the day is over. You will be on your way in three days' time. There's no more to be said. Be you greeted.'

It took them some time to find their way through the smoke back to the passage and the staircase leading into the open. Not until they were standing outside the temple did they feel how dizzy the smoke had made them. They were as if bewitched and had to support each other. An image of a woman kneeling appeared in Ish-a-tar's mind. The woman was holding a human skull in one hand and a book in the other. The sound of drums and bells came up from below, forming strange rhythmic patterns that followed them on their way back to the harbour.

They saw a man running towards them from the harbour and recognized one of Ben Nari's servants. When he got close to them he threw himself to the ground gasping for air and saying:

'I've been looking for you everywhere. You must follow me immediately. My master has risen from his sickbed, but we don't know him any more and we are all afraid that we are

269

going to lose our jobs on board. He keeps asking for you. You must come and heal my master.'

Lamu could not help laughing.

'Get up my good man and go back and tell your master that we are on our way.'

Having bowed and scraped and thanked them in a confusing flow of movements and words the servant disappeared back where he came from.

At the harbour a crowd of people followed the unloading of the ship. The smell of spices mixed with the pungent smell of dried hides, which were being carried ashore and stacked in the long warehouses.

Ish-a-tar and Lamu were walking up the gangway to the *Isis* shortly after – for the second time.

*

A drop of rain.

I heard the sound of it and felt it as it hit my helmet right in the middle of the crown centre. It felt like a finger from on high reaching down and knocking lightly on the top of my head.

I lifted my head in order to see where the drop came from. At that moment another drop fell. It felt like an explosion when it hit my pineal centre in the middle of the third eye.

Open.

Immediately I realized that these were the two initiating steps in a baptism to my new life. The third and last step was yet to come. But in my heart I had a clear sense of what this baptism was about and what the purpose of it was.

I suddenly understood the hidden truth about the legend of the Grail saying that the Grail was a gem, which at the dawn of time had fallen out of the tiara on the forehead of the rebellious angel Lucifer when he was expelled from heaven. This gem symbolizes the third eye and the monadic consciousness possessed by all people before they incarnate into this life. I realized that the bearer of light, Lucifer, is archetypal man who has lost his true vision, the awareness of his true origin: the certainty that we are all children of the Heavenly Source, God – or ☉. And when the old Cathar legend tells us that the saint of the Cathars, Esclarmonde, during the siege by the Inquisition of Montségur, threw the Grail, the gem of Lucifer, into the mountain in order to prevent it falling into the wrong hands, then this was the Cathars' allegorical interpretation of one of the deepest and most important truths about the condition of man, his potentiality, means and purpose.

'How are you?'

Bart's face appeared in the entrance-way. My whole body felt light as a feather. I felt a lively, electrical activity around me. But I couldn't find any words to match the situation.

'You look as if you feel very well. Are you ready to continue further into the cave?' he asked slightly worried.

I must have looked silly sitting there squatting with a transfigured smile on my face and a scratched climber's helmet on my head. I pulled myself together then and tried to say something. But I couldn't find the words. Instead I sent him a thought asking him not to worry. Immediately his face also lit up in a smile and he withdrew from the entrance and left me sitting in peace. In the following silence I heard a voice whispering:

'You've found what you were looking for: the heart on your true Mount Carmel.'

It was an unbelievable moment. Every cell in my body was filled with joy. I understood that each person is a sensitive field of energy that is constantly surged by numerous kinds

271

of powers, which it cannot always transform and recognize. And I understood that it is the degree of ability, willpower or courage to acknowledge and awaken these powers that is decisive for the way they manifest and become expressed through man. Exactly there, at that moment, I surrendered to the flow, and for the first time in my life I, more than ever before, felt in agreement with that which was real in me. For the first time ever I felt in agreement at a higher level with the task that I had taken upon myself before I was sent into the terrestrial reality. Everything the angel had told me opened up into my innermost being and, sitting there in the cave, I realized that the transfigured certainty within me perhaps consisted of this one single element:

Grace.

I silently spoke the Aramaic prayer of Heaven, thanking the angel and crawled into the open.

Outside Bart was sitting in blessed meditation. Ba-Bé was smiling at me as if she was fully aware of what I had been through. She then kissed me on my forehead and crawled into the cave.

*

Ben Nari received them in his saloon. He looked completely different and one might have thought it was a stranger talking:

'The good ship *Isis* will be unloaded in a couple of days. It will then hoist anchor and head for Massilia with no other cargo on board than those who are looking for the holy Mariam Magdal. It is my hope that you shall be among the travellers.'

Ben Nari took a step in front of Ish-a-tar. He was not pretending when he said:

'Thanks to you a new human being was born last night. It is this human being standing in front of you at this moment wanting in all humility to give you just a fraction of all that you have given me. Without any cargo we'll be able to make the journey before the autumn storms really set in.'

He knelt down before her. Ish-a-tar put her hands on his shoulders:

'Stand up, today the prayer of man has been heard by God.'

*

'Are we going any further?'

Bart stood up, came over and sat on a rock beside me.

'I don't think so,' I said. 'Only if Ba-Bé wants it. I have found what I came to find. What would we find further in?'

Bart was scratching the back of his neck as if he didn't quite understand why I didn't want to see it all when we had taken the trouble of crawling all the way up here. Shortly after he said:

'You crawl about five metres along quite a narrow passage. Then you enter a large room about fifteen metres in diameter and about twenty metres high. From here there are two openings, one on each side of the room, leading into an intricate system of passageways where you can walk about for hours. I've no idea how big it is or where it leads to and I don't know of anyone who does. When I have investigated the passageways on earlier occasions, I stopped when the thread I used for security ran out. But I'm convinced that you can really get lost there.'

Bart stopped talking. We were looking at the entrance to the cave, waiting for Ba-Bé to turn up.

I couldn't help thinking that the innermost cave that Bart had just described was an image of man's latent need to complicate everything, a kind of matrix of our neurotic

273

need to get lost each time we are unable to differentiate, or for some reason do not want to. I had no doubt that what I had experienced in the antechamber was the essence of everything that I at this moment was able to contain. And I was equally aware that this experience was part of a plan to make me step out from my hiding place, which up until now perhaps had kept me from being found by God.

Although I felt totally centred and rested in my heart, I also felt how sensitive and vulnerable I was. I could feel the sensitivity and vulnerability of all mankind. Thinking about what we put ourselves, and others, through, and at the same time wasting all our best qualities and possibilities on nothing, made me more than sad.

I waved my sadness aside. What good was it? Instead, I followed a sudden inclination once more to try the chariot of fire. I closed my eyes, lost myself in my breathing, and briefly described my goal, which this time was a bedridden client I had worked with in Denmark for a while. I had a prickly sensation on my forehead and immediately I found myself sitting at the sickbed. My client cried out in surprise, 'What are you doing here?' As though it was the most natural thing in the world I put my left hand on my client's chest. Shortly after I heard myself saying, 'I honour you. I respect you. I love you. Be you healed!' I then lifted my hand and once more I was sitting in front of the hidden cave on Mount Montségur in the Pyrenees.

My left hand was warm and the right one was cold. This was a very strange form of precision. There was no nonsense about it. And the self who spoke the words was not my own little self but something bigger and inexplicable. It had all taken just a few moments and it left me wondering and filled with gratitude. I sat for a while but then decided to contact Sylvia. Having done the necessary simple act of focusing, and having felt the familiar prickly sensation on my forehead, I was standing face to face with Sylvia. However, we were not in her living room in Charlottenlund in Denmark, but in a shapeless floating space.

She smiled at me in acknowledgement:

'As you can see, you shouldn't play with fire.'

Her golden laughter filled the ethereal space with a life-giving electricity.

'Remember Venus,' she whispered.

Shortly after she disappeared again, and once more I was sitting on the mountain at Montségur.

Venus?

So close and yet so far away.

Where should I go from here? There were so many questions I wanted to ask Sylvia, but apparently this was not the time for it. There was so much to remember and so much to understand in order to work out the puzzle. If there was a puzzle at all? At that moment I remembered Sylvia's reminder that I should also visit the church in Montségur.

Shortly after Ba-Bé appeared in the entrance to the cave. She was also visibly marked by the experience of this place.

Bart looked closely at her. Then he looked questioningly at me, and I knew what was going on in his mind. I therefore asked Ba-Bé if she was ready to crawl further into the cave. She answered immediately:

'Why? We already got what we came for, didn't we?'

Bart was confused and looked from one to the other. I couldn't help smiling at her direct ways.

'I suppose that ends the matter,' I said to Bart.

We then started the descent, which was even more difficult and more dangerous than the ascent had been. The only difference was that I had much more energy now.

We came down whole, tired and sweating, but with a totally new and different kind of energy than the one it normally takes to crawl up and down mountains. We quenched our thirst with a couple of lukewarm cans of beer before driving Bart back to Roquefixade.

We paid him, thanking him for his assistance, and once more set out towards Montségur.

'We now have only one problem,' I said.

'And that is?' Ba-Bé asked, casually.

'How do we get the key to the church in Montségur?'

'Oh, that. Don't worry about it.'

I looked at her. As usual she was sitting with her legs on the dashboard over the glove compartment looking at the landscape passing by outside.

I parked outside René's house. Before I could take off my seatbelt, she was halfway out of the car:

'You go on down to the church. I'll be there shortly.'

Then she was gone. As I stood on the road I tried to catch a glimpse of her, but she was nowhere to be seen. I started walking down through the village. The distance from René's house to the church is not very far and although I took my time, it didn't take more than ten minutes before I was standing in the little square in front of the church. I couldn't see the door which was hidden in the shadows from the trees, and I was about to sit down when I heard Ba-Bé's voice:

'Why don't we go in?'

I squinted and could then see her standing outside the church door waving a large key in the air.

'I'll be . . . ! Where the devil did you get that?'

'From the Norns,' she laughed secretively.

It was obvious that she didn't want to tell me more, but I couldn't help wondering what she knew about the Three Norns, representing past, present and future whose presence

I knew all about here in Montségur. However, I didn't ask her about it.

The key made a rusty, grating sound as it was turned in the lock. We helped each other push the door open and it squeaked so much on its hinges that it was clear that it hadn't been opened for a long time. We were met by a pungent smell of chalk and mouldy wood. It was pitch-dark. I found a switch to my right, which lit a naked bulb that turned out to be the only light in the church.

We stepped inside.

*

One early autumn morning the *Isis* finally arrived in Massilia after 26 days of hard sailing.

They were not allowed to leave the ship before they got permission from one of the officials of the Roman proconsul. They waited most of the day without getting any kind of information at all. Ben Nari then sent a messenger to Herod's palace in the Jewish part of the town. This worked. Ben Nari and Herod had been involved in many business transactions over the years. They went ashore an hour later with all the necessary permits. Furthermore, Ben Nari and his entourage had been invited to dine with Herod himself, who was here in order to relax.

'Would you please join me as my guests?' Ben Nari asked Ish-a-tar and Lamu.

And thus it happened that they got lodgings and were about to dine with the richest man in Massilia.

Herod was a well-proportioned man in his prime with obvious Jewish, aristocratic features. He seemed quite surprised at the sight of the re-born Ben Nari who bore no resemblance at all to his old, smirking and promiscuous self.

But Herod, who could appreciate a profitable deal himself, had always liked Ben Nari, if nothing else then at least because he was the most cunning and the most gluttonous of them all. Anyone in the company of Ben Nari immediately turned into a saint. Slightly insecure, Herod embraced the great merchant who now appeared to be humility itself, showing signs of true joy. Herod was wondering what was going on, but he just didn't understand.

Ben Nari was virtue itself and if Herod had doubted his sincerity, he had to admit that the gratitude and humility which the merchant showed his two guests were unmistakable and beyond any doubt.

'Herod my dear friend,' Ben Nari said. 'I would like you to meet these Therapists from Alexandria to whom I owe my life.'

He called Ish-a-tar and Lamu, who came forward before Herod and greeted him the way you are supposed to greet a royal personage.

'I greet you, you who are dressed in white,' Herod said and asked them to the table.

When, shortly after, according to Roman tradition, they lay on soft couches around a well-provided table, Herod clapped his hands and four musicians started to play softly.

'Be my guests and eat heartily,' Herod laughed while he studied Ish-a-tar with curiosity.

It was clear that he had noticed her beauty. They dined in silence until Herod asked:

'What brings you to Narbonensis?'

Ben Nari answered: 'A holy woman by the name of Mariam Magdal. Do you know where we may find her?'

Herod looked at Ben Nari in surprise:

'What do you want from her?'

'We really want to meet her. Do you know her?'

Herod nodded:

'I should say so, since she came to Narbonensis aboard one of my ships. But do tell me what you want from her?'

'Well, it is really my two friends here who are looking for her. So many stories are told about this Mariam that I myself would like to meet her.'

Herod now spoke directly to Ish-a-tar:

'What do you expect from Mariam Magdal?'

Ish-a-tar placed her slice of bread on the table thinking about Herod's question. After a while she answered:

'Everything. The only thing I want is to become a student of this holy woman.'

Herod was feeling increasingly insecure in the company of Ish-a-tar. He was very impressed by this remarkable, beautiful woman.

'Haven't I seen you before?'

The question had an ominous ring to it. Lamu looked tense and Ben Nari had raised himself on his elbows and looked equally uncomfortable at the situation. Then he intervened with another question intending to dissolve the tension:

'I don't think so. Sister Mar-Iona has never before been outside Alexandria.'

This answer seemed for a while to move Herod's attention away from Ish-a-tar, in whom he could hardly suppress his interest.

'I suppose that dancing would be inappropriate,' he said. 'I have some of the best female dancers in all of Gaul.'

Ben Nari uncomfortably shook his head:

'No, no, there's no need for dancing. Let us dine. Now, tell us about this Mariam Magdal.'

Herod got up from his pillows:

'Mariam Magdal is the most learned woman that I have ever met. As far as I can tell she knows more about the deepest

Mariam Magdalene lecturing the King and Queen of Marseilles. (From a painting by René d´Anjou, 1408–1480)

secrets and the highest sciences than any man. Few only, however, understand her teaching, which is a continuation of the wisdom of the well-known magus and messiah Yeshua Ben Yoasaph. She prophesies and preaches, she heals and teaches.'

'Is she here in Massilia?'

'Apparently she lives not far from here. But even I do not know where since she lives a very secluded life. It has been quite a while since she was seen and heard teaching. It is said that even aristocrats, rabbis, druids, even alchemists are among her students. Some say that she lives in a castle, which has been put at her disposal by a princely vassal south of Narbo-Martius.* Others say that she lives in some desolate

---

* Present-day Narbonne.

caves in the wilderness. But tomorrow I shall send out messengers in order to obtain more information about her.'

'Is Narbo-Martius far from here?'

Ish-a-tar now also sat up. Herod looked at her as if he contemplated putting aside all his inhibitions. But Ish-a-tar's white gown made him control himself:

'It is situated several days' travel from here. Narbo-Martius is one of the largest and oldest Jewish settlements in Narbonensis and in all of Gaul. I have vineyards down there, but I have never been there myself. They say it is supposed to be quite tolerable. The wine from my grapes is quite good. That is all I can say with any certainty. And for that we thank the powers in heaven. Thank God we are not and shall never be Romans. However, we do owe our safety to the power of Rome.'

At these words Ish-a-tar remembered what Salome had said, 'a choice is always between ROMA and AMOR'.

She now had to control her impatience and wait until morning.

17

We closed the door behind us and stood in the faint light from the single bulb, which lit up only part of the small church.

I saw her immediately. She was placed on a pedestal against a pillar to the left of the aisle.

Joan of Arc?

I walked right up to the figure and looked at the brass tag on the pedestal. As I suspected it was Joan of Arc. But it was hardly her fault that the village church wasn't being used any more. There had to be a connection to my quest since Sylvia had both mentioned Joan of Arc and, at the same time, reminded me that I ought to visit the church at Montségur. Was there a specific connection between this saint and the village, I wondered?

*Saunière's glass chapel, Villa Bethania, Rennes-le-Château
(Note the figurines of Mariam Magdalene and Joan of Arc)*

I tried to remember if there were other churches where I had seen a similar figure of Joan of Arc but I couldn't remember one.

Then it struck me that I had seen a similar one once before. It happened when the Seer and I had visited Rennes-le-Château for the first time, years ago. It was placed in the small glass chapel built by the legendary priest, Saunière, in connection with the building of 'Villa Bethania' at the beginning of the previous century. The story about the priest who had found something during the restoration of the church in Rennes-le-Château, which was so valuable that from that day on he became extremely wealthy, was known by most people. At least by the millions of people who had read *The Holy Blood and the Holy Grail.* In spite of numerous attempts no one has yet succeeded in solving the riddle of what it was the priest found and from where he got all his money.

The glass chapel had been built at a time when Saunière had been temporarily suspended from celebrating Mass in the church itself because of disagreements with his bishop. According to myth, it was to this chapel that some of the great personalities, like the diva Emma Calvé, came from far away in order to participate in Saunière's Masses. What had taken place during these Masses that was so popular?

When the Seer and I had visited the chapel several of the window-panes had been missing and the interior was clearly marked by wind and weather and the passing of time. Somehow, however, this only added to the ambience of the place. The chapel, like almost everything else in Rennes-le-Château, was dedicated to Mary Magdalene, and on the altar of the small chapel a large, beautiful sculpture of her was placed. As far as I remember, the sculpture of Joan of Arc was placed below Magdalene.

Inside the church of Montségur

Joan of Arc, Black Madonna and Mariam from the church of Montségur

I wondered if there was a Magdalene sculpture in the church of Montségur? Or a Black Madonna? According to my sources you would always find Joan of Arc in the company of either Magdalene or a Black Madonna.

I walked further up the aisle but saw only the usual sculptures of saints like Notre-Dame-de-Lourdes, Francis of Assisi, Teresa, Joseph and the mother of the Virgin Mary, Anna. I threw a casual glance at the altar and could hardly believe my eyes.

On a dais under a canopy at the centre of the altar and with three candelabra on each side was a Black Madonna with child. It was pitch black and plated with gold foil. Apparently my sources had been correct. But what was the connection between the Madonna and Joan of Arc?

To the left of the altar I could see a sculpture of a young girl. There was no name on the pedestal. Was this supposed to be Magdalene?

I started to look more closely at the altar and to my surprise I noticed a fresco on the ceiling above the Black Madonna, depicting an occult symbol: a burning pyramid with the tetragram YHVH within it on a pale blue background. The burning pyramid is also seen in other ecclesiastical contexts but never before had I seen it depicted like this. The figure of a black woman with a black girl beside her was painted above the left side altar. Above the right one was a white man.

No matter what had taken place in this church, one might assume that those responsible for the decoration must have worked on the basis of a specific idea. Either this, or it was the result of a bizarre sense of humour or perhaps simply religious confusion.

I continued my investigation but at first failed to find anything of interest. Only the baptismal font seemed interesting since it was shaped like the cup of the Grail and was situated just inside the door. It was, however, hard to say if it was different from any other baptismal font.

Just then, I turned and looked at Ba-Bé who stood smiling behind me pointing to the stone floor. I looked down and immediately knew that those who had decorated the church had been fully aware of what they were doing.

On the floor just inside the door two diamond shapes were carved in the tiles.

They overlapped forming a third, diamond shape just as two overlapping circles form a mandorla: the almond shape symbolizing Venus and the vagina.

I was just thinking that we ought to go to Rennes-le-Château when Ba-Bé said:

'Why don't we go to Rennes-le-Château?'

When we were sitting in the car shortly after on our way to Saunière's village I was wondering why Ba-Bé had suggested

The Mandorla in the church of Montségur

that we go there at this exact moment? In spite of the fact that she was a total stranger I had only known for a couple of days, so many striking things had happened between us within those days that it seemed that we really knew each other at a deeper level. Yet she still remained a stranger to me in a worldly sense. It was a real paradox.

From where did she originate and what did she want from me?

If she was the virgin that Sylvia had talked about who would come to me, was it the Board Upstairs who had sent her? And what was it all about?

I couldn't help thinking that she might be a guide pointing to the signs I myself couldn't see as she had just demonstrated in the church at Montségur. And we were now on our way to Rennes-le-Château.

We drove through Quillan. I went faster as we drove out of the last curve heading towards Couiza. The answers would come soon. She couldn't go on hiding her true identity from me.

*

They were awakened in the middle of the night. It was Ben Nari himself, dressed in his tunic only, standing outside the guesthouse where Ish-a-tar and Lamu were staying. He looked very worried:

'You must continue your journey immediately. You must leave before dawn.'

'What is it that is worrying you so much?' Lamu asked slightly worried himself.

'It is Herod. I could see it in his eyes, and I know him all too well. He wants Ish-a-tar, and when he wants something he just takes it. One of my servants will take you to a person who is familiar with the area to the south of Narbo-Martius. I have already told him that you are on your way there.'

'Aren't you coming along?' Lamu asked.

'No. I shall stay here and try to make Herod change his mind. I shall join you later.'

The three parted in friendly fashion and before the sun had risen they had left Massilia together with a middle-aged Jewish wine merchant whom Ben Nari had paid to lead them on their way south. They preferred to travel by lesser known paths, not only to ensure that Herod's men didn't find them, but also because the Via Domitia, running all the way from Rome to just south of Narbo-Martius, was tough on the horses' legs.

In spite of a storm, which was quite normal in Gaul during the autumn, they reached Narbo-Martius within two weeks. Ish-a-tar insisted that they should continue but their guide convinced them that they should stay in the town in order to find someone who knew the whereabouts of Sister Mariam.

The size of Narbo-Martius and all its facilities were a result of the Roman presence over about a hundred years. But although the town was in a Roman province, with mainly Roman inhabitants, there was also a major Jewish community within the town's limits. This was where the wine merchant led them. The town was filled with lively activity and the inhabitants were busy with their own affairs and thus the travellers passed through unnoticed.

They found an inn where both they and their horses could be refreshed, while the wine merchant went to look for some relatives who could help them further.

They were sitting in the inn looking out at the bustle of the town when Ish-a-tar, having collected all her power in her heart to ask for a sign, suddenly saw a big middle-aged man at the other side of the square. The man wore a gown, which very much resembled the white robes of the priests of the Chaldeans with the characteristic signs of the lion, bull, eagle and angel embroidered on the chest.

'When you open your heart and ask from the innermost chamber an answer will always manifest itself,' Salome had told her and she now experienced how it worked.

'Do you see what I see?' she asked Lamu as if to make sure that the old Chaldean wasn't a dream.

Lamu looked inquiringly at Ish-a-tar:

'The Chaldean?'

'It is probably best that you talk to him. I'm certain that he knows the whereabouts of Sister Mariam.'

Ish-a-tar stayed in her chair watching how Lamu greeted the Chaldean priest who looked more and more worried as the conversation progressed. When he shook his head Ish-a-tar nearly got up and ran to the two men. Instead she took a deep breath. 'Faith, faith and more faith,' that was what Salome had always said. It was now or never.

The man looked in the direction of Ish-a-tar. His gaze felt like pure fire burning its way into her innermost being.

*

The gearbox moaned when I put it into second and started to climb the five-kilometre-long road to Rennes-le-Château. Considering the time of year there was more traffic than usual. Soon we drove into the town and turned into a car park. I was pleased to see that only one other car was parked there.

We went directly to Saunière's house, which, together with Villa Bethania, the garden and the Tour Magdala, has now been turned into a museum of the mystery of the priest and his assumed treasure. I bought tickets and immediately

290

went up to the first floor from where you have access to the garden and the glass chapel outside Villa Bethania, while Ba-Bé saw the exhibition in Saunière's original home on the ground floor.

Stepping into the garden gave me my first surprise. The glass chapel had been restored with new coloured window-panes and was totally changed. I practically ran to it and tore the door open. Inside, everything was very neat and newly painted. The sculptures of Mary Magdalene and Joan of Arc were gone. I hurried back to the ticket office and asked the woman there if she knew where the sculptures had been taken. But she didn't. She didn't even seem to know of their existence. I suddenly doubted whether or not I had seen them in the glass chapel. But they had actually been there. Who had moved them and why? And what difference did it make? Was it at all important?

When all was said and done, external circumstances interested me only to the extent that they provided delivery from or acknowledgement of inner experience. But something told me that precisely the fact that the sculptures had mattered to Saunière and the cult he apparently had been a part of, was not a clue to an external, tangible treasure but more an important piece of knowledge about man's possibilities in the spiritual realm. I was, however, convinced about one thing: Mary Magdalene and Joan of Arc were somehow significant parts of this knowledge.

I didn't need anything else in Rennes-le-Château and went back to the museum in order to find Ba-Bé. She was neither downstairs nor upstairs. I went back upstairs, through the garden to the Tour Magdala, but she was not in the tower or at the balustrade outside. I quickly went back through the garden and through the glass chapel to see if she was in Villa Bethania.

She wasn't.

On my way back to the ticket office I met an elderly couple and asked them if they had seen a young woman fitting my description of Ba-Bé.

They hadn't.

At the ticket office the woman there couldn't remember if she had seen Ba-Bé passing by or not. I was getting slightly panicky.

Before walking over to the church to see if Ba-Bé was there, I asked the woman at the ticket office to tell her, should she turn up again, that I would be waiting in the car park.

Having made sure that she wasn't in the church I hurried back to the car park, but she wasn't by the car either.

I opened the door of a public toilet and shouted her name but there was no response. I ran back towards the museum to check the souvenir shop, but they hadn't seen her. Then she had to be in the bookshop. I was completely out of breath as I opened the door and almost fell down the stairs and into the shop.

'Have you seen a woman of about 28 years old? She is tall, slender and blond.' I stuttered while trying to catch my breath. My heart was pounding and I thought that everybody in the shop could hear it.

The young man looked absent-mindedly at me and said dryly:

'The young woman was here just a moment ago.'

I breathed a sigh of relief. Then nothing had happened to her. On the other hand, what could have happened?

He then added in a neutral voice while at the same time writing something on a note pad:

'She bought a map of Durban-Corbières.'

I thanked him and walked back to the parking place through the narrow streets. Why did Ba-Bé want a map of

Durban-Corbières I wondered? I had never heard of the place before.

I still couldn't see her anywhere and decided to wait in the car. She was bound to appear soon.

I didn't see it until I was sitting in the driver's seat. It was tucked behind one of the wipers like a parking ticket.

The map. The sight of it worried me.

I opened the door quickly and took hold of it.

It was a map of the area Durban-Corbières Leucate.

I unfolded it frantically. It covered the area from south of Narbonne to just north of Perpignan. What did she want with a map of this area? And why had she left it here? I was about to fold the map again when I noticed a town, which had been circled by a pen.

Périllos.

*

The two men said their good-byes and shortly after Lamu again sat next to Ish-a-tar.

'Good news,' Lamu said, 'The priest, who is not a Chaldean but a druid and whose name is Gisbart, will take us to Sister Mariam. She is staying at a monastery to the south by the name of *Salveterra* situated at *Terresalvaesche*, a plateau outside the town of *Oppidum*.'[*]

'Did he have anything else to say?'

Ish-a-tar could hardly control her curiosity.

'He is a man of few words. But you may get him to say more than I can. He undoubtedly knows Sister Mariam. He said that she had withdrawn from any worldly activity and spends a lot of time in the desert near the monastery. She regularly

---

[*] Present-day Opoul.

293

sees pilgrims of whom there seem to be more and more. The rumours about her are spreading and she attracts not only Jews, but also Romans, Gauls, Celts and people from the south. I do feel that we may safely put our trust in him.'

'When are we leaving?'

Lamu laughed:

'You are incorrigible. We leave today. Gisbart had just one thing to do before we leave.'

*

Périllos!

Wasn't this the surname of the waitress at the 'Belo Bar' in Narbonne?

Marie Périllos.

Was this a coincidence or . . . ?

I began studying the map more closely and now saw that a route was marked from the town of Périllos to a point not far from it, which had been marked with a red star and the name *La Caune*. The whole area seemed quite desolate. I found yet another penmarking to the south of Périllos. It was just a little more difficult to see. Next to this mark the name *Château d'Opoul* had been written.

I slowly went over the whole area on the map but couldn't find any more marks.

It was obvious that Ba-Bé wanted to tell me something. But what? And where was she? Had she for some reason or other continued to the town on the map? The map had to be a suggestion for me to go there.

The sun was setting behind the mountains on the horizon and gave the whole landscape a red hue. While I was waiting I got the idea that I might try to contact Ba-Bé by way of *the chariot of fire.* I closed my eyes and concentrated on my breathing. 'On to Ba-Bé' I whispered to myself. The familiar prickly sensation on my forehead was followed by the just as familiar, ethereal sound of hissing around me. I opened my inner eye and found myself in a totally desolate landscape. It was dark, foggy and bleak with no one in sight. There was an oppressive feeling about it all. I whispered her name once more but she didn't appear.

When I opened my eyes again I saw the last rays of the setting sun.

Had it all just been a dream? The whole meeting with Ba-Bé did seem rather unreal. And now she had disappeared as suddenly as she had appeared.

'Who are you? All of you?' I heard myself saying. 'Speak to me. Show me the way!'

But there was no answer. The only other presence was the empty air. Had everything up until now been a figment of my imagination?

No, the experience in the cave at Montségur had been very real. The being that had spoken to me there had been very real, just like the experience of light with Ba-Bé had been in Roquefixade. No doubt about it.

It was too late to do anything about it now and I decided to drive down into God's valley, *Valdieu*, just below Rennes-le-Château where I knew I could find a small hotel.

*

A few hours later they were on their way. As Lamu had already said, Gisbart was a man of few words. But that didn't stop Ish-a-tar. As soon as they got away from the Via Domitia and came into a more peaceful area in the shade of some oak trees she rode up next to the druid.

'Excuse me for intruding. I do not know anything about the faith of the Celts or the Gauls and nothing at all about the rules of the renowned druids. I myself, however, have been taught by the Therapists in Alexandria and I sense a kinship between us.'

'Hm' was all Gisbart said keeping his eyes on the path in front of him.

Such an answer might have discouraged anyone else, but not Ish-a-tar. She simply considered his response as encouragement to continue.

'Your gown resembles that of the Chaldean priests. How is that?'

Gisbart turned his face towards Ish-a-tar. He looked closely at her and their eyes met. Ish-a-tar felt a deep sense of warmth at this meeting and she knew that she was right. Then Gisbart said:

'The Chaldean priests and we druids have co-operated on many occasions. You ought to know that as a Therapist.'

Ish-a-tar looked at him uncomprehendingly. Then Gisbart continued:

'A great deal of the Therapists' knowledge of the stars and herbs comes from the Chaldeans and the druids. And as you very well know, sister Mariam was also trained by the Therapists in Alexandria.'

Ish-a-tar nodded eagerly. Gisbart now looked more obliging. Ish-a-tar almost thought that she had seen a smile in his eyes. This encouraged her further:

'Tell me, how is Sister Mariam?'

He was pondering her question for a long time. After a while he said in a low voice:

'She is different from any other person I have ever met. She is not of this world. That is all I can say.'

It was very clear from the tone of his voice that he was speaking about something very special.

They were rocking along in their saddles when finally Ish-a-tar broke the silence:

'Do you think she might receive me and my fellow traveller?'

'She might. However, at the moment Sister Mariam is in the desert going through forty days of fast. While this is going on it is only her closest sisters who may contact her. No man is allowed near her.'

At these words Ish-a-tar exclaimed, not knowing where the words came from:

'But I am one of Sister Mariam's closest sisters!'

'We'll see,' was the laconic answer.

*

A giant dog came running towards me, barking, as I stepped out of the car in front of the Hôtel Les Labadous in Valdieu. The threatening animal was about to jump up at me when a voice called it back into the darkness. The light from the hallway shone on to the car park and a face appeared.

I booked a room for one night and went into the dining room to get supper. The place was very cosy and there was a fire in the open fireplace. A small, round man about my own age was seated at the refectory table. I nodded and sat down opposite him. It would have been awkward not to. He shook my hand across the table:

'André,' he said, and shook my hand again.

'Lars,' I replied.

He turned over one of the glasses from the cluster of wine glasses in the middle of the table.

'Would you care for some wine?'

'Yes, please, a glass of wine is just what I need.'

'What brings you here,' he said pouring wine into our glasses.

For a moment I thought about telling him about the disappearance of Ba-Bé but decided against it. Instead I said:

'I'm about to finish my latest book.'

'Oh,' he smiled almost indulgently, 'you're one of the writers trying to solve the riddle of Rennes-le-Château, then?'

'No, not at all. I . . .'

I hesitated. Why did I feel the need to justify myself to this person whom I didn't know at all.'

'I write books with an esoteric content,' I said, 'and right now I'm on my way to Périllos, a small town on the coast.'

He nodded approvingly:

'Have you been there before,' he asked, suddenly seeming quite interested.

'Never,' I said.

'It is a very unusual place with an equally interesting history. Do you know it?'

'I'm afraid not, but I would like to hear it.'

Suddenly I had forgotten all about my evening meal. He got up and signalled to me:

'Come on,' he said. 'Bring your glass. The food will be late anyway.'

Shortly after, when we were comfortably seated in a couple of oversized arm-chairs at the fireplace, he poured more wine and started to talk:

'For centuries the area around Périllos remained unexplored for unknown reasons. Until the eighteenth century it was still marked as "white, empty space" on the map that the contemporary head of the observatory in Paris, Cassini, had made. Today, Périllos is an abandoned village surrounded by cliffs and a few, low, desert-like bushes. The last inhabitant left the village towards the end of the Second World War and moved to the village of Opoul near where several of the old families from the original Périllos now live. The whole area has always been seen as quite mystical and there is no doubt that it was once considered to be holy land. The ruins of an old castle, Château Opoul, are situated on a plateau above Opoul. This plateau was once called *Terresalvaesche*,[*] the anointed, blessed and deified land. It is also known that a chapel used to be where the castle was later built and that a small town or some buildings were situated there at the time of Christ, and some people think that it was a monastery named *Salveterra*.'

He stopped and lifted his glass:

'Well, we mustn't forget to drink.'

His brown eyes looked happy. It was clear that he was very pleased to have found someone who was interested in his information about the area. It was quite clear that he knew something about the subject. He continued when we had tasted the wine:

'The village still looks more or less the way it was when it was abandoned. Of course the houses deteriorate with the passing of time but the people from Opoul try to keep it in order. The church is not very big but still intact and each year on the first of May they celebrate Mass there. By the way, the church is dedicated to St Michael, St Katarina and St Barbe.'

I leaned forward in my chair:

'Excuse me, but what was the name of the last of the saints you mentioned?'

'St Barbe,' he said, 'it is short for St Barbara.'

'Yes, of course.'

---

[*] In the oldest legends of the Grail the Grail castle, *Montsalvaesche, the anointed, blessed or deified mountain*, was situated in the Pyrenees.

For a moment I thought he had said Ba-Bé, but you usually hear what you want to hear just like you usually say what is in your heart.

'Perhaps it is not very strange that the preferred saint is St Michael. There is a legend about a dragon-like monster, *Babaos*, ravaging the area, which is as old as the area itself. It is told that the Babaos came up from the underworld. The ravaging of the dragon was at its peak when the master of Périllos went on a crusade to Palestine in 1270. By the way, he was also Grand Master of the Order of Malta. When he returned from the crusades he had to face the dragon in order to reinstate peace and order. It is also said that he defeated it and that it is now chained in the depths of one of the numerous bottomless pits in the area.'

He lifted his glass once more before continuing his story:

'The well-known prophet Nostradamus, furthermore, made a prophecy connected to the town of Tuchan which is situated very close to Périllos.'

He brought out a piece of paper from his wallet and unfolded it:

'This is what the prophecy sounds like:

At the foot of the new sect,
The earthly remains of the Great Roman are to be found,
A shrine covered with marble shall come forth,
The earth shall shake in April, wrongly buried.'

He folded the paper once more and laughed slightly embarrassed at the words he had just read out loud. They certainly echoed momentously. But what they meant was another matter.

'Do you know a place in the area called *La Caune*?' I asked him, thinking about one of the markings Ba-Bé had made on the map.

'Yes. And as the name implies it is not *any* cave. *La Caune* is simply *the* cave. As far as I'm concerned it is and has always been a very holy place. The cave has been in use for thousands of years and many interesting things have been found in it. Among others, sculptures depicting alien-like beings, sculptures which have been dated as far back as 3000–4000 BC. It is also in *La Caune* that they found the oldest Black Madonna as far as we know. Unfortunately, the shepherd who found it painted it so that it now appears white. The shepherd, however, is still alive and he himself has explained where in the cave he found it and how he later gave the Madonna a "new colour of the skin".'

'Where in the cave did he find it?'

'In a small recess behind what is now called "the Altar". If you find the cave you'll soon see that "the Altar" is the holy of holies and the natural place for various rituals and initiations. Among other things the Altar was decorated with old, equilateral circle crosses.'

'Is it difficult to find the cave?'

'That must be a yes. I must also tell you that you have to find it yourself. If you find the cave it is meant to be. If you do not find it I'm afraid you must accept the fact that the time is not yet ripe for you to find it.

We were silent for a while, then he said:

'There are those who think that Périllos fits into the legend of the Grail. In one of the oldest stories of the Grail, *Perlesvaux*, it is said that the one who is seeking the Grail ought to visit the "Chapel of Périllos". The Knight of the Grail is the "Chosen One" or "Christ", who places himself in the empty seat, the *Seat Perilous*, at the Round Table of

301

King Arthur. When we consider that the legend of the Grail originates in the mystical figure of Kyot, who apparently lived in Narbonne, it is perhaps not so very strange that we are also talking about the area of Périllos.'

André's tale made me dizzy.

Kyot, alias Kansbar, the old magus, who wrote the manuscript of the Grail, which the Seer had placed in my hands. Kyot, the old master, whom I had contacted in my dreams in Toledo a few years ago.

'There is more,' André said looking curiously at me.

I nodded affirmatively although it was difficult to get an overview of all the information.

'Regarding the mystery of Saunière and Rennes-le-Château, new pieces of information have appeared which also point towards Périllos. Before the death of the priest he ordered a plaster of Paris model of a landscape. This landscape had a very specific topography. Two tombs are shown in the landscape.'

'What kind of tombs?'

'Hold your breath now,' he said. 'One tomb is marked down as belonging to Joseph of Arimathea and the other one as the tomb of Jesus Christ. Unfortunately, Saunière died before the model was finished. Now, however, it has appeared from its hiding place and is becoming the cause of new considerations.'

The proprietor, Yoke, came into the dining room carrying a large pot.

'Time for dinner!'

18

They rode into the interior and reached the Salveterra Monastery after two days of riding through almost impassable terrain. They had to leave the horses at the foot of the magnificent cliffs of Terresalvaesche, 'The Holy Land'.

The monastery was inhabited only by women and Ish-a-tar was surprised that all the sisters introduced themselves with the title *Magdal* following their personal initiation names. Only a few very young novices used their first names. Apart from a short ceremonial welcome all the sisters kept silent, which created an atmosphere of contemplation and harmony.

When the travellers had washed and eaten they were quartered in a small annexe where each of them got their own cell.

After the first communion of the evening, Ish-a-tar went to find the head sister. Being so close to her goal she could hardly control her impatience. But the sister put a finger to her lips indicating that Ish-a-tar should calm down. The sister was a mature woman and Ish-a-tar immediately felt devoted to her. She therefore folded her hands and silently gave her face the appropriate expression. This was met by a warm smile from the older sister who shook her head resignedly and went up to Ish-a-tar and kissed her on her forehead. She then whispered into Ish-a-tar's ear:

'Tomorrow.'

Ish-a-tar twisted and turned on her couch all night long in the small cell. Several times during the night she got up on her couch to look out of the window and get another glimpse of 'The Holy Land' which lay bathed in the mystical glow from the full moon. She tried to imagine in which direction Sister Mariam would be at this moment. She imagined what she would say to her when she stood face to face with the woman she had wanted so much to meet and for such a long time. But her thoughts wandered and she once more tried to fall asleep.

Ish-a-tar had just fallen asleep when one of the young novices woke her up again. Ish-a-tar screwed up her eyes, looking into the flickering light from the oil lamp that the young girl held in her hand. The full moon still bathed the plateau when the two figures moved across the large atrium courtyard situated like an oasis between the annexe and the monastery itself. The older sister who had sealed the fate of Ish-a-tar with a kiss the previous evening was sitting in a lotus position waiting for her in deep contemplation. Ish-a-tar sat down beside her. Shortly after this sister started the ritual:

Give me strength to step out of all the old things,
So that I may be re-born totally pure.
Laying everything transient down,
I ask for strength to dress in Your eternal gown.
May that which belongs to the earth fall where it belongs.
And may that which belongs in Heaven be guided in order
to find its way home now.
Amen.

They got up and the sister handed Ish-a-tar a cup of unfermented wine. She then said to Ish-a-tar, pointing to the young novice:

'Jehanna will guide you to Sister Mariam. When you get there she'll show you what to do. Give yourself over to the care of Heaven and it shall come to pass as it must. Goodbye.'

She kissed Ish-a-tar lightly on her mouth after which Jehanna and Ish-a-tar got on to their donkeys and set off.

Riding across the plateau, they watched the sun rising from the sea on the horizon, slowly lighting the white desert with its blood-red fire. Ish-a-tar repeated the first lines of the morning prayer to herself:

'Give me strength to step out of all the old things, so that I may be re-born totally pure. Give me strength to step out of all the old things, so that I may be re-born totally pure. Give me strength to step out of all the old things, so that I may be re-born totally pure.'

Again and again she repeated the sentences like a mantra when suddenly she noticed that the sun was rising in the east as the moon was setting to the west so that they formed a completely balanced scale. She took this as a sign of the new kind of life of which she had been dreaming for such a long time and which now seriously was about to begin.

After riding down the path from the cliffs, they went through the Gate of the Wind and on to a desert-like plain.

While she was praying, Ish-a-tar looked at the young novice, whose face radiated with an inner power, and she thought that this young girl had long ago left all the old behind in order to possess such a fine light in her. And in that face she momentarily caught a glimpse of her own face, as a fifteen- or sixteen-year-old who had already tasted the rotten fruit of the world. She wondered if Jehanna had also tasted it?

They continued on the red carpet of the sun spreading out in front of them and showing the way. After half an hour's ride Jehanna turned off the path and headed for some cliff formations further into the desert. Apart from the faint wind, not a sound was heard. After a while they stopped at a low tree under which a watering trough was connected to a well.

'We are not going any further,' Jehanna said in a low voice.

They got off. Jehanna untied a small bundle from her saddle and handed it to Ish-a-tar.

'Give this to Sister Mariam when you get to the cave. It is just up there.'

She pointed to the cliffs not far from them.

'Just follow the narrow path there. But be careful, there are many bottomless pits in the area.'

Ish-a-tar wanted to embrace the young girl, but Jehanna took one step backwards whispering:

'I'm not worthy yet.'

Shortly after she added:

'I'll come back for you in three days.'

Ish-a-tar watched the young girl ride back towards the path further down the slope until the two donkeys and the rider faded into the surroundings and disappeared in the red light. Then she started walking towards the cliff.

*

I dreamt about the great dragon, the Beast from Revelation, that night. I saw how the dragon was thrown into a bottomless pit in the desert where it was to be bound for a thousand years. And I saw it being lifted up when the thousand years had passed, and I saw a woman dressed in a purple and scarlet gown decorated with gold and precious stones mounting the dragon. And I saw that she was the woman they called '*the great whore of Babylon*' and '*the mother of all whores*'. I saw that she was really the one who, through 2,000 years, had had to bear the burden of the sins that the Roman Church had given Christ the honour of having atoned for us. I saw that she was the one who had lifted the dragon, which symbolized the repressions of man, from the bottomless pit of the subconscious. Not in order to let it run wild but in order to tame it and to transform it. That is why she had mounted it. And I saw the number of the beast – 666 – written on the forehead of the dragon. And I saw that the sum of the digits of this figure – 9 – is the figure of death, transformation, resurrection, perfection and the Great Mother.

It was still dark outside when I woke up. But I was wide awake. I clearly felt the presence of the strange being which by now wasn't all that strange any more. I prayed the Heavenly Prayer within myself. Then I got up and prepared myself for the journey ahead.

André was not up yet when I went down for breakfast, and I had my breakfast alone and wrote him a note on a postcard thanking him for his help.

I then drove back to Quillan and continued by the D 117 towards the coast. The sun was rising and gave a virgin-like, rose-coloured hue to everything. Just before Estagel I turned left towards Tautavel, through Vingrau and then headed for Opoul. There was a sign showing the way to the Château Opoul. I followed the road in that direction and caught my

*The plateau of Terresalvaesche;
note the almost Judean topography*

*The ruins of the old château on the site of the former
Magdalenian monastery, Salveterra, on Terresalvaesche*

breath at the sight of the enormous plateau of cliffs in front of me, which had to be Terresalvaesche.

André was right. It was a bare and quite desolate landscape. But there was something grandiosely open and opening about it.

I parked my car in a gravelled space at the foot of the plateau and stepped out into the fresh air. A wooden gate indicated the beginning of the path to the castle ruins. The ascent was not that difficult, but a wind was coming up from the west and into my face when the path turned around the plateau and continued along the northern side further up. When I got to the end of the northern side the path suddenly became steep, leading towards a natural gate between two rocks. I really felt the strength of the wind when I passed through it. It was as if it had decided to concentrate all its strength here in order to protect 'The Holy Land' against intruders. I leaned against the wind for a short moment and felt how it carried me and held me in a tight grip. I really had to struggle in order to break through this 'wall'. The wind didn't let go of me until I had passed through the gate between the two rocks and I could step on to Terresalvaesche where once a cloister-like society by the name of *Salveterra* had been situated according to André.

If the view of the cliff as seen from Opoul had almost taken my breath away, it was nothing compared to the sight waiting for me on the plateau itself – in front of me the remains of the castle and behind it, as far as I could see, the Mediterranean and the endless horizon. To the south the peaks of the Pyrenees reached towards the sky. It was a divine sight.

I stood for a while enjoying the magnificent view and the remains of the castle ruins. Then I started to investigate the plateau in order to find out where the old monastery, Salveterra, had been situated. After a while I found a spot where the energies seemed to flow the most. I stood still with my eyes closed waiting for something to appear. As usual I began with the Heavenly Prayer. After a while and as I have experienced so often, I heard some fine, soft and bell-like sounds around me. This time, however, the sounds also seemed to be followed by a sweet, rose-like smell. I slowly opened my eyes and surrendered to the 'far sight'. Shortly after, small, flickering lights appeared and started their life-giving dance. I saw in a vision a figure resembling Ba-Bé hovering above the ground past me and into the blue air heading north. Each and every cell and each and every atom within me joined in the unbelievable song of life, which joyfully danced towards the sun.

When, about half an hour later, I walked back towards the *Gate of the Wind*, I turned around to get a last glimpse of this holy site and saw that a pure, radiating crystal pyramid hovered in the air above Salveterra.

*

'III … AAA … OOO … III … AAA … OOO … III … AAA … OOO.'

The sound of a woman's voice singing was heard through the low growth embracing Ish-a-tar as she got closer to the place pointed out by Jehanna. She was immediately filled with an unbelievable, joyful feeling of expectation which was incomparable but which might be described as a wave seizing you and dissolving everything at the peak of divine lovemaking.

She continued towards the sound and was led towards an opening in the rock. A mouth seemed to open in the ground in front of her and she saw a light, which made shadows dance on the walls of the cliff further down. The smell of incense reached her nostrils. She put one foot on the first step of the staircase leading down to . . .

The song stopped. Two oil lamps created small haloes in the enormous cave. She had to let her eyes get used to the faint light before she spotted the shape of a woman wrapped in a red cloak sitting in the lotus position facing an altar-like formation of rocks from where a thurible threw an unreal glow on to her face.

'Sister Mariam.'

Ish-a-tar stood still at the foot of the stairs waiting for Sister Mariam to react. It seemed like an eternity. Slowly she opened her eyes and looked in the direction of Ish-a-tar:

'Welcome.'

Ish-a-tar felt a stab in her heart at the sound of Mariam's golden voice, which was both warm and soft, clear and precise.

Ish-a-tar kept silent. She had completely lost her voice. Mariam smiled at her:

'Good that you finally got here. Come and sit down.'

She pointed to the fleece in front of her. Ish-a-tar obeyed and sat down. At first she kept her eyes downcast but then slowly lifted her head and looked into the most intense eyes she had ever seen. They were like glowing mirrors burning into the eyes of the one looking into this wonderful universe. A deep, compassionate power, which made any restraint and any fear disappear. She then gave Mariam the small parcel, which Jehanna had given her for Mariam. She took it and put it beside her saying:

'Do you know why you have come?'

Ish-a-tar's voice shivered slightly when she answered. However, there was no doubt in it:

'I have come to obtain the knowledge which may set mankind free.'

'It is obvious that Salome hasn't taught you in vain,' Mariam answered smilingly. 'Good, let us begin.'

Mariam sat up and Ish-a-tar followed her example.

'I just made the initial preparations before you came. Did you hear my song?'

'Yes,' Ish-a-tar said. 'It is the most wonderful sound I have ever heard. It reminded me of something we were taught to sing by the Therapists at Alexandria.'

'This is true. However, the song I'm using now I learned from my beloved friend and teacher, Rabbi Yeshua. Have you heard about him?'

Ish-a-tar nodded:

'Many stories are told about him in Galilee and Judea. I have heard the most unbelievable stories about the wonders he has done. Who is he?'

'He was a true master. He was the one who reopened the women's door to the mysteries. Without him, you and I wouldn't have been sitting like this. I owe him my life.'

Mariam became distant for moment.

'He knew about the deepest mysteries and he knew how to unfold them for everybody, high as well as low. Never before have I known such a sensitive person with the ability to see behind any kind of foolishness and any kind of lie. He taught me about the highest of all sciences. I gave him everything that only a woman can give a man. Together we read and we wrote in *The Book of Love*.'

'What were the mysteries he taught, and what is *The Book of Love*?'

'*The Book of Love* is the secret about the mystery of the fire. Yeshua belonged to the brotherhood of water and fire. Born of the lineage of David but of the order of Melchizedek. He was raised on Mount Carmel by the Essenes but broke away and formed the brother – and sisterhood – of the Nazarenes. This was what offended the priests of both Qumran and Jerusalem and turned the country upside-down. He first came into this world as the consciousness Adam. When he ended this life he came back as Enoch. Later he came as Hermes and as Melchizedek. Then followed the consciousnesses Yehoshua, Asaph and the master of fire, Zarathustra. The series of lives ended and it was crowned with the consciousness of Yeshua, Son of Man. He is Metatron, the angel who rules the seven Elohim[*] in the world.

Mariam's eyes were like diamonds shining in the semi-darkness.

'You see, Brother Yeshua was the long-awaited Messiah. He was the Anointed One, whom our world had been awaiting for hundreds of years. His earthly remains are now buried here but his spirit will always be where people invoke him. He was the master above them all. Even the seven Elohim will bow to him for ever and ever. He did not want an earthly kingdom. His kingdom was of a different world.'

Ish-a-tar thought that she saw a tear on Mariam's cheek and spoke in order to lead the conversation to other subjects.

'I heard in Jerusalem that some of Yeshua's disciples are forming a congregation in his honour. Some of them are building synagogues where they worship him and heal in his name. Others live celibate lives in the desert. It is said, however, that a man named Petrus goes forth with fire and brimstone attacking anyone who does not submit to the right faith.'

'Well, Petrus,' Mariam sighed. 'I'm very sorry to hear that. Petrus has always been an ox who does not understand the deeper meaning behind the science. He has only one goal: the dream of honour and power. It is just like him to create

---

[*] The seven archangels.

313

a worldly hierarchy where he himself may sit on the highest throne.'

Mariam's voice lost for a moment its golden sound and Ish-a-tar regretted having turned the conversation on to that subject. She tried once more to change tracks:

'What then is the deeper meaning behind the science?'

'The understanding of man. The understanding of the powers which are always at the disposal of the Sons and Daughters of Man.'

'What kind of powers?'

'The seven Elohim. When you know the power of the seven Elohim your eyes and ears are opened and you see everything in a new light.'

'What do you then see and hear?'

'You dissolve what is false and see what is true. You hear the Heavenly Sound, which surges through everything within and without. You see, the truth comes into the world naked but veiled in images and archetypes, otherwise it wouldn't be understandable. Rebirth happens through the archetype of rebirth. This is the only way to be reborn. This is the resurrection.

'Entering this image, the groom is led to the truth, which is the renewal of everything in its integrity. This is valid for those who do not just know the names of Father/Mother, Son/Daughter and Spirit, but who have also integrated them in themselves. The one who hasn't integrated these names in his innermost being, his name shall be taken away from him.'

'What kind of names and what does it all mean?'

'Everything that cannot be expressed in words can be expressed in sounds and movement. The one who hasn't vitalized the true names of the Father/Mother, the Son/Daughter and the Spirit must lose his own true name. This means that the one who does not know the Power behind them must stay in front of the veil of the world and only see the external movements. Only through the knowledge of the seven abilities of the Power may man become a true co-creater in the seven worlds of the Pleromas.[*]

Mariam looked at the young woman sitting opposite her. She contemplated the basic qualities of the woman for a time. She had followed Ish-a-tar for a while through various visions, uniting with an angel who guided her. She knew of the contrary powers which had torn Ish-a-tar's heart apart, but she also saw the simple, uncompromising yet loving power which could walk the road of untruth no more.

'We invoke the seven Elohim with sound. The angel of peace, Michael, is invoked with the sound A.'

Mariam sang out the tone and signalled to Ish-a-tar to do the same. Shortly after she stopped and said:

'The angel of grace is Gabriel who is invoked with the sound of E.'

The two women again sang the sound together.

'The angel of power is Raphael who is invoked with the sound H.[†] The angel of willpower, Uriel, is invoked with the sound I. The angel of truth, Raguel, is invoked with the sound O. The angel of light, Anael, is invoked with the sound Y, and the angel of healing, Saraphuel, is invoked with the sound O which in this case means Omega.'

Together they then sang all the sounds in succession, AEHIOYO.

'When you are familiar with the sounds and the qualities behind them you may synthesize them all in the three sounds IAO. This holy mantra, apart from the invocation of

---

[*] Cosmos.

[†] Pronounced AE.

315

the Elohim, is also a confirmation of: I AM ALPHA AND OMEGA.'

Mariam softly began singing IIIIIII. Then she changed to AAAAAAA and ended with OOOOOOO.

Ish-a-tar joined in and they repeated the mantra again and again until the ethereal level opened itself for them.

'IAO is the most effective sound with which to open the ethereal level. You may use it in connection with the seven gates of your holy star-body. Let the sound rest in your womb and you'll activate the Snake of Fire that is curled up at the foot of the Tree of Life which has its origin there. When this is set free, be prepared, for it will tear everything impure up through the trunk of the tree, combining the seven worlds in your star-body. Only through serious preparation may you make certain that the awakening of the Snake of Fire may pass painlessly. If you cannot tame it, it'll devour you. The Snake of Fire is either creative wisdom or total destruction. Only if your motives are pure should you choose to mount the dragon. The choice is yours.'

They sang all day long. Day and night became one. The holy mantra gave them strength. They needed no other sustenance than ethereal light.

They rested off and on, but not for long, then they would sing the holy mantra once more. Ish-a-tar felt how her physical body and her star-body slowly got more and more enlightened.

Having rested, Mariam said:

'If you have any questions feel free to ask them.'

Ish-a-tar sat for a while trying to think of something. There was so much she would like to know and yet she felt that it was all contained in the holy mantra.

'We met Herod in Massilia. He gave us the impression that he and you know each other quite well.'

316

Wisdom of the Snake
(The last painting by Maria Struzik-Krull,
reproduced by kind permission by Hans Krull)

Mariam smiled:

'Well, here is cause for gossip. You see, Herod has always appreciated the Essenes at Qumran very much. He knows about the secrets and he has been a good man for the mystery societies. However, since he pretends to co-operate with the Romans, there are many militant groups in Palestine who hate him and want him dead. But Herod is a diplomat. Without his help I would probably never have reached Salveterra. He was also the one who arranged for the remains of Yeshua to be buried here. He owns many vineyards in Narbonensis and he helps many Jewish immigrants.'

They sat in silence for a long time. There really wasn't anything to say but still Ish-a-tar's heart burned with a fire which could not be quenched. She could not hold back the words:

'Please initiate me into the mystery of the Fire and give me my true name.'

Immediately the energy in the cave dissolved. It was as if a void appeared in the wake of Ish-a-tar's words. As if the invoked Elohim stepped aside to make room for something else. Was it really time? Had Ish-a-tar finally reached her goal?

Mariam got up and went over to a circle of rocks, which had been placed on the floor between two phallic-looking pillars. She stepped into the circle and sat down in it.

'Have you ever heard about Merkabah?'* she asked Ish-a-tar.

But Ish-a-tar looked uncomprehendingly at Mariam.

'Merkabah is a chariot of fire written about by Ezekiel many years ago. When your star-body and the chariot of fire become one you may travel in the worlds of the Elohim. You may get in contact with the Elohim through your breathing and the holy mantra IAO. You must throw a circle of light around you. Until you can do that by the power of your thoughts you can help the process along by making a circle of rocks around you like the one I have made here. The circle will centre you at the earthly level while the fire in you will seek upwards through you and towards the Heavenly level. You may lift yourself above everything earthly and move wherever you want to go.'

She got up and made room for Ish-a-tar who sat down in the circle. Mariam continued:

'Now imagine that you are sitting between two pyramids. One upright below you and the other one upside down above you. Now, let the two pyramids unite until they form the

---

* *Merkabah* = carriage, vehicle. The term belongs to the oldest part of the Enoch tradition and the Jewish Kabbalah tradition. See Ezekiel 1, 1–26 and Isaiah 6, 1–8.

Merkabah – The Chariot of Fire

seal of King Solomon and Queen Sheba, the six-pointed star. You activate the fire with your breath, and the fire shall move upwards from your womb and through the seven gates and into the Heavenly spheres. You may now move through any one of the seven gates. However, the higher you want to go the more gates you must open. When you can invoke the Elohim with certainty, the rest is easy. The Merkabah is the highest wisdom. Here Solomon and Sheba become one. The radiating eye in the tiara of God.'

Mariam taught Ish-a-tar everything that she herself had learned with and from Yeshua. Day and night disappeared once more. After yet another rest, Mariam continued:

'Throughout time, Logos has been looking for Sophia the way Kether has been looking for Shekhinah. However, Sophia has always had more than one face. Behind them all, the great mother, Anyahitha, the Guardian of the Heart, is resting. She is Venus. From her came Innana, Ishtar, Isis, Hathor, Athene, Diana and Cybele, as well as many, many others, known and unknown to the world. Her secret being, however, is known by a few only. She is Miriam, the precious companion and prophet of Moses, who sang *The Song of the Sea* with him. Miriam was the daughter of the water who made a fountain of miracles spout. A fountain that nourished everything and never dried out. She is Sheba, the daughter of the fire and the black bride of Solomon, who sings the most beautiful song with him. The secrets of the highest possibilities are hidden in The Song of Songs. Like a pearl in a lotus flower. Anyahitha, Shekhinah and Sheba. Together they form the threefold, Heavenly Goddess. Her number is three times six, 666. In the old writings you may read about the time when King Solomon received 666 talents of gold. It is the allegorical tale of the wisdom that Solomon received through the union with the Queen of Sheba. It is the Heavenly Marriage, which must also take place in each human being. Each one of us is the bride who must prepare the bridal chamber for the arrival of the groom. As above, so below. Do you understand?'

Ish-a-tar nodded and Mariam continued:

'When Venus unites with Mercury in the sky, the Pleroma offers man precious gifts and invites man to follow the example of Heaven. Yeshua was my groom and I was his bride. Together our souls reflected each other like the sun enlightens the moon and the moon reflects it. Let us now together meditate on the unification of Solomon and Sheba in our innermost chambers of the heart. Then I shall give you your true name.'

Once more day and night melted into one and on the third day the two souls came back and united with the bodies sitting in the lotus position in the cave.

When the eyes of the women met, the gaze of the two equal sisters united and became one revealing sight.

'As you can see,' Mariam said, 'the great mother, Anyahitha, and the women of the earth are heading for hard times. When, therefore, I give you your name you accept the obligation of passing this knowledge on to our sisters you meet on your way and who are mature enough to receive it. Only thus may the wisdom continue to live in the world. Only thus may the world survive. You must at any time be ready to go to the bottomless realm and lift the dragon from the depths. When Solomon and Sheba have united in you, you will possess the power with which you may tame the Beast. From now on you shall be known by the name Mariona Magdal. But your hidden name shall, from this day on, be BARBELO!'

Tears were running down the cheeks of Ish-a-tar who had now received the name of Mariona Magdal. Then she whispered:

'Barbelo?'

'You are Barbelo. The scarlet- and purple-clad whore from Babylon whose task it is to tame the dragon.'

They each got up from their couch. Mariam took the small bundle, which Ish-a-tar had brought from Jehanna. She now unwrapped it and brought forth a milk-white crystal.

'This crystal, the first one I found in this cave, has been waiting for you at Salveterra. Take it. It will protect you and guide you.'

They embraced, kissed each other on the mouth and departed.

'Do not look back,' Mariam whispered.

Mariona Magdal turned around and began the long journey back to the world.

19

The wind became stronger and it alternately pushed and carried me down from Salveterra. A piece of paper whirled through the air and stuck to the windscreen as I got to the parking place and was about to get into the car. I removed it and took a hasty look at it. It looked like a label from a winegrower's box with a colourful print of grapes. Below the illustration and the name of the grower the following line was printed in capital letters, '66600 Opoul-Périllos.'

It was almost too much of a cosmic joke to be a coincidence that the postal code of the area contained the sign of the Beast, 666.

I turned the car on to the narrow road and drove towards the abandoned village of Périllos and the La Caune cave. Ba-Bé's map lay open on the passenger seat. The landscape became more harsh and it struck me how much it resembled the topography around Jerusalem in Israel. After fifteen minutes of driving, the village appeared at the end of a winding, single-track road leading up to a small mountain top on the horizon. I stopped the car and studied Ba-Bé's map. According to her markings I would find La Caune by following a path to the right not far from the place I had stopped. I put the car in reverse and rolled back to something that might be the path. I parked, put the map in my pocket and started walking up the path, with a vineyard on one side and barren, stony ground on the other. The path soon became full of holes and uneven, and at places it seemed to disappear and then reappear from the stony ground further ahead. When I reached a path that crossed mine I saw a man carved from stone at the place on the map marked by Ba-Bé where I was supposed to turn left. I followed Ba-Bé's markings step by step until I reached a small open space in front of a low piece of rock. A clear path in the grass lead in between two bushes. I found the entrance to the cave on the other side of them.

I held my breath as I got closer. I stood still and took a few deep breaths; then I went inside.

If I have ever in my life experienced the feeling of being guided then it was here at this moment. How do you describe something like that? Everything around me was so quiet that you could hear the proverbial pin drop. Even the wind had died down. A flash of light to the right. Then one in front of me. Like a spark jumping between electrical poles. The Being had entered. I stood for a moment waiting for something to happen, but something told me that I should go on.

Although André's story was fresh in my memory nothing could have prepared me for the sight, which met me when I looked down at the holy cathedral. The size of it in itself was enough to make you catch your breath. At various places on

The author in La Caune

The altar in La Caune behind which a Black Madonna and two 3,000-year-old figurines were found

the cliff wall, crystals shone in the light coming from a large hole in the ceiling at the other end of the cave. The hole gave a pleasant light and lit up most of the cave.

A fireplace had been built in the middle of the cave. Around it some strange, phallus-like pillars were placed reaching almost to the ceiling. I partly slipped and partly walked the rest of the way down the path, which ran at an angle down into the cave. I slowly walked around investigating everything. I finally found the 'altar' that André had mentioned, as well as a small depression next to it where the old shepherd had found the Black Madonna. I found the circle crosses on the altar as well as other signs, which I couldn't, however, interpret.

I had finally reached my goal and slowly sank to my knees in front of the Holy of Holies. The moment was filled with an indescribable peace. There was no more to search for and no more to be found. There was only this moment. A breath. A now.

Then the being started to speak:

'Be you greeted. If you have any questions, then ask.'

The voice was indeterminable. Like balm. It was – and it wasn't. My thoughts went to the altar. I heard my own voice saying:

'What is it about this place that makes it different from other places?'

'Only the fact that you have made it special in your own mind.'

'But aren't there places in the world that are holier than others?'

'No.'

'Can you be more specific?'

'Places are not holy. They are just part and parcel of the great time-space illusion. Only the conscious NOW is holy. A conscious now may only be created by a person who can free himself from

the earlier mentioned illusion. This may be created anywhere and at any time you want it. It is a choice.'

'But history is filled with saints, gurus and avatars who have attained enlightenment in holy places. For thousands of years pilgrims of all traditions have sought these places where some of them have actually had extra-sensory experiences. The Mary revelations for example.'

'It has always been important for the human mind to arrange its so-called "spirituality". For far too long it has needed to create extraordinary circumstances in order to believe. This is all right as long as the individual is able to see through the illusion. Let's call it a tool which may sometimes help to open the mind to deeper acknowledgements.'

'Some people think that the energy is more intense at places where believers have practised and prayed for centuries and that this may be good for other believers.'

'If this is what you think then this is how it is. However, the eternal now offers awareness irrespective of time, place and specific conditions.'

Silence.

'Is it not pure fatalism to think that everything is an illusion?'

'Only if the material reality is so important that man is unable to imagine a reality created by SPIRIT. It is not material reality but man's interpretation of it which is twisted. It is the mind of man which is creating the illusion. The curse lies in man's total identification with the body, his job, social status and all other external things.'

'But why has man been placed in an earthly reality if it is an illusion?'

'Remember that it is your own interpretation of earthly reality which keeps you ignorant, not earthly reality in itself. It simply constitutes an enormous possibility.'

'It seems to me that human development happens extremely slowly.'

'*That depends on the position you take. Everything is and has always been accessible and open to man. EVERYTHING! But man has forced himself into a corner from where he can see no other way out than looking after number one. You have chosen a very limited interpretation of reality and that is why you see nothing but limitation. You see, there is no language, which can put this into words. Words, imagination, beings and life are all symbols. Everything is a symbol of something behind it which cannot be expressed in any other way.*'

'What is going on when I have experienced my reality being turned inside out?'

'*You are then experiencing the other side of illusion. There may be other laws here but it is still the same illusion because you experience it as a contrast to your normal reality. But nothing is separate. Everything is one. It is simply a different interpretation of the eternal now.*'

'How do you step out of this illusion?'

'*Through the understanding that there is no "outside" or "inside".*'

Silence.

While I was meditating on what I had learned, Mariam Magdal suddenly appeared in my consciousness and once more I heard my own voice speaking as if it came from outside of me:

'Who was Mariam Magdal?'

'*An old soul. A sister who woke up from the dream and liberated herself from her "destiny".*'

'"Liberated herself from her destiny", what does that mean?'

'*What you understand by destiny is your limited interpretation of the simple life. Mariam Magdal started her long journey from a misinterpretation of a series of lives which have continued up until now.'*

'What lives?'

Silence.

'If this was explained it would only give rise to more mis-understandings.'

'Or it may be of value to a lot of people who are trying to break through these illusions?'

'As you wish. Sister Mariam was among the first souls. The basic identity is IO from Venus. This identity has among others been expressed as Queen Tiyi, Miriam, the Queen of Sheba, Mariam Magdal, Guinevere, Esclarmonde de Foix and Joan of Arc. It is an identity that has always had a great personality. It has been the turning point of what you understand as good and evil. As Joan of Arc it received its baptism of fire. It was, however, not until your own time that the identity as Noor Inayat Khan completed the so-called Way of Christ. However, at the same time as it lived its life as Noor Inayat Khan the Magdal idea also expressed itself as Helen Schucman, who received and wrote the message about forgiveness and freedom from Brother Yeshua.'[*]

I contemplated these words for a while.

'I don't understand that. How can a soul incarnate in two personalities at one and the same time?'

'"Magdal" is not and has never been a personality. It is a state of mind, like your idea of Christ.'

'Then there were more Magdals?'

'That is one way of putting it. The bestowed name Magdal, says something very important about the person that has it.

---

[*] Noor Inayat Khan, 1914–44, died in France after having been tortured by the Gestapo. Helen Schucman lived from 1909 to 1981, about ten years after having finished scribing *A Course in Miracles*, a series of channellings from Yeshua.

Magdal can be compared to the Aramaic word for master, Mara, that's to say an initiated one. Mariam has both given names. She was both Mariam Magdal and Mariam Mara. The Exalted One and the Master.'

'Where is the identity now?'

Silence.

After a while the being continued:

'It is here. Now! Mariam Magdal is the all-dominating new female Sophia archetype that, after more than 1,700 years in the dark, has appeared out of the depths in order to regain its rightful place, on an equal footing with the Logos principle, Messiah/Christ. Since the establishment of the church its leading men have oppressed this archetype, with ensuing serious and painful consequences for mankind. Now, however, the time to put the record straight has come when the great swindle must be uncovered. The church elders were afraid of the idea that a woman could come to stand in the forefront of the new church. And rightly so. For Mariam was Yeshua's chosen disciple and his beloved equal. Therefore, she had to be eliminated, and was, in one fell swoop, made out to be a whore. She is that wisdom that Yeshua, with the words: "Be as wise as the Snake and as innocent as the Dove," encouraged you to follow. The Dove is the symbol of the Holy Spirit, Agape and the Virgin, which represent man's three highest chakras, whilst the Snake symbolizes Wisdom (Sophia/Hochman), Eros and Magdalene, which represent the three lowest chakras. And that is maybe the church's greatest crime against mankind, that, by condemning the Magdalene aspect, it has made the whole life-giving foundation for mankind's incarnation on earth, sinful. Mankind has only been half present. Now it's time for you once again to be complete people.'

I do not know if another being took over communication here, but deep inside me something told me that this was Helen Schucman speaking:

'There are no missing links. Everything is certain. All that has been hidden will become obvious. And it happens NOW! Therefore, take all the exhibits and present them openly. The circumstances will never be better. The ideas of "Days of Yore" and "The End of the World" are limited states of mind just like "Birth and death" are. There are no such limitations in reality. The Primal Sea is without limits and the Primal Sea is identical with the enlightened consciousness. It is, however, not continuous. There are no other lives than the one within the One. We are all a part of this One Life and this is how it shall be for ever and ever. The enlightened consciousness is NOW in all of eternity. It is Eternal Life. Eternal Life embraces all forms of existence at all levels, including all temporary transitions that we erroneously interpret as stagnation and separation. Have no doubts. There is no room for doubt in healing. Unite with the light. Step into it without fear. Be it, give it and receive Eternal Life.'

My whole being was filled with quiet joy and deep gratitude and I thought that this was the creative stillness I had always sought but which I had never been able to find and unite with. In silence I sent the identity Helen Schucman my warmest greetings.

It was more than quiet. There was an openness that I had never experienced before. It was as if a large abyss appeared around me and in a moment of panic I shouted:

'Are you still there?'

Silence.

Somewhere in the cave a drop of water hit the stony ground. An answer? The great nothing? ⊙?

But suddenly the Nameless One appeared again:

'Do you, from the bottom of your heart, want to be able to see and hear?'

'Yes,' I replied immediately.

'If you really want to see and if you really want to listen you must accept that deep in your being you are already the eternal, unchangeable joy that you seek outside of yourself. Give up your position. Give up your special status and your dreams of it. Give up your dreams of becoming anything at all but beware that this giving up does not just open to another illusion of becoming something special. If you can manage this you will obtain a true relationship with Θ who lives in your heart.'

'You spoke last time about we, the people, hiding from God or Θ. How do we hide?'

I immediately felt that the question was naughty and that it exposed me as particularly ignorant. However, there was no judgement in the voice when it spoke again:

'Do not blame yourself for this. The hiding-place may be called judgements, prejudices and projections. If you let them go – and do not let yourself be seduced into exchanging them for new prejudices and projections, which will always remain what they are although they may be "ennobled" because you are now "holy" or "spiritual" – then you have made an important acknowledgement.'

'You spoke the last time about the fifth dimension being Grace. What does that mean?'

'This may only be explained by way of an idea which most people know but which is only understood by very few.'

'Which idea is that?'

'Forgiveness.'

Once more I felt a stab of unpleasantness poking its head into my solar plexus. But I realized that there was no way around this concept which had been flogged to death in spiritual, Christian and Buddhist circles and had lost its meaning. It had been reduced to a word, a banality and an empty phrase without any meaning.

Once more I was met with empathy.

'There is only one way, and I repeat one way only, in which to understand the word forgiveness. By practising it. And while practising it, it is important to be aware that another judgement is not hiding within this forgiveness of the person or thing that is forgiven. For example, are you able to forgive yourself?'

I could feel that I was balancing on a knife's edge between fear and total surrender. The abyss around me opened into eternity.

'Be not afraid. There is nothing to be feared. But be aware that every thought, every word and every action has an impact in the cosmos. Remember that a wrong word said on one side of the globe is all it takes to create a tidal wave on the other. Step outside fear.'

'Help me to understand how. Show me a way I can go.'

I was losing my balance.

'Are you sure you are ready to know?'

'Yes!'

A long silence, like a light-year, a free fall into endless space that made me dizzy. It was as if I was clinging to the outermost edge of the world, and of reality, with my fingertips. Then the being took pity on me:

'You yourself are the abyss opening below you as well as the bridge you must cross. You are the path you must follow. You are the mountain you have to climb. You are the cave you must find and enter. And when once you are sitting there you'll realize that you are the cloud above you in the sky, you are the Heavenly song and you are the rain falling and evaporating again, you are the drop of water uniting with the sea. No more will you have the need to know anything, because you will then be the knowledge of Heaven and the sea, the stars and the Universe. No more will you be separated from ⊙.'

Silence.

'In time, you may become a path that others may follow, a gate to walk through, a mountain to climb and a cave that anyone may enter.'

'Is this the Grail?'

'In a way. What you call the Grail is a state of mind connected to the opening of the Third Eye, the Sapphire in the Tiara of the Forehead, the Jewel in the Lotus flower. It's a state that is directly connected to travelling in the Fire Chariot. The Fire Chariot's and Power of Thought's ranges are directly proportional to how firmly the Forehead Centre's flower is planted in the Heart Centre's earth. Just as the plant's roots must be anchored in the Sacral Centre. That is the marriage between the masculine, Thought, and the feminine, Feeling. Take note of that: Thought is the vessel and Feeling is the fuel. Thought in itself has only a limited range. Thought calculates, defines possibilities and sets conditions, before it acts, whilst the Heart immediately and intuitively knows what should be done or not done in every situation, and acts on that. The Heart has no need of any insurance or confirmation after the act. The Heart doesn't seek others' approbation. It's only concerned with one thing: to accumulate unconditional love.'

It was very simple and yet very moving. And at that moment I understood that this certainty is the *Grace* that the Nameless One had spoken about earlier. And this made it easier to accept that the teaching was over for now. A sigh went through me and through the cave.

'Be you greeted. Call us when you need us. We are always CLOSE.'

I saw a small milk-white piece of crystal in front of me. A sign? A talisman?

I silently thanked this being, got up and began my climb towards the world outside.

The sun was shining through drizzle. I followed the path back to the car. When I turned around in order to look at the cliffs with the cave one more time, a rainbow stood like a giant gate around the place.

I parked the car shortly after outside Périllos. I walked through the narrow streets between the derelict, empty houses. Only the small chapel stood fully intact. Then I noticed the salamanders in various colours which were printed everywhere in the village.

A golden laughter sounded in the empty streets. It was Sylvia:

'Remember, the door is on the inside. Remember that the key is on the inside. As of today there is no intermediate stage between man and God.'

I went into the desert in the rain. The branches of the low bushes were heavy with water and here and there small puddles appeared in the depressions on the stony ground. I carried an image inside of me. It was an image of a world where man is born, lives and dies in tears and laughter, in poverty and riches, in anger and forgiveness.

This was the picture I held up towards Heaven, completely sure that it would be received.

'If you will come to meet us, we shall bend down and lift you.'

There was a flickering light around me in the wind:

'Heaven and earth are my parents. Consciousness is my home. Lack of selfishness is my work. Simplicity is my way. Humour my only weapon. Attention and honesty my emblem. Forgiveness, faith, patience and belief my true strength.'

May the eye rest only on that which is new.
May the hand no longer take, but give.
May thought in the future be free in the service of the Exalted.

The heart is the mirror of the universe.
The heart is the true Grail.

*

The train cut like a knife through the European dusk. The rain whipped against the windows of the compartment.

'God is peeing,' said a small boy, sitting on the seat opposite me with his sister.

'Carl!'

Their mother looked apologetically at me while she leaned towards her son and wiped his mouth with a paper napkin.

'God doesn't pee,' his sister answered, 'He cries.'

It was not a fanfare of a statement. Just a quiet establishment of a fact with a faint exclamation mark behind it. Like a stifled breath with an immediate, checkmating effect.

'He must be very sad, then,' the mother sighed resignedly with an empty look at the steamed-up window, before hiding once more behind a women's magazine.

The girl put her head on her brother's shoulder, uncomplaining. Sitting there, they constituted the silent protest of a whole generation against the thoughtless rejection of that Holy of Holies: people's divine and frail ability to be present.

I smiled sympathetically at them and leaned back in my seat hoping to get some sleep. The old Spanish manuscript *San Gral* was burning in my heart.

AUM
OM
☉

In a time characterized by war and unrest, economic instability, religious extremism, global environmental problems and spiritual estrangement, His Holiness the Dalai Lama is travelling around the world with his simple message of inner peace and compassion. Whenever he visits the West, he urges all those brought up in the Christian faith to remain Christians and deepen themselves in the esoteric aspects of Jesus' teachings.

An increasing number of Christians, however, seek this esoteric wisdom in vain. Fortunately, there is now help at hand. In Lars Muhl's book, *The Law of Light*, one can, through the psychology underlying the Aramaic language, get an insight into Jesus' hidden wisdom, as expressed in the New Testament.

If not us, then who?
If not now, when?

Otherwise known as the Grail Trilogy, *The O Manuscript* includes *The Seer*, *The Magdalene* and *The Grail*. This is the compelling full account of Lars Muhl's spiritual awakening, written with extraordinary energy, candour and humility. It is a personal and philosophical quest that challenges conventional wisdom and takes the reader on a mystical journey through ancient history and modern times.

A work in three volumes, the book begins with the author at a crossroads, suffering from debilitated health, his personal and professional life disintegrating around him. Bedridden for three years, Lars Muhl was put in touch with a seer who helped him, over the telephone initially, to recover his energy and brought him back to life. The Seer became his spiritual leader, teaching him the inner truths of existence.

The second and third parts of the trilogy cover the Female principle, followed by that of the Bridal Chamber, a Sufi concept, in which both the Male and the Female meet to form One Unity. This trilogy is not only a spellbinding introduction to the ancient vision of cosmic interconnectedness, but also a critical evaluation of a long list of limiting New Age dogmas.

WATKINS
Sharing Wisdom Since 1893

The story of Watkins began in 1893, when scholar of esotericism John Watkins founded our bookshop, inspired by the lament of his friend and teacher Madame Blavatsky that there was nowhere in London to buy books on mysticism, occultism or metaphysics. That moment marked the birth of Watkins, soon to become the publisher of many of the leading lights of spiritual literature, including Carl Jung, Rudolf Steiner, Alice Bailey and Chögyam Trungpa.

Today, the passion at Watkins Publishing for vigorous questioning is still resolute. Our stimulating and groundbreaking list ranges from ancient traditions and complementary medicine to the latest ideas about personal development, holistic wellbeing and consciousness exploration. We remain at the cutting edge, committed to publishing books that change lives.

DISCOVER MORE AT:

www.watkinspublishing.com

Read our blog

Watch and listen to
our authors in action

Sign up to
our mailing list

We celebrate conscious, passionate, wise and happy living.
Be part of that community by visiting

 /watkinspublishing   @watkinswisdom

 /watkinsbooks   @watkinswisdom